Models of Leadership in Plato and Beyond

Models of Leadership in Plato and Beyond

DOMINIC SCOTT AND
R. EDWARD FREEMAN

OXFORD

UNIVERSITY PRESS

OXFORD
UNIVERSITY PRESS

Great Clarendon Street, Oxford, OX2 6DP,
United Kingdom

Oxford University Press is a department of the University of Oxford.
It furthers the University's objective of excellence in research, scholarship,
and education by publishing worldwide. Oxford is a registered trade mark of
Oxford University Press in the UK and in certain other countries

Published in the United States of America by Oxford University Press
198 Madison Avenue, New York, NY 10016, United States of America

British Library Cataloguing in Publication Data
Data available

Library of Congress Control Number: 2020952995

ISBN 978-0-19-883735-0

Printed and bound by
CPI Group (UK) Ltd, Croydon, CR0 4YY

Acknowledgements

We would like to acknowledge the support of the Alexander von Humboldt and Carl Friedrich von Siemens Foundations, as well as Lady Margaret Hall, Oxford. We have benefited from ongoing support from the Institute for Business in Society at the Darden School of Business, in particular Executive Director Joey Burton and the following researchers: Sergiy Dmytriyev, Megan Juelfs, Rebecca Little, Jenny Mead, Andrew Sell, Logan Spangler, and Salem Zelalem. We are grateful to Harry Lloyd for further research assistance.

Thanks also due to: Thom Little and Steve Lakis from the State Legislative Leaders Foundation; Professors Gregory Fairchild, Mary Margaret Frank, Jared Harris, Tim Rood, and Ben Wempe; Jennifer Hicks from the Darden Executive Programs; Jamie Dow and Christopher Megone from the Inter-Disciplinary Ethics Applied Centre, University of Leeds.

The development of this book would not have been possible without the support and encouragement of the Oxford University Press, especially Peter Momtchiloff and Adam Swallow. We are also grateful to Jenny King for seeing the project through to the end. An earlier draft was seen by three anonymous readers for the Press, who provided us with incisive comments. Their advice helped transform the book into a much larger project than was initially conceived.

Finally, David Newkirk originally suggested that we work together. He has been a constant source of insight over the years.

Contents

Introduction

Studies of leadership have proliferated in recent years, drawing on a wide variety of disciplines, among them history, management studies, political science, economics, and psychology. This is predominantly an academic phenomenon, but it exists alongside more informal, 'self-help' books, as well as autobiographies written by former CEOs and others. In the course of all this, a vast number of definitions and theories of leadership have been proposed, such as 'transformational', 'servant', 'responsible', 'ethical', and 'thought' leadership.

In this book, we adopt a very different approach, by going back to one of the greatest thought leaders of all time, the Greek philosopher Plato, and using his insights to throw light on contemporary theory and practice. The book combines an account of his thought with applications to modern case studies and leadership approaches. Plato wrote extensively on political philosophy, where he puts a great deal of focus on leadership: what kind of leaders there should be, how they are to be trained, and what kind should be avoided.[1] Our view is that what he said about political leadership carries over well to other spheres, notably business.

His views on leadership are interesting in part because of the time in which he lived. Athens in the fifth century BCE, when he was born, was a place of extraordinary innovation—cultural, intellectual, and political. But it was also a roller-coaster of a time, the highest achievements of the human mind matched by periods of extreme violence and chaos. All this gave him the opportunity to witness leadership at its best and its worst. It should also be said that he was not just a theorist, but an institutional leader in his own right: he created a vehicle for the dissemination of his ideas, called the 'Academy', a centre for teaching and research that was in many ways the inspiration for the modern university.[2]

Plato left behind around thirty books on a wide range of topics, ethics and politics being two of the most prominent. Although some of his writing is quite technical, it has a friendlier side, capable of tapping into the intuitions of his readers and appealing to their imagination. This is certainly the case when he writes about leadership. Across a number of his works, he uses the following models to understand the phenomenon:

- the shepherd
- the doctor
- the navigator
- the artist
- the teacher
- the weaver
- the sower.

Even before you read any of his works, you can see the appeal of these models. Each one points to certain features of leadership, which we intuitively recognize to be important. To compare a leader to a shepherd is to stress the notion of care; as someone who tends the flock, protecting it from dangers, the leader is the servant of their followers. The doctor is also at the service of his or her patients, focusing first and foremost on their well-being. This model also makes us think of various social or institutional ills that the leader might have to remedy. The navigator is someone who steers the passengers and crew through choppy waters. There is the idea of danger here, especially unpredictable dangers. Like the doctor model, there is also the idea of a specialized skill practised by the leader. This raises the question of exactly what expertise the leader will have, how they acquire it, and from whom. So too with the leader as teacher: now the idea is that you lead by informing and educating people. The relation between leader and follower is more intellectual than in the case of the shepherd, perhaps also the other two models as well: after all, we don't think of navigators instructing their passengers, or even doctors their patients (though in this case we might).

The model of the artist emphasizes the importance of vision: just as a painter or a sculptor might look to a model and organize materials in its image, the leader is guided by a vision, which may be moral, social, or technological. The model of the weaver is all about cohesion: a weaver selects and then unites several different strands of wool into a single garment; likewise a leader needs to recruit the right people and, despite their very diverse talents and temperaments, bring them together into a unified team. Finally, the sower is someone who takes a more hands-off approach to leadership. Their aim is to generate ideas and initiatives for others to take up and then develop. The leader plays an important part in nurturing these ideas, but they are also happy for others to take the lead.

You might agree that these models have intuitive appeal. But perhaps they are *too* intuitive: some of them might feel like dead metaphors or clichés. But what Plato did was to take a set of homely images, some of them already in wide circulation (like the shepherd and the navigator), and give them a very distinctive twist. Sometimes he did this by honing in on specific details in a model, e.g. particular facts about disease, navigation, or weaving, and then using them to make the model illuminate features of leadership that would otherwise have gone unnoticed. Sometimes he problematizes a model: for instance, he shows that modelling a leader on a doctor—someone who prescribes unpalatable treatments—raises awkward questions about how such a person will ever persuade their followers to take the cure. These are just two of the ways Plato deepens the salience of his different models; we shall encounter many more as we go on.

All these models bring out very different aspects of leadership. And this brings us to another feature of Plato's approach. As a philosopher, he is often associated with the idea of finding a single definition for something, e.g. of justice, love, or knowledge—a 'one-size-fits all' approach. But, for some reason, he tended not to take this approach with leadership. When we think about his list of models, the question is not which *one* of them is correct. They might all be, in the sense that they capture certain aspects of the extraordinarily complex phenomenon of leadership. Each model may have its place in different contexts. Some situations require an educator; others a leader to navigate between various obstacles. No one leader imitates all the models all of the time; but each model may be apt for individual episodes in a leader's career. Different cultures and contexts require different qualities; it is impossible as well as fruitless to boil leadership down to a single formula. The variety exhibited by Plato's models helps bring out the sheer diversity of what may be involved.

The advantage of this approach is that it reflects the fact that 'leadership', like many terms that matter in human life, is so complex that it is almost impossible to pin down. The philosopher Ludwig Wittgenstein claimed that it is impossible to give any kind of simple definition of the word 'game', familiar though it is. No one formula will fit all cases. Give it a try: 'a game is a pastime, involving competition between two or more players.' But this doesn't work for all cases. Some games involve multiple players, but others, like patience, do not. Not all games involve winning and losing. Some are pastimes, but not all: think of professional chess players. For Wittgenstein, concepts like games involve whole lists of features, some, but not all, of which will crop up in any one instance; different games share some features with each other, but not all games have exactly the same features.[3] To capture the point he used the term 'family resemblances': there might be a string of features, and different members of a family might have some on the list, but not others. Or it is like a rope that seems continuous, but is in fact made up of several overlapping strands, no one of which extends its whole length.

We take a similar approach with leadership: don't expect there to be a single formula; the point of the models is to highlight different features. That said, there is plenty of overlap. The notion of care is very prominent in the cases of the shepherd, the doctor, and the navigator; expertise is essential for the doctor, the navigator, and the teacher; both the teacher and the sower enable others to become like themselves. The doctor and the artist have a prescription or model that may well be at odds with their followers' desires or expectations, which means that leadership may require the willingness to challenge and confront.

All this helps to explain why Plato is such an attractive figure to use when thinking about leadership. However, most of the ideas we shall discuss comes from his political writings, which raises the question of how far one can use politics to throw light of other areas of life, especially business.[4] Readers will be able to judge for themselves whether the models Plato used to understand political leadership can carry over to other fields. We see no reason why they should not: in all cases, we are dealing with the way human beings interact in groups focused on a common goal, and politics is only one arena in which this takes place.

Indeed, we shall argue that in some cases Plato's models fit other areas of leadership better than politics. Besides, many relationships in business are political: leaders have to work with people who are not necessarily employees; they have to find ways of influencing external stakeholders not unlike the way politicians have to win fellow citizens, lawmakers, and international partners over to their cause.

Outline of the book

Since Plato's views on leadership were so influenced by the times in which he lived, we start in Chapter 1 with a sketch of the historical backdrop to his philosophy. After that, we proceed through the models one by one. In each case, we begin by exploring Plato's use of the model, and discussing what was innovative about it, what may be problematic, and how it might be developed beyond the political context in which he originally proposed it. We then apply his thinking to our case studies: usually one from politics, the other from business. We close in Chapter 11 with a comparison between four of the most prominent modern theories of leadership and the Platonic models. At the end of the book, in Appendix 3, we have included extracts from Plato's works where he sets out the models.

This book presupposes no prior knowledge of Plato and is designed to be accessible to readers new to his ideas. At the same time, we hope that those familiar with his philosophy will find it a fruitful way of re-reading his work. We have tried to represent his views accurately, but on occasion have felt free to adapt or amend them in the interests of making them more relevant to the present. As for our case studies, we have looked for examples to match the Platonic models, and tried to ensure that they really do map on to the key principles of the models we have chosen. Of course, matching theory to practice, the general to the particular, is a messy business (as Plato would have been the first to acknowledge). So we are not claiming that our case studies match the models point for point. But we do think that they illustrate some of the core components of the model in question. And we hope that the exercise of matching actual leaders to Plato's models will stimulate readers to think of further examples for themselves.

Notes

1. The centrality of leadership to Plato's political thought is the theme of Anton (2011).
2. See Meinwald (2020): 'Plato's Academy, founded in the 380s, was the ultimate ancestor of the modern university (hence the English term *academic*); an influential centre of research and learning, it attracted many men of outstanding ability.'
3. Wittgenstein (1967) §66.
4. We are certainly not the first scholars to have looked to Plato to throw light on business leadership. For some article-length studies, see Klein (1988), Takala (1998), Cragg (2012), Cox and Crook (2015), and Bauman (2018). However, to our knowledge, no one has looked systematically across the different models and metaphors Plato provides for understanding the phenomenon, though Klein (1988) does focus on the model of the weaver.

1
Setting the Scene

The historical background

The Athenian empire

Born in 428/7 BCE, Plato worked mainly in the ancient Greek city of Athens until his death in 348/7. It is important to realize that the Greece in which he lived was not a single political unit as now, but a region that included many smaller political entities, or 'city states'. Athens, one of the largest, probably had around fifty thousand male citizens at its height, but most were much smaller. They were scattered around the region now called Greece and in some cases beyond, e.g. in Asia Minor on what is now the western side of Turkey, as well as in Sicily and North Africa. Some of them occupied sizeable areas on the mainland, like Sparta; others were on islands, such as Lesbos, Thasos, and Naxos.

Far from being united, Greece was often torn apart by inter-state rivalry and, sometimes, war. But certain things held them together, e.g. a common language and a common religion. Sometimes they were also held together by a common enemy: the Persians out to the east, who occupied a vast territory, now including Turkey and Iran, and were always on the look-out for opportunities to increase that territory, notably by invading the Greeks. Between 480 and 478, five decades before Plato's birth, several Greek states managed to unify themselves sufficiently to beat back the Persians. In the aftermath of their success, they wondered how they might sustain it. The answer was a defensive alliance, now known as the Delian League, which involved all its members pooling their resources to create a permanent fighting force against any future Persian attack. The leader of this alliance was Athens, which was one of the two most powerful Greek states. The other was Sparta, who decided not to participate.

The way in which this alliance was set up would have huge importance over the next few decades. Instead of having each member contribute troops, ships, and equipment to the force, it became the practice that most states would contribute money to a single fund, to be administered by the league's most powerful member. In other words, Athens was given a war chest to create the largest fighting force the Greeks had ever known. But it was not long before the Delian League turned into an Athenian empire: the other states had given Athens the resources not just to defend them from the Persians, but also to make them bend to its will. What was originally intended as a contribution to the defence fund became a system of enforced taxation to the Athenians. If an individual member decided they did not like the way the 'league' was going and wanted out of it, Athens could simply use its military power to bring them back into line. This they did on a number of occasions, when individual states tried to secede: the Athenians invaded their land and took a series of retaliatory measures, including financial penalties (indemnities), the demolition of defensive walls, internal political interference, and expulsions. (The most extreme example was the city of Scione, which revolted in 423: the Athenians killed the men of fighting age and enslaved the women and children.) So, under the guise of shepherding its fellow Greeks into a defensive alliance, the Athenians had turned itself into a tyrant—and indeed some of them admitted as much.[1]

The empire meant an influx of wealth into Athens. It became a vibrant metropolis and a hub of innovation, with some extraordinary achievements to its credit—in architecture, literature, science, and philosophy. Despite these achievements, Plato was a stern critic of the empire, as we shall see—not so much because of the treatment meted out to the subject states, but because of the moral harm it did to the Athenians themselves. He likens them to a sickly patient, bloated by wealth and leading a life of excess.[2]

Athenian democracy

The most important Athenian innovation for our purposes was political. In the decades before Plato's birth, Athens developed a system of democracy. Its emergence was a gradual process, but a decisive point came in 462, when two politicians, Ephialtes and Pericles, enacted a series of reforms. The democratic system they entrenched has been celebrated as one of the most extraordinary experiments in political history. At its heart was the Assembly, the supreme body responsible for legislation and particular decision-making. Any male citizen, whatever his background or status, could turn up to listen to a debate and vote. They were also entitled to speak in it. This was a direct democracy, not one in which you elect representatives to do your voting for you. In addition, there was the Council, a group of five hundred citizens, chosen by lot and (among other things) charged with drawing up the agenda for each meeting of the Assembly. At any one time, they had ten 'generals' (*stratēgoi*), chosen by election rather than lot, charged with day-to-day decision-making and (as their name suggests) military operations. The law courts were also democratically managed, with sizeable juries chosen from among the citizens. The courts were an important part of political life, as people could use them to eliminate political rivals by hauling them up on charges of corruption.

The fortunes of the democracy ebbed and flowed, and its fate was very much bound up with the military fate of Athens. In running its empire, Athens came into conflict with Sparta, the other main power of Greece. Shortly before Plato's birth, in 431, the two started a war, known as the Peloponnesian war, which dragged on for over two decades. Sparta was eventually the victor, and the defeat led to political chaos in Athens. When it surrendered in 404, its democracy was replaced by a dictatorship—the rule of the so-called Thirty Tyrants. (It had also been temporarily replaced with an oligarchy in 411.) But their regime was so brutal and divisive that they lasted only a year. Democracy was restored in 403 and remained in place for the next few decades, the period when Plato was most active as a philosopher.

There is plenty of room for debate as to how democratic the Athenian system actually was. Although all male citizens, whatever their background, were entitled to vote, women were completely excluded; there was also a huge slave population in the city. It is even a matter for debate how much power the male citizens wielded: the historian Thucydides said that, when Pericles was general, Athens was in name a democracy, but in reality was ruled by its foremost citizen.[3] But what matters for our purposes is Plato's view. To judge from some of his works, he was in no doubt that the system put power in the hands of the people; he explicitly denies that Pericles was master of the people: on the contrary, he just pandered to their whims.[4]

In taking this position, Plato was emphasizing the political importance of rhetoric. For him, this gave rise to the phenomenon of political demagogues: those who work out what the people want to hear and say it back to them. For him, such figures were not leaders, but followers. True leadership requires someone to confront the will of the people.

Even from this brief sketch, we can see why some of the leadership models mentioned in the Introduction appealed to Plato. If imperial Athens was like a sickly patient, the task of the leader would be akin to that of a doctor. The political chaos that marked the first thirty years of Plato's life—the collapse of the democratic regime, the rule of the Thirty Tyrants, and the subsequent restoration of democracy—would have made the navigator an appropriate image: a leader who can steer the ship of state even through the worst of storms. The experience of tyranny in 404–403 would have made Plato attracted to a model that character-izes the leader in the very opposite way: the shepherd, wholly devoted to the well-being of his flock. And amid all the chaos, leaders need the courage and independence of mind to think outside the box and form their own vision of how the state should be run; hence the model of the artist. Finally, since the Athenians were tearing themselves apart, an appropriate model of leadership is the weaver, capable of uniting all citizens into a single web of state.

The intellectual background

Because of the importance of public speaking in democratic Athens, people started to ask how they could acquire the art of rhetoric. To meet the demand, a group of professional teachers arose, called the sophists. Travelling around Greece, but with a special interest in Athens, they professed to teach young men hungry for power how to succeed in politics. One of them, Gorgias of Leontini (in Sicily), professed only to teach rhetoric. Other sophists, like Protagoras of Abdera, also taught their students how to argue their case in law courts. What he and his like were offering was the ability to help even those who had all the odds stacked against them. This meant the ability to 'make the weaker argument the stronger', as they put it. All this gave the sophists a reputation for twisting the truth and manipulating their audiences; they were also accused of 'corrupting the young'—i.e. all those who spent their money trying to acquire forensic and rhetorical skills. But, for all the criticism, they were also intellectuals of a more serious kind: they wrote books on rhetoric, truth, and the relation between law and morality, among other subjects. Though the evidence is fragmented, they were clearly an intellectual force to be reckoned with.

Amid all the controversy surrounding the sophistic movement was another intellectual, the philosopher Socrates. Unlike the itinerant sophists, he never left his native city of Athens except to go on military campaign a couple of times, as required by the law. He was born forty years before Plato, and spent his life in philosophy, especially moral philosophy. He wrote nothing down, and claimed not to know anything, although he certainly held strong views about ethics, politics, religion, and human psychology. Instead, he went round questioning others, especially those who claimed expertise for themselves, his favourite quarry being anyone who claimed to have ethical knowledge. For instance, on one occasion he interrogated two Athenian generals about the nature of courage, only to reveal their ignorance on the matter;[5] likewise he showed the sophist Protagoras, who claimed to teach virtue, that he had no understanding of the subject.[6] For him, such conversations were a way of disabusing others of their ignorance and forcing them to interrogate their own beliefs. He likened himself to a gadfly buzzing around a horse that wanted to go to sleep. In a similar way, he tormented his fellow Athenians with questions, trying to stop them falling into a state of intellectual complacency.[7]

In one sense he was extraordinarily successful. Young men, including the rich and talented, flocked to join his circle. Although they presumably received the same interrogatory treatment he meted out to others, it was doubtless entertaining to see him knocking the great and the good off their pedestals. The great and the good, however, were not so pleased.

Over time, momentum began to build against him. In the end, he was prosecuted for 'corrupting the young', as well as holding unorthodox religious beliefs. Although he had always tried to distance himself from the sophists, he was in effect grouped with them in the minds of his contemporaries and considered just as dangerous. He was tried at the age of 70, in 399, and found guilty. His sentence was death by drinking hemlock. Views differ on exactly why he was accused of corrupting the young. One explanation is that the young men who followed him around learnt to imitate his methods of interrogation and humiliate their elders, rather as he had done.[8] Their victims therefore blamed him for leading the young men astray. Another explanation is that he was perceived as having influenced a group of younger politicians who had been complicit in some of the worst anti-democratic plots of recent years. Notice that his trial happened in 399, when democracy had been restored after the rule of the thirty tyrants in 404–403, and those leading the charge against him were prominent democrats. The younger politicians associated with Socrates included Alcibiades, who had not only helped undermine Athenian democracy in 411, but also betrayed the city to the Spartans in the later stages of the Peloponnesian war. Two other members of Socrates' circle, Critias and Charmides, had been among the Thirty Tyrants in 404–403. Seen in this respect, Socrates' dealings with the young appeared downright sinister, at least to the Athenian democrats.

Plato

His works

Plato was born into a wealthy and well-connected family, but it was his association with Socrates that really determined the course of his life. He joined his circle while young, following their conversations and engaging in philosophical debate. For Plato, Socrates was an object of fascination—and love. As well as being a great philosopher, he also saw him as a leader—a political leader, no less:[9] though never elected to office, Socrates lived his life as a public intellectual, engaging directly with his fellow citizens—stirring them out of their slumbers like a gadfly.

This idea is what lies behind another of our models: the leader as teacher. Even if Socrates ultimately failed, for Plato he still left behind an ideal of how leaders should interact with their followers.

After the death of Socrates, Plato devoted himself wholeheartedly to philosophy. He did so in at least two ways: first, as an author of the thirty or so works that have come down to us; second, as the founder of a philosophical school, the Academy, which served as a training ground for future generations of philosophers.

A striking feature of his works is that they are almost all dialogues—conversations between two or more people. Interestingly, he never appears as one of the speakers, and in the great majority of cases Socrates is the lead interlocutor: he does most of the talking and, when there is an argument to be won, he almost always wins it. This is part of Plato's tribute to his mentor, but it raises a number of problems for his readers. When Plato has Socrates speak, is he reporting what the historical figure actually said, or is he using Socrates as the mouthpiece for his own philosophical views, on the grounds that it was Socrates who inspired him to take up a life of philosophy and to form his own theories and ideas?

A fairly standard answer to this question is that in his earlier works Plato does remain faithful to the historical Socrates, not reporting his words verbatim, but certainly capturing his distinctive way of doing philosophy and showing the reader the kinds of views he held and the arguments he used to defend them. As he developed, Plato went on to form his own views, over a wider range of topics than Socrates had ever investigated, but until the last years of his life still retained Socrates as the principal spokesman.

At any rate, the dialogues range over a very large number of themes, but ethics and politics are some of the dominant ones. It is here, of course, that we find his discussions of leadership.[10] He retained an interest in the subject throughout his life, and in this book we shall be looking at a range of dialogues that are thought to span the early, middle, and later stages of his career.

His most famous work is the *Republic*, which is also one of his longest. It was probably written in mid-career, and, although Socrates is the main interlocutor, the views he expresses are most likely those of Plato himself, not the historical Socrates. As its title suggests, it is a work of political philosophy, and is best known for its account of what Plato considers to be the perfectly just state. In constructing this 'ideal' state, he directs much of his attention to the kind of rulers it needs, and those whom it should avoid, and it is here that some of the most famous proposals of the work are to be found: for instance, his view that women should be allowed to rule alongside men, which was very radical for its time.

Because the work is full of passages about leadership, it contains several of the models that we shall be discussing: the doctor, navigator, shepherd, artist, and teacher. There is also a dialogue written somewhat earlier, the *Gorgias*. In this work he contrasts the true political leader with the demagogue, and puts the doctor model centre stage. Later on, we shall look at three dialogues Plato wrote after the *Republic*. Two are overtly about politics: the *Statesman* and the *Laws*. In the first we find the model of the weaver, while in the second (written right at the end of Plato's life) we find the doctor and the teacher from before, but now synthesized into a composite model.

The other dialogue we consider is the *Phaedrus*, whose primary topic is the use of words, whether spoken or written, to influence others. It is here that we find the model of the sower, a thought leader who manages to use words not just to change the present, but to create an enduring legacy for the future.

The *Republic*

Since we shall be focusing so much on the *Republic*, it will be useful to have a brief introduction here. Consisting of ten 'books' (i.e. chapters), this is a work about justice. It begins with an attempt to define justice and quickly leads into an argument between Socrates and one of the sophists, Thrasymachus, who has a highly distinctive take on the value of being just. Justice, despite all the fine words that have been spoken in its praise, is a mug's game: when you fulfil your obligations, like keeping your promises and paying your dues, it is usually your loss and someone else's gain. Anyone who knew their own interest, and was skilled in achieving it, would avoid justice like the plague. The only truly happy person is someone who is unjust, a point epitomized by the tyrant: someone who manages to enslave others to his own will. Throughout the argument, Socrates takes the opposite point of view, and tries to persuade his Thrasymachus that justice is in fact in our interest.

For our purposes, the importance of this argument lies in what it has to say about a leader's motivations: for Thrasymachus, the leader acts purely in his own self-interest. To this end he creates rules of justice for his subjects obey, but only so that they will better serve his interests. (Hence it is not in their interest to obey such rules.) By contrast, Socrates insists several times that true leaders rule only in the interest of their citizens, and to make this point he appeals to the figures of the doctor, navigator, and shepherd, whom he thinks also act only for the benefit of those in their care (patients, passengers, sheep).

At the end of Book 1, Thrasymachus gives up: he is unconvinced, but unable to find a way of refuting his opponent. Yet it seems that Plato was dissatisfied with Socrates' defence of justice here, because from Book 2 onwards he has two other interlocutors (his brothers, Glaucon and Adeimantus) press Socrates for a more convincing defence of justice. So they start all over again, first trying to define justice and then explaining why we should care about it. The subsequent discussion operates at two levels, sometimes focusing on what it means to be a just individual, at others on what it is for a state to be just. In the latter case, this means describing an ideal state, and it is this aspect of the *Republic* that we shall be examining.

To see what justice in a state is like, imagine trying to found one that is completely just. What would it look like? What sort of constitution would it have? Would it be a democracy, for instance? Who would its leaders be, and how would its resources be distributed? What sort of education would its citizens have? What differences, if any, would there be between the way men and women are treated? Plato begins his account of the ideal state in Book 2 by arguing that, since no one is self-sufficient, states exist in order to serve our mutual needs (369a–b). But these needs are best met if each person specializes in one task (rather than diffusing their energies over several), and this task is the one for which they are best suited by nature and temperament. In general, Plato thinks there are three kinds of task—economic, military, and ruling.

Hence the state has three corresponding classes of citizen, called 'producers', 'auxiliaries', and 'guardians'.

This arrangement, in particular the principle of specialization, explains one of the most notorious features of Plato's political philosophy: his rejection of democracy. Everyone will contribute to the state according to their natural abilities: if, at root, your talents lie in one direction, you will be trained in that profession and serve the interests of the state that way, whether as a soldier, farmer, or doctor. But you will not be allowed any share in political decision-making simply because you are a citizen. After all, we wouldn't hand over decisions about how to make ships to just anyone, only to those with the appropriate skill. So why should we think any differently when it comes to matters of the greatest importance—political decision-making?

As a result, whenever Plato discusses leadership, as he does very frequently in the work, he puts a great deal of emphasis on the need for expertise. This leads into the question of what exactly the leaders' expertise consists in (Books 5–6), and how they acquire it (Book 7). The need for expertise will be a recurrent theme in this book, especially with the models of the doctor, navigator, and teacher. It also raises problems: the leaders' expertise creates a gap between them and their followers. The gap may be so large the leader might seem alien to their followers; and the decisions they make on the basis of this expertise may appear incomprehensible and unpalatable. What will induce the followers to accept them?

Another feature of the ideal state is the importance of harmony and unity among its citizens; for Plato, this explains what makes it ideal. The citizens will all be focused on the common good, empathizing with each other's pleasures and pains, like a single body where pain felt in one part is felt throughout (V 462a–464b). The question arises as what will ensure such harmony among the citizens, and many of Plato's detailed proposals about education (Books 2–3 and 10) and the distribution of resources (Books 3–4) are intended to answer it. In the light of his own experience, he was painfully aware that such an ideal might seem impossible to realize. But this vision of social harmony was one he thought should be pursued—hence his interest in the leader as artist, who works with his materials to make them approximate his model as closely as possible. Also, because Plato's vision is all about harmony and balance between the different elements in the state—the parts of the 'body politic'—it also fits with the model of the doctor: as we shall see in the next chapter, the Greeks thought health lies in the correct balance or harmony between different bodily elements (the four 'humours').

This is only a quick sketch of the ways in which the *Republic* will be relevant to us. We shall dip further into the work as appropriate: the importance of social harmony will be important in Chapters 2 and 4 (the doctor and the artist); expertise in Chapters 3 and 5 (the navigator and the teacher). We do not wish to overload our account of each model, so when it comes to narrating Plato's views we shall stick to what is strictly necessary in the main part of each chapter, but then provide interested readers with more details in Appendices 1 and 2.

Plato's biography

These are the different dialogues we shall be discussing. But not all the works that have been handed down under Plato's name are dialogues. We also have a collection of thirteen letters, all purporting to be written in his own person, and often containing biographical information. The problem is that we cannot be sure if they are authentic or if they were forged (a common practice in antiquity). Some are definitely fakes (because they contain highly improbable or anachronistic claims), but there is one that has long fascinated scholars: the Seventh Letter. In it, the author (Plato?) explains why he went into philosophy in the first place.

As a young man he intended to enter public life, but abandoned his ambitions after experiencing the political chaos following the end of the Peloponnesian war, especially the rule of the thirty tyrants and the appalling treatment of Socrates by the restored democracy in 399. Instead of going into active politics, he spent his time reflecting on how a state should be governed, who should lead it, and what kind of leaders they should be.[11]

But most of the letter is taken up with a different tale—about how, much later on, Plato was invited by a politician in Sicily to educate its young ruler, Dionysius II. Here was an opportunity to implement the proposals he had made in the *Republic*. Would he take the bait and finally venture into practical politics? In the event he yielded to temptation, with disastrous results: Dionysius proved to be shallow and corrupt, wholly incapable of fulfilling Plato's ideals of political leadership. He eventually fled the island in despair, and the politician who had invited him was eventually assassinated.

We do not know how much of this is true, even if it makes a good story. But if we trust the letter, we would have to conclude Plato's attempts at political leadership were a disaster. Perhaps he was just not cut out for the role; or maybe the task of reforming Sicily would have defeated anyone. Either way, he would have been better off staying in Athens. The moral of the story might seem to be that Plato was great as an other-worldly intellectual, but he should never have dipped his toe into the 'real world'.

Actually, this is not quite true. We mentioned above that Plato's philosophical career included not only his intellectual work (in a narrow sense), but also the establishment of the Academy, an institute of higher education and research. The range of disciplines included philosophy of course, but many others, e.g. mathematics, astronomy, and cosmology. Given this breadth of interests, it is quite appropriate to see the Academy as a small-scale university. What is so interesting about the Academy is its legacy. One of his first batch of students was Aristotle, and long after Plato's death his school continued to have a deep influence on the development of philosophy. So it has to be remembered that Plato, whose views on leadership are the inspiration for this book, was himself a leader who managed to create an institution that endured for about three hundred years (until it was disbanded after the Roman invasion of 88 BCE). In this respect, Plato was the archetypical sower.[12]

Notes

1. According to Thucydides, Pericles described the Athenian empire as a tyranny in 2.63, as did Cleon in 3.37.
2. *Gorgias* 517a–519b.
3. 2.65.
4. *Gorgias* 516d–517c.

5. At least, according to the evidence of Plato's early dialogue, the *Laches*.
6. This encounter is depicted in Plato's *Protagoras*.
7. Plato *Apology* 30e.
8. *Apology* 23c–d.
9. *Gorgias* 521d.
10. Plato uses different Greek words to describe a leader. One is *hēgemōn*, which parallels our word 'leader' by coming directly from the Greek verb for 'lead' or 'guide'. Another term is *archōn*: a ruler, or one who holds office. A less common word is *prostatēs*, which can also mean a 'protector': someone who stands in front a group and defends their interests. Plato uses the word in this narrower sense when he says a tyrant, however powerful, is not a *prostatēs* (*Republic* Book 8, 566d).
11. 324b–326b.
12. This chapter has given only an outline account of the background to Plato's philosophy. Readers in search of further introductions to some of the topics discussed here will find plenty of resources available. For an overview of Athenian history in the fifth and fourth centuries BCE, see Cartledge (2011) ch. 8, esp. 72–9. A useful introduction to Athenian democracy can be found in Lane (2014) 95–115, esp. 103–8. On the sophistic movement and its historical context, see Dillon and Gergel (2003) ix–xix and Adamson (2014) 77–83. The literature on the historical figure of Socrates is vast, but Adamson (2014) chs 13–14 and Lane (2014) 133–50 provide good entry points; Cartledge (2016) 175–80 discusses Socrates' run-in with Athenian democracy. Some biographical details about Plato can be found in Adamson (2014) 102–8 and Thesleff (2012). For overviews of the *Republic*, see Lane (2014) 155–71 and Scott (2008); there is also a book-length introduction by Pappas (1995) and an engaging account of the work, with particular reference to its legacy, in Blackburn (2006).

2

The Doctor

Plato

Overview

Plato first develops the model of the leader as doctor in one of his early works, the *Gorgias*. But it is also important to the *Republic* and resurfaces in his final work, the *Laws*. In this chapter we shall focus on the *Gorgias* and the *Republic*, leaving the *Laws* until later.

One point the doctor captures is that a leader is someone who serves the interests of their followers: it is clearly built into the very nature of the medical profession that doctors work for the good of their patients. Plato insists on this at the beginning of the *Republic*, when he is attacking the view that true political leaders serve only their own interests (341c–342e). It is to counteract such cynicism that he deploys the doctor as a parallel: it is simply not in the nature of the medical profession to work for anything other than the good of its patients. The same, he argues, applies to professionals in the political realm. Plato also invokes the ship's captain to make the same point: again, they work purely for the safety and well-being of their passengers and crew.

We shall pick up this theme again when we look at the captain in the next chapter, and especially in Chapter 7, when we turn to the model of the shepherd (protector of the flock). But in this chapter we shall concentrate on features specific to the doctor model. Most pressing is the following question: if the leader is analogous to the doctor, what are the analogues of health and disease in an institution or in the people who constitute it? Once this is answered, we can ask what exactly it is that the leader as doctor does to promote and maintain institutional health.

Institutional health as balance

The *Gorgias*

In the *Gorgias*, Plato deploys the medical analogy at two levels: in the individual and the state. For our purposes, it is the institutional level that matters most, but to follow Plato's train of thought we need to start with what he says about the individual. His point is that, just as there is a good condition for a person's body, there is also one for their mind—or psyche, to use the Greek word. Certain things bring pleasure in the short term, without being necessarily good for us. Psychic health consists in desiring things only in so far as they benefit us. Psychic disease, conversely, involves having desires for the wrong things (certain kinds of pleasure) and being unable to restrain them. It is the job of the doctor of the psyche to help us restrain such desires and reduce their strength, if not eradicate them altogether.

Plato expresses this idea by saying that the doctor attempts to impose order (*kosmos*) on our desires—or, to put it another way, find the appropriate balance between them (see e.g. 503d–508a). In ancient Greek medicine, health was very much a matter of achieving the right balance between different bodily elements. Called 'humours' (blood, yellow bile, black bile, and phlegm), each one had a different nature, and a different effect on the whole system. If one of them was too dominant or too feeble, the body as a whole would suffer. Plato is taking this idea and applying it to the moral and psychological health of the individual.[1]

He also applies this reasoning at the level of the state. As a collective, the citizens might be pursuing the wrong goals, or at least certain goals too strongly at the expense of others. The role of the 'doctor', now standing as an analogue for the political leader, is to moderate such desires, and refocus the citizens on more sustainable goals. This is where Plato's critique of the Athenian empire comes to the fore (as mentioned in Chapter 1).[2] The supposedly great leaders of Athens, such as Pericles, pandered to the citizen's desires for imperial expansion, and with it the increasing amounts of tax that the subject states were forced to pay. This actually had the effect of making the state yet more aggressive and its citizens increasingly intractable. The 'leaders' failed to lead in the true sense (they were effectively led by the people); they failed to rein in the citizen's maximizing desires and achieve an orderly balance of objectives that would have kept Athens secure and sustainable. They allowed the city to pursue short-term gratification, whose effects only became known long after those leaders had died (515e–519b).

The *Republic*

In the *Republic*, Plato continues to apply the medical analogy to the moral and psychological well-being of both individual and state. In the case of the individual, he argues that each of us is a complex of different elements, psychological humours, if you like. We have physical desires or appetites (typically for food, drink, and sex); we experience emotions— pride and anger, for example; but we also have the power of reason to form judgements and intentions about what is best to do for ourselves and others. It is all too easy for these different forces to come into opposition: our appetites are sometimes too strong, perhaps destructively so, as are our emotions. Both can easily come into conflict with reason and each other. Rationalist as he was, Plato thought that our lives go best when we use our reason to work out our good, and then keep our appetites and emotions in tune with this. Such is the life of psychological health—a harmonious balance between the different elements within us (cf. Book 4, 444b–e). This involves a life of moderation, where appetites are pursued only within strict limits, and emotions follow the call of reason—not the other way around. Allowing our appetites and emotions to grow too strong is self-destructive, and a form of disease. The more they are indulged, the stronger they become, and the more they disrupt reason's ability to deliberate about what is really in our interest. Indulging in strong emotions or appetites feels good in the short term; but there is always a price to be paid later on.

As in the *Gorgias*, the *Republic* also applies this type of analysis at the collective level. Plato describes a state (sounding suspiciously like Athens) that is forever increasing its 'appetites'—the range of pleasures its citizens can indulge, and their variety and novelty (372e–373e). He is clearly thinking of the way an imperial metropolis like Athens could continually import ever-increasing and exotic enjoyments for its citizens. This maximizing approach leads the state to annex neighbouring territories, requiring ever more military adventures, and so inviting counterattack. Such a city Plato describes as 'diseased',[3] just as he had done in the *Gorgias*. By contrast, a healthy state would be one that lives within its means, keeps its population from growing too large or too small, and insists on harmonious relations both within and without (372c).

In all this, the *Republic* continues the thought of the *Gorgias*: political health involves the balance and moderation of the citizens' desires. But in the *Republic*, Plato also applies the analogy of civic health and disease in a slightly different way. Any state will include a great diversity of citizens, with different temperaments, skills, professions, and so on. In the ideal state examined in the *Republic* there are, broadly, three types of citizens: the 'producers' (charged with securing the material necessities of life), the 'auxiliaries' (the military, responsible for the state's defence), and the 'guardians' (the leaders of the state). The health of the state consists in each group sticking to its prescribed role, co-existing in a spirit of mutual trust. No one group should feel that the others are encroaching upon it in a way that undermines its well-being. Conversely, a diseased city (or indeed any kind of organization) would be one in which one group becomes too dominant and so undermines the successful functioning of the whole.

If this is Plato's conception of political health, the task of the leader as doctor is all about finding a balance. On the first version of the model, there are different and competing goals that need to be balanced: if the state is suffering from some kind of disease, the problem may be that it is too fixated on one goal (or set of goals) at the expense of others. The political doctor needs to balance the citizens' desires, taking particular care to restrain those that arise naturally, but are focused on short-term satisfactions.[4] On the second version of the model, a balance needs to be found between groups within the state. These might be factions within it: some have become too powerful and are inhibiting the functioning of the others. So there is a need for establishing harmony between them. In fact, when he stresses this point, Plato goes beyond the need for mere harmony and order. As he makes clear in a number of places in the *Republic*, the ultimate goal is the *unity* of the state.[5] This idea will be important to one of our case studies below.

So the leader needs to find a diagnosis; to do this they take stock of competing goals or conflicting groups, assess their relative importance to the state, and then do a health check on the current balance of power between them. This requires working out which ones have become too dominant and which need building up.

This process is especially important when we apply Plato's notion of the doctor as leader to modern businesses and non-political organizations. Every one of these organizations have groups and individuals who are outside the organization who can affect whether or not the organization is successful. Leaders of the organization must balance or harmonize the interests of these groups, called 'stakeholders', if it is to achieve its objectives or purpose.

The problem of persuasion

Of course, it is not just a matter of reaching a diagnosis; the leader has to find some way of implementing it. They need to get the citizens to take the cure. At this point, we run into an obvious practical difficulty, one that Plato takes almost masochistic pains to expose. The leader has probably identified strong but damaging desires in the citizens, or groups among them that are too strong. These all need to be confronted so that the appropriate balance can be restored. It is inevitable that any leader who attempts this will run into opposition, possibly vehement. How can it be overcome?

In the *Gorgias*, Plato highlights this problem, but without offering a solution. As well as using the dialogue to propose the model of the doctor confronting the patients with a diagnosis they will not like, he also articulates the opposite viewpoint. According to this, it is never a good idea to obstruct the will of the people; anyone who did so would incur their wrath and be left defenceless against the onslaught that would inevitably follow. Instead, one should adopt the opposite strategy and assume the role of flatterer. Like the doctor, the flatterer is keenly aware of what the people desire, but takes the opposite step, indulging rather than confronting them. This is the figure of the political demagogue, whom we mentioned in Chapter 1. Much of the *Gorgias* is concerned with the contrast between the demagogue and the true political leader. In fact, Plato has another analogy: the chef who, instead of curing the body and promoting its good (health), gratifies it and promotes its short-term pleasure. In response to those who think this a promising model of leadership, Plato points out that demagogues eventually become unstuck: they may indulge short-term desires, but the result is that the people become more demanding and less tractable as time goes on (515e–516c).

But if we are not to go down the route of the demagogue, do we instead bravely persevere with the role of the doctor? In the *Gorgias* there are several warnings about the dangers of opposing popular opinion, and the dialogue alludes to Socrates' own fate (his trial and execution, described in Chapter 1). Towards the end of the dialogue he actually claims to have been almost the only Athenian who practised the true art of politics (521d), presumably referring to his own role as a public intellectual and would-be reformer. Knowing what was eventually going to happen to him, the reader can draw the obvious moral: you take on the role of political doctor at your peril.

In the *Republic*, Plato is also pessimistic. If you live in a democracy like Athens, and have any principles, you would stay out of politics, because attempting to put your principles into action would be met with violent resistance. Instead, you should stay out of public life, like someone sheltering behind a little wall in a storm (Book 6, 496d). This is not so much an answer to the problem of persuasion as an admission of defeat. Fortunately, Plato returns to the problem in the *Laws* and seems more optimistic about a solution. More on that in Chapter 6.

Objectivity and expertise

There is one more implication of the doctor model that we need to highlight. Medicine is a science, and it is a matter of objective fact whether a certain state of the body constitutes health or not; that something is bad for us, medically speaking, means that it tends to promote disease, and this too is a matter of objective fact. If the leader is analogous to a doctor, and there are institutional equivalents of health and disease, the implication seems to be that these too are matters of objective fact.

Where the institutions are political, this assumption involves some controversy. Put strongly, the point might be that there are certain ways of life that are better or worse for the citizens than others, and it is the job of the political leaders to ensure that people live the lives they ought to. Plato certainly signed up to this approach; when he castigates his fellow citizens for having the wrong desires, he does so as if they are objectively wrong. But more the liberal-minded would venture to disagree. Surely it is up to individuals to determine what sort of lives they lead (within limits), not the state. Even here, though, one might say that certain kinds of political organization are better than others at allowing citizens to pursue their own ends autonomously. So there is still room for objectivity in how the state should be managed: some kinds of educational provision, for instance, are better than others at ensuring that the citizens flourish (in whatever paths they choose to pursue).

A closely related implication is that, on the doctor model, the leader needs expertise. Doctors are scientifically trained; they pass exams and obtain qualifications from recognized bodies; many of them continue to do research while still practising. How well does this apply to leadership? Once again we walk into controversy where political leadership is concerned. In what sense are politicians experts? Experts in what, exactly? People can of course take degrees in political science, sociology, law, and economics. Perhaps these are the analogues of biology, physiology, and anatomy. But the link seems less tight. Someone could be a successful political leader without any degrees in the social sciences; and another person with a distinguished track record in them might be useless in politics. As far as business is concerned, leadership in most modern organizations is rarely a scientific or objective matter. And yet, according to the doctor model, a leader must simultaneously have specialist expertise as well as deep organizational knowledge. Without such expertise, the leader will simply not be credible to the members of the organization or to external stakeholders.

For the moment we are just flagging up these issues. But we shall give some examples of what might count as a leader's expertise in politics and business in our case studies below; and we return to the theme of leadership and expertise in the next chapter, where it is a central feature of the navigator model.[6]

The doctor. Key principles:

D1. The leader works for the benefit of their followers, not to pursue their own self-interest.

D2. The leader has to find a balance: either between the various objectives of the organization, or between groups that constitute it.

D3. The leader confronts the tendency to favour short-term goals.

D4. The leader needs technical expertise.

D5. The leader faces a difficulty in persuading people to accept the cure.

Case studies

Plato's model of the leader as doctor, caring for patients, based on expertise and a view of health, and being detached from the pressure to conform, is very relevant as we look at our modern institutions. His worry about the philosophy of maximization without constraints is alive in our current conversations about business and politics. To illustrate let's examine two modern leaders who exhibit some of the characteristics of the doctor.

Roy Vagelos and river blindness

Roy Vagelos was CEO of Merck and Co. Born in 1929 to Greek emigrants in New Jersey, he received a partial scholarship and left his family's small restaurant to pursue a career of a doctor.[7] He trained as a biochemist and surgeon, obtaining his M.D. from Columbia

University. After becoming a university professor, he authored more than one hundred scientific papers and was elected to the American Academy of Arts and Sciences and the National Academy of Sciences. Upon joining Merck, he became the head of its research laboratories.

Merck is a very large and successful pharmaceutical company, originally German, but now based in the United States. In the 1980s, its scientists had recently discovered a compound that could be used to alleviate the symptoms of river blindness, a disease that affected tropical areas of the world, especially in Africa and Central and South America. At that time, there were about 85 million people in thirty-five countries in Africa, the Middle East, and Latin America at risk. Over 300,000 people had already become blind because of the disease, and a million more suffered from different degrees of visual damage; 18 million were infected but without serious symptoms so far.[8]

> The cause: a parasitic worm carried by a tiny black fly which bred along fast-moving rivers.... When the flies bit humans...the larvae of a parasitic worm...entered the body. These worms grew to more than two feet in length, causing grotesque but relative innocuous nodules in the skin. The real harm began when the adult worms reproduced, releasing millions of microscopic offspring, known as the microfilariae, which swarmed through body tissue. A terrible itching resulted, so bad that some victims committed suicide. After several years, the microfilariae caused lesions and depigmentation of the skin. Eventually they invaded the eyes, often causing blindness.[9]

The testing, development, and distribution of Ivermectin (the potential drug for people struggling with river blindness) would require tens of millions of dollars in investment over ten to fifteen years. Unfortunately, the people suffering from the disease lived mainly in small settlements in developing countries and could not afford it.[10]

Roy Vagelos, head of Research and Development and himself a doctor, decided to go ahead with the project. Once it was completed, he was sure that he could find sponsors in governments to help Merck deliver the drug so that they could recoup at least some of their costs. As the project progressed so did Vagelos, becoming Chairman and CEO of Merck.

After much effort to find partners with little success, Vagelos decided that the problem was so severe that Merck had to fund the distribution of the drug on its own. Since 1987 Merck has given away more than 2.9 billion doses of the drug, and eventually found a number of partners to help. 'Today, the MDP [Mectizan Donation Program] is the longest-running, disease-specific drug donation program of its kind.'[11] However, the financial burden of manufacturing and distribution has fallen largely on Merck.

The role of balance (D2); the leader confronts the tendency to favour short-term goals (D3).

Looking at Vagelos' handling of this crisis, we can find many similarities with Plato's leadership model of the doctor. To start with, there is the notion of corporate (or, more broadly, societal) disease. The leadership model of the doctor is only applicable when there is some sort of illness at issue. In this case, corporate America was suffering from a disease that conceptualized business as primarily about profits, money, and share-holders. But what about the other stakeholders who were affected by the choices of business leaders? Should leaders care for these stakeholders as well? Economist Milton Friedman famously said that the only responsibility of the executive was to maximize profits for shareholders.[12] Merck had not fallen prey to this disease as it had a history of both increasing profits and pursuing a purpose that stated that 'medicine is for people not profits'. However, even in a well-managed and high purpose-driven company like Merck, there was pressure to make profits.

Vagelos argued that most of the time a drug like Mectizan had applications in the developed world that could financially carry the application to the developing world. However, in this case there were no applications in the developed world, and the areas where river blindness was severe were among the economically poorest in the world. Vagelos had to take on this corporate disease for ever increased profits in deciding what to do with Merck's potential cure for river blindness.

Corporate health, Vagelos knew, was more than short-term financial health. While Merck was very profitable, there were signs of trouble as a number of patents were on the waning end of their lives. Vagelos understood that the research process at Merck was its lifeblood, and he had to reinvigorate that process. In doing so Vagelos believed that businesses must take care of those groups and individuals who can affect them and whom they can affect, i.e., their stakeholders. Like Plato's doctor, Vagelos could not give in to the rhetoric of the day, which was that business had no responsibility to anyone but shareholders. He knew that Merck's health depended on continuing to live its purpose. Profits, necessary for any business, were an outcome. In his own words:

> Corporations, no less than individuals, need to be good citizens and should be held to a high moral standard. Our policy on Mectizan and other gifts made Merck a place where people were proud and excited to work because they wanted to make lives better around the world. It helped us recruit the best people and build company morale. It was consistent with Merck's fundamental corporate philosophy of doing well by doing good. It served the global society Merck serves. It also served Merck's stockholders because corporate social generosity is often followed by higher profits as the corporation becomes a better, more attractive workplace for the best talent.[13]

As a corporate 'doctor' (as well as a doctor in the literal sense), Vagelos found a balance between revenue maximization and social responsibility; he found the right balance between the different stakeholders, and their different goals or aspirations. In doing so he probably boosted long-term company health and profitability, because he created the right 'culture' at Merck to attract talented scientists (who had a social conscience too!) and 'build company morale'.

The importance of expertise (D4)

Expertise is central to Plato's model of the doctor. Vagelos had expertise along two dimensions that were crucial in helping him lead Merck through this period. First, as a business leader, he developed organizational expertise that gave him the leadership ability to be successful in a large complex organization like Merck. He saw himself as responsible for helping to cure the disease of corporations that focused only on profits, a disease encouraged by Friedman and colleagues. As he set about this task, he brought to it a deep understanding of the role of the corporation in society, its relation to its stakeholders, and the factors that make a company truly successful in the long term—factors that promote corporate health.

Second, as a doctor and a medical researcher, Vagelos had technical expertise that was both recognized and admired. So in addition to using his organizational expertise, he also deployed his medical knowledge in making his solutions work. His specialist understanding informed him, first, of what scientists inside Merck required in order to do good work, and second, of how to attract and keep top talent at Merck. He also had inside knowledge of the company, just as a doctor has inside knowledge of the body.[14] Overall, his expertise allowed him to balance both the internal issues at Merck, and the external issues among its stakeholders, including its shareholders.

The problem of persuasion (D5)

We also discussed the problem of persuasion when looking at Plato's account of the leader as doctor. He acknowledged that such a leader will struggle to persuade patients to take the prescribed medicine. Unlike the pastry chef, who simply panders to people's desire to maximize pleasure, the doctor typically offers a medicine that is unpleasant but good for the health. In confronting the Friedmanesque corporate culture, Vagelos was in an analogous position. He needed others to help, but as Plato would have anticipated, he couldn't initially persuade his multiple stakeholders to work with him in addressing river blindness. The US Government and the World Health Organization initially turned down requests to help Merck. As a result, Vagelos and Merck had to take most of the burden on themselves. Not only did they give away the drug, but they had to take the initiative in establishing a committee of world-class scientists to work with individual programmes aimed at distributing the drug to hard-to-reach areas. It was only after years of going it alone that Vagelos was able to persuade the World Bank, World Health Organization, and the Carter Center to join forces to help Merck.

So Vagelos certainly struggled to sell his idea to agencies (and Merck itself) that would help him to make it work, just like Plato's doctor who struggles to persuade patients to take their prescriptions. But here there is the promise of a solution, which we did not find in Plato's account of the doctor. Sometimes the leader-as-doctor can succeed by initially going it alone. When the success of their ideas become apparent, it will be easier to persuade others to take the medicine.[15]

The leader works for the benefit of their followers (D1).

Finally, we said at the beginning of this chapter that for Plato the doctor exhibits care and serves the interests of his subjects focusing on their well-being. This is not peculiar to the doctor; it also applies to some of the other models as well. But it is worth emphasizing the salience of this feature to Vagelos' case. He spent time actually participating in the river blindness project, going on trips to deliver the medicine to people with former President Jimmy Carter and others. In addition, he constantly gave back to university communities by making charitable contributions and spending time with young business leaders.

Jean Monnet and the European Common Market

The role of balance and the 'disease' of nationalism (D2)

Our next example is the Frenchman Jean Monnet (1888–1979), one of the main architects of the EEC, the entity that developed into the EU. Throughout its history, Europe had suffered from wars and conflicts among its various nations. For Monnet, a root cause was excessive nationalism, a problem that he spent much of his life trying to solve. His efforts culminated in the ever-increasing integration of Europe, and his example of leadership fits Plato's medical analogy very well. The symptoms: a seemingly endless cycle of war and conflict, stretching back centuries; the disease: an excessive tendency towards nationalism, often militant nationalism. The balance between national identity (itself perfectly understandable) and other considerations, such as security and economic welfare, had gone seriously awry; the aspiration towards national pride had grown too strong and needed to be restrained. The cure: a pooling of economic interests and ultimately political power, initially in the EEC and ultimately in the EU. It was Monnet, perhaps above all, who saw the diagnosis and worked out the means to implement it. Though the European Union (EU) came into being only in 1992, some years after his death, its establishment became possible mainly because of the earlier integration efforts led by Monnet resulting in the Common Market.

Monnet said, 'nothing is made without men; nothing lasts without institutions'.[16] He believed that the common economic and political institutions in Europe could solve the problem of conflicts and wars:

> There will be no peace in Europe if States re-establish themselves on the basis of national sovereignty, with all that this implies by way of prestige policies and economic protectionism.... The countries of Europe are too small to give their peoples the prosperity that is now attainable and therefore necessary. They need wider markets...to enjoy the prosperity and social progress that are essential, the States of Europe must form a federation or a 'European entity' which will make them a single economic unit.[17]

The Common Market became the key economic platform for large-scale European economic integration—for instance, the European Monetary System was launched in 1979, which later grew into a political union (the EU) with an elected supranational European parliament and its executive body, the European Commission.

There is a specific respect in which Monnet reflects Plato's ideas about the leader as doctor. As we saw above, the *Republic* (unlike the *Gorgias*) expects the leader to go beyond just balancing the appropriate elements; he goes as far as creating a unity out of the state. This is similar to a point Monnet himself makes in his memoirs:

> All too often I have come up against the limits of mere coordination: it makes for discussion, but not decision. In circumstances where union is

necessary, it fails to change relations between men and between countries. It is an expression of national power, not a means of transforming it: that way, unity will never be achieved. At the same time, I had come to realize that the quest for unity, even if it were limited to material problems such as production, armament, and transport, had effects far beyond administrative matters and involved the whole political authority of the countries engaged in a common struggle.[18]

Monnet's aspiration towards seeing Europe united stemmed from his desire to prevent wars once and for all and promote freedom:

It seemed to me, looking back, that I had always followed the same line of thought, however varied the circumstances, and no matter where I was. My sole preoccupation was to unite men, to solve the problems that divide them, and to persuade them to see their common interest.[19]

The importance of expertise (D4)

Like Plato's doctor, Monnet was a man of deep expertise: an exceptionally skilled diplomat, who had spent years honing his craft through relentless hard work, experience, and single-mindedness. It was this skill that enabled him to build trust with the political leaders who would help create the EU.

His experience began very early in his career, when he started working in the area of international politics:

As the First World War broke out, Monnet...threw himself into the effort to get France and England to work together closely, especially in the joint purchase and distribution of materials.... From his experience Monnet learned that alliances were strengthened when the parties could work together on a concrete economic initiative from which each felt it was getting its fair share.[20]

His political experience also included working at the League of Nations at various points between the two world wars,[21] and helping the governments of Poland and Romania to reorganize their currencies, as well as the government of China to organize its finances for railroads.

Monnet was exceptionally determined in his goal of developing much closer ties among European nations. This determination was well described by Edward Heath, the Prime Minister of Britain, when it joined the Common Market in 1973: 'I think there are few men in the world more persistent than he is.'[22] This single-mindedness allowed Monnet to develop a specialized expertise in diplomacy that would not have been possible if he had scattered his energies more widely. He says:

> My life so far had involved a series of actions at the level where contemporary issues are decided, whether by men's willpower or by default. I had constantly been concerned with public affairs; but my work, unlike that of the quintessential politician, had not required an endless succession of fresh choices to be made in the infinitely complex situations that face the Governments of States. What I had undertaken, at every turning-point in my life, had been the result of one choice and one choice only; and this concentration on a single aim had shielded me from the temptation to disperse my efforts, as from any taste for the many forms of power... my role for a long time past had been to influence those who held power, and try to ensure that they used it when the opportunity arose.[23]

As a result, Monnet was admired for his expertise and skill. John F. Kennedy (1963) acknowledged his 'wisdom,... energy in persuasion,... tested courage, and... earned eminence in Europe'.[24] George Ball, a former US Undersecretary of State and a close friend of Monnet, described him as 'the supreme practitioner of personal diplomacy. And he practices that art with unfailing perception on the loci of power and with an extraordinary singlemindedness.'[25]

The problem of persuasion (D5)

Needless to say, Monnet met with fierce resistance as he tried to implement his cure to Europe's ills: at the time, people were used to living in closed-border communities and it was unthinkable to unify with those they had been fighting for so long. Of all the opponents during his lifetime, one of the most interesting is his own (better-known) compatriot, Charles de Gaulle:

> De Gaulle constantly criticized Monnet and ridiculed his idea of a single Europe. 'Dante, Goethe, and Chateaubriand belong to Europe only insofar as they are respectively and eminently Italian, German, and French. They would not have served Europe very well had they been without a country, if they had written some kind of Esperanto.'[26]

However, in the struggle between the two men, it is Monnet's ideas that prevailed, and his role in building a united Europe is well described by Kennedy:

> For centuries, emperors, kings and dictators have sought to impose unity on Europe by force. For better or worse, they have failed. But under your inspiration, Europe has moved closer to unity in less than twenty years than it had done before in a thousand. You and your associates have built with the mortar of reason and the brick of economic and political interest. You are transforming Europe by the power of a constructive idea.[27]

Of course, when we say that Monnet's ideas prevailed, we should not exaggerate. There has been significant push-back against his project, Brexit being the most obvious example. Whether the EU will survive in its current form is a question many commentators still ask. For advocates of Monnet's project, there is more work to be done; for sceptics, the project has already gone too far. It is not our job to arbitrate between the two. But we should make one point. Even if one is critical of Monnet's desire to unify Europe, it is still useful to view the whole issue through the lens of Plato's medical analogy. When Monnet started, he was surely right that Europe suffered from a disease of excessive, militant nationalism, and the aspirations of its leaders and citizens needed drastic rebalancing. In the end, though, the question is whether this rebalancing went too far—and, with it, the suppression of nationalism. As we said above, a sense of national identity is no bad thing—one of the bodily humours that has its place in political life. Too much of it led to the chaos of two world wars; too little of it may bring dangers of its own, even an undoing of the whole project. For both sides of the debate Monnet can be seen as a doctor; the question is whether he went too far with his prescription.

Finally, whatever assessment one makes of Jean Monnet, there is one more similarity with a doctor: like a doctor who is doing his job well, but who is mainly known by his colleagues and patients, the name of Jean Monnet is often forgotten today by the general public.

Notes

1. Plato gives his own account of the origins of disease in a later work, the *Timaeus*, 82a–86a. The beginning and end of this passage (82a and 86a) are especially clear about the connection between disease and the excess of some bodily element. A useful account of Plato's interest in Greek medicine can be found in McPherran (2012). On Greek medicine more generally, see Adamson (2014) ch. 11.
2. 515e–519b. At 519a, he refers to the accoutrements of empire—naval shipyards, defensive walls, and the tribute paid by subject states—as 'trash'.
3. 372e: more specifically 'festering', suffering from excess phlegm.
4. The *Republic* does not explicitly refer to the leader as a doctor after Book 1, except once in Book 8, 564b–c. (Here the political leader is called 'a doctor and legislator of the city', whose job is to purge it of excessive 'phlegm and bile', i.e. criminal characters and would-be tyrants, who would imperil the state.) Nonetheless, the doctor remains central to the *Republic*, because Plato characterizes justice and injustice as health and disease respectively (Book 2, 372c–373a and Book 4, 444b–e). If justice in the state is a matter of 'health', its maintenance requires the analogue of a doctor, exactly as stated at Book 8, 564b–c.
5. *Rep.* Book 4, 422e–423e, Book 5, 462a–b, and Book 7, 520a. The same applies at the level of the individual: 443c–444a. The dangers of disunity feature at Book 4, 444b, Book 8, 554d–e, and Book 9, 577e and 588e–589a.
6. When Plato discusses expertise in the *Gorgias*, he sometimes contrasts it with experience, which he disparages as being insufficiently theoretical. By contrast, medical and political expertise grasp the underlying causes of the phenomena they study. (This is apparent from the extract we quote in Appendix 3, 462b–465b, especially 465b.) In the *Republic*, however, he acknowledges that leaders need experience as well as more abstract knowledge. (See Book 6, 484d,

Book 7, 539e–540a, and Book 9, 576e–577b.) So experience and theoretical expertise go hand in hand together. It is important to us that experience is not denigrated, because a number of our case studies put some emphasis on it, e.g. Monnet in this chapter and Douglass in the next.

7. Johnson (2004).
8. Bollier, Weiss, and Hanson (1991).
9. Bollier, Weiss, and Hanson (1991) 1–2.
10. Bollier, Weiss, and Hanson (1991), teaching note, p. 5.
11. https://www.merck.com/about/featured-stories/mectizan.html.
12. Friedman (1970). Cragg (2012) 30 also uses Plato's concept of justice as balance and harmony against this view.
13. Vagelos and Galambos (2006) 169.
14. One might venture that Plato would have preferred internal corporate promotions over the use of headhunters in hiring new executives.
15. Relevant here is the Chinese proverb, 'Not the cry, but the flight of the wild duck, leads the flock to fly and to follow', quoted by Adair (2013) 18. See also Mandela (2011) 146: 'It is absolutely necessary at times for the leader to take an independent action without consulting anybody or to present what he has done to the organisation.'
16. Gardner (2011) 264.
17. Monnet (1978) 222.
18. Monnet (1978) 35.
19. Monnet (1978) 221.
20. Gardner (2011) 252–3.
21. Smith (1979).
22. Smith (1979).
23. Monnet (1978) 229–30.
24. Kennedy (1963).
25. Smith (1979).
26. Gardner (2011) 254.
27. Kennedy (1963).

3

Captains and Navigators

Plato

Overview

On 24 June 2016, just after the referendum to leave the EU, David Cameron addressed the nation. He had campaigned to remain, and was now announcing his resignation as Prime Minister:

> The British people have made a very clear decision to take a different path and as such I think the country requires fresh leadership to take it in this direction. I will do everything I can as Prime Minister to steady the ship over the coming weeks and months but I do not think it would be right for me to try to be the captain that steers our country to its next destination.

The words 'ship' and 'captain' fall effortlessly from his lips. No surprise: the idea of the state as a ship is well-worn in our political discourse.[1] It has an ancient lineage, and existed in Greek thought long before Plato.[2] He himself uses it in the *Republic* and invokes the analogy of a captain or navigator in two other political works, the *Gorgias* and the *Statesman*.

The core idea is that the ship stands for the state, the passengers for its citizens, and the navigator or captain for the leader. The citizens have decided upon a destination; the leader's task is to work out a plan for getting them there and to implement that plan. Reaching the desired destination will involve overcoming obstacles, some of them expected, others not, and the leader has to maintain course despite all the perils that lie ahead. This makes the concern sound very much outward-facing, but there is also need for internal discipline, unity, and even self-sacrifice on board the ship, something that is up to the captain to inspire (or enforce).

It is not difficult to see how to apply this in specific cases, both in politics and beyond. For David Cameron, the public had decided on a certain course—life outside the EU—and it was the job of the Prime Minister to lead them to that destination. 'Navigating' the journey involves anticipating specific obstacles, dealing with unintended consequences and unexpected threats. It therefore requires considerable expertise: detailed knowledge of EU institutions, trade agreements, and numerous issues involving security. There is also the need for expertise in dealing with the public—building their trust and managing their expectations.

The image is obviously applicable whenever the electorate decides to take the state on a new course, but it applies in all sorts of contexts outside of politics. Imagine a company that decides changes in technology require it to operate in a completely different manner in order to be viable. Perhaps it needs to enter a new market and target a different kind of customer; or to position itself as more ethical or environmental. Not only does it need to make tough decisions, but someone needs to decide on the means to get it to the new destination, trying to anticipate the problems that lie ahead. When the going gets rough, the leader needs the resolve to persist and the skills to inspire the rest of the company's stakeholders with that resolve.

All this may seem relatively intuitive. But Plato also uses the navigator model and the ship of state to make a series of deeper points about leadership, specifically about the sort of expertise it requires. To do justice to this, we need to examine the exact way he describes the ship of state image and see how it supports the account of leadership he develops in the *Republic*, which will be our focus here.

Plato's ship of state

Before we turn to the ship of state in *Republic* Book 6, we should just register one point Plato has already made about the leader as navigator or captain in the work. In the previous chapter, we saw how he argues that the political leader resembles a doctor in being focused solely on the good of those in his charge, rather than on his self-interest (Book 1, 341c–342e). In the same place, he reinforces the point by comparing political leaders to sea-captains.³ We shall take this theme up again in Chapter 7, when we look at the model of the shepherd. But in this chapter we focus on the way the navigator model is incorporated into the more complex ship of state as described in Book 6. The passage is worth quoting in full:

Imagine something like this happening on board one ship or several: there's a shipowner who's larger and stronger than everyone else on board, but slightly deaf and short-sighted, and his grasp of navigation is no better. The sailors are fighting with each other to be captain of the ship. Each one thinks he should be captain, but has never acquired the skill, nor can point to anyone who taught him, or when he learnt it. What's more, they claim it can't even be taught; and they're ready to cut to pieces anyone who says it can. They're always crowding around the shipowner, pleading with him and doing everything to persuade him to let them take control of the steering oar. Sometimes, if they fail and others succeed instead, they kill them or throw them overboard. They overpower the noble shipowner with drugs, drink, or something else; they take over the ship and sail along much as you'd expect such people to do, helping themselves to the supplies on board, feasting and drinking. On top of all this, they praise anyone who's clever at working out how to control the shipowner, whether by persuasion or by force; they call him a seaman, a navigator, or someone who knows about ships. Anyone who's not like this they dismiss as useless. But they understand nothing about the true navigator—that he needs to pay attention to the time of year, the seasons, the sky, the stars, the winds, and everything that pertains to his skill if he's really going to be the leader of a ship. They don't think it's possible to acquire the skill or the practice of how to steer the ship (whether people want them to steer or not), along with the art of navigation. When things like this happen on board, don't you think that the true navigator will be dismissed as a star-gazer, a babbler, and of no use by people who travel on ships managed like this?   (*Republic* Book 6, 488a–489a)

Before going any further, we need to be aware of some basic facts about nautical leadership in ancient Greece.⁴ There were actually three different roles required on board: first, the navigator, who deter-mined the course to be followed; second, the helmsman, who knew how to operate the steering oars to follow that course; third, the captain, termed a 'ruler' of those on board in *Rep.* Book 1 (341c–d), whose role was to maintain discipline among the crew and passengers. In Plato's mind, these roles were all combined into one (although it is the navigator who is uppermost in his mind at the end of the passage).

An image of democratic politics

Now return to the image. The passage describes the rough and tumble of Athenian democratic politics, as seen through Plato's eyes. The first figure mentioned is the shipowner, who stands for the demos, the people. The description is not entirely flattering: the implication is that the demos is deficient in political expertise. (Plato was not one to celebrate the 'wisdom of the crowd'.) There is one silver lining: at least Plato acknowledges that the demos 'owns' the state; it exists for the people. This is part of his revulsion against any form of tyranny, where the ruler treats citizens as slaves, i.e. his property. By contrast, Plato thinks that the members of the demos are the principal stakeholders, and this ties in with the point stressed in *Republic* Book 1: rulers lead for the sake of their subjects, not themselves (341c–342e). If the demos is conceived like this, the most obvious way to understand the image is that they have decided on a certain destination, and it is the job of the captain or navigator to get them there. In political terms, the people decide the ends, and the politicians work out the means.[5]

The next group, the sailors, stand for the unruly politicians of democratic Athens. In the space of a few lines, Plato fires off a whole volley of criticisms, but three points stand out. First, they have abso-lutely no competence to rule: they have not learned the science of political leadership; in fact, they do not even think it exists, and go out of their way to deny that there is such a thing. Second, all their energies are focused on persuading the demos to let them rule. But this persuasion amounts to no more than low-level, manipulative rhetoric.[6]

Finally, the problem with these 'leaders' is that they are completely inward-focused. While the real challenges lie without—the weather, the rough seas, the threat of pirates—they are solely interested on who is winning the battle to be elected; note also the sheer violence involved in such conflicts.

This third point raises an all too familiar problem in politics: an obsession with leadership contests, ignoring the real problems that need to be addressed. It is also a problem with all sorts of organizations that become inward-looking and parochial. Plato's point is that there is a desperate need for the skills of a captain—in addition to those of the navigator: someone whose specific goal it is to instil unity and a sense of common purpose on board. This is particularly important when we move to business. There are many conflicting stakeholders who are only voluntarily associated with a particular company. It is easy for such situations to turn into battles between 'roving gangs of stakeholders' with the loudest being the winners. The astute captain has to tread carefully among what are usually conflicting demands, getting stakeholders to rethink their positions and their interests, so that a harmonious direction can be achieved. The challenge is to engage with stakeholders and get them to see that 'we are all in the same boat'.

The ideal navigator

The final section of the passage is about what navigators ought to be like. Standing aside from all the power struggles on board, they turn their gaze in another direction entirely. Literal navigators require knowledge of the weather and, in Plato's time, they needed 'navigational astronomy': it is only by checking their position in relation to the stars, especially the north star,[7] that they could steer the ship safely on its course. To anyone who actually knew about seafaring, this would have been obvious. But in the image, the point is completely lost on the crew members on board, too busy squabbling for control of the ship. For them, the focus is on who is doing or saying what in relation to the shipowner, while the true navigator looks in a completely different direction. This is what the crew find incomprehensible: why, they ask, would you look to remote objects in the sky when you're trying to steer the ship across the sea? Hence they dismiss the true navigator as a 'star-gazer and a babbler'—an irrelevance. And this is Plato's deeper point in applying the well-worn ship of state image to political leadership: practical decision-making requires a kind of knowledge that will seem abstruse and irrelevant to those who misunderstand the true nature of politics. More generally, any leader requires a deep expertise, utterly different from the kind of quick-wittedness that enables rival competitors to grab power within the organization.

Looking at the image as a whole, we can see that Plato begins with the realities of political life in Athens, but at the end turns his thoughts in a utopian direction: to what politics could be like at its best, in the ideal state. For him, this would be a perfectly just state, and as such would require moral expertise in its rulers—a deep understanding of highly abstract principles, e.g. about justice. This is mainly what leads him into one of the most notorious proposals in the *Republic*: that the guardians of the state should be philosophers. For readers who want to know more, we shall explore this further in Appendix 1. But the force of Plato's image is not confined to the specific (not to say eccentric) way he conceived of political leadership: the underlying point is that any leader requires a specific expertise, which may appear to their followers as abstruse and irrelevant.

To an extent, Plato has won the argument here. To us, it sounds obvious that a good leader cannot perform their role without drawing on technical expertise. No one, for instance, could doubt the need for expertise in economics. True, people have wondered whether our economists are up to the job, given their failure to predict the economic crisis in 2008; but the appropriate reaction to that is that we need better understanding of economics, not that there is no understanding to be had. Economics is a good example because it involves highly abstract mathematics: it is not merely the sort of head for business that an individual practitioner might have. And, of course, economics is not the only case, even if one of the more obvious. The environmental crisis shows an urgent need for policy to be informed by good science and, again, that may reach up towards the most abstract areas of physics, etc. Decisions about healthcare likewise depend on a range of scientific disciplines (e.g. biomedical statistics), education policy ought to be informed by academic work on the subject (including cognitive psychology). The list is endless. In all these cases, we cannot set a limit on the degree of rigour and abstraction that may ultimately be required. Stargazing is now firmly entrenched in the decision-making process.

But if Plato has won the argument, it may only be a partial victory. It is difficult to deny that leaders need to *draw on* experts; but do they need to be experts themselves—in economics, biostatistics, and educational theory? Where Plato goes wrong, you might say, is in failing to distinguish between leaders and the experts who advise them. But he still has a come-back. The navigator image can be used to argue that they should be experts of some kind, not merely that they need to draw on other people's expertise from time to time. It is all too obvious from the COVID crisis that leaders need to know how to deal with the advice they are given. In this instance, there has to be some sort of interface between scientific experts and their political masters. Don't leaders need some sort of scientific training in order to be competent in weighing up often conflicting pieces of advice—navigating through scientific disagreements? The challenge Plato laid down will not easily go away.

A similar challenge arises in business. In essence, we can use Plato's image to reject, or at least question, the idea of a generic leadership skill. One of our case studies from the previous chapter helps to illustrate this. Roy Vagelos was a doctor who specialized in medical research. His expertise gave him the knowledge to proceed with the project to alleviate river blindness. This is what enabled him to empathize not only with the people who had the disease, but also with the scientists in Merck's lab, whose motivations he understood, hence his decision to give away the drug.

The fact that decision-making requires quite abstruse forms of expertise recalls the problem that we were considering in the last chapter: the problem of persuasion. In the *Gorgias*, Plato highlights the difference between the true politician and the demagogue: one aims at the good, the other at gratification. The medical analogy brings out the problem that the right policy, like the right treatment, may be deeply unpalatable to the subject. So how do you persuade them to take the cure? Plato offers no solutions, and we are left with a sense of pessimism. The ship of state image points in a similar direction. The true navigator is a remote figure, ignored or scorned by everyone else. The problem is that no one understands the point of his expertise. So how could he possibly persuade them to be subject to it? Both the doctor model in the *Gorgias* and the navigator in the *Republic* paint the same gloomy picture: whether it is because his remedies are too painful, or because people consider his expertise irrelevant, his advice risks being ignored.

The distinction between captains and navigators

Plato's image of the ship of state makes two rather different demands on the leader. One is outward-looking: we need a navigator with specialist expertise to guide the ship in the right direction and antici-pate external threats. But the problem of persuasion shows that the leader also needs to be inward-looking—to control what happens on board. This relates to a distinction we made at the beginning of this section, between the different roles required for nautical leadership: aside from the literally hands-on skills of a steersman or helmsman, we need someone with the external focus of a navigator, but also a captain with the ability to control passengers and crew. The passage we have discussed ends by describing the work of the navigator, whose eyes are fixed on the beyond; but the central section, with its description of the chaos on board—the sailors all at each other's throats—points to the need for a captain.

As we turn to our examples, this distinction becomes crucial: we shall look at an example of someone who used his knowledge of the stars, his moral principles, to maintain unity on board, and then someone who acted as a great navigator, but was less successful as a captain at main-taining internal unity.

> ## The navigator/captain. Key principles:
>
> N1. The citizens (or stakeholders) have decided on a destination; the leader's task is to devise and execute a plan for getting them there.
>
> N2. The leader is not self-interested, but concerned with the well-being of the followers.
>
> N3. The leader requires expertise.
>
> N4. To some followers, the leader's expertise may seem irrelevant or ill-suited to the task.
>
> N5. The leader is not afraid to stand apart from the crowd.
>
> N6. While being outward-facing, the leader must also be inward-facing: someone who creates a unified sense of purpose on board.

Case studies

Frederick Douglass and the end of slavery in the United States

Charting a new course (N1)

The ship of state was in disarray. The Civil War was the result of the conflict over slavery in the United States. While we can see Abraham Lincoln as Plato's navigator, it is perhaps a bit more subtle to look further and see how Lincoln himself was influenced by other leaders. Lincoln knew where he wanted the country to go—towards a slave-free society. He needed the practical knowledge of navigators or captains such as Frederick Douglass if he had any hope of ending slavery and creating a more just society.

Looking at Douglass' extraordinary achievements as a whole, one could see the potential for other models of leadership: he addressed a social disease and fought to implement a cure; he was a social visionary (anticipating Martin Luther King, Jr) who sought to transform society. We do not deny the appropriateness of these models (great leaders may well embody more than one model). But here we want to show how well he illustrates some of the features of Plato's seafaring model.

As a former slave, Frederick Douglass played a pivotal role in putting an end to the institution of slavery in the United States. His life was full of hardship but also of great accomplishments. It is in part due to these hardships, the very experience of slavery, that makes Douglas a navigator or captain. He helped the whole country, and Lincoln, navigate through difficult times to build a better and more sustainable society. Douglass was one of the leaders of the anti-slavery movement who developed and shared his strategic thinking on why and how to abolish a deep-rooted institution during his public speeches, articles in his own newspaper, the *North Star*, and in his books. On several occasions, Douglass provided President Lincoln with critical advice that prevented the country from going in the wrong direction.[8]

The navigator has to lead in times of danger, much of it unforeseen, and this was obviously true in Douglass' time. He lived and worked amid many dangers, at all layers of the society: the whole country suffered from growing instability and the threat of collapse. Douglass had to help steer the anti-slavery movement, and society in general, through some decidedly choppy waters.

Douglass saw that the way forward demanded something drastic. Many abolitionists believed that slavery in the United States could be ended through peaceful means, such as persuasion, election, and legislative changes. However, Douglass was one of those who realized that the institution of slavery had sprouted such deep roots in the South that the Southern states would never peacefully abolish slavery. Half their wealth was comprised in its slaves: the market price of the slaves had doubled within ten years, from 1850 to 1860, thus 'the personal assets of slave owners rose accordingly'.[9]

Douglass was extremely bold about what was required to end slavery, realizing that peaceful discussions would only give more time for the 'monster' to expand:

> The only true remedy for the extension of slavery, is the immediate abolition of slavery. For while the monster lives he will hunger and thirst, breathe, and expand. The true way is to put the knife into its quivering heart ....[10]

For it is not light that is needed, but fire; it is not the gentle shower, but thunder. We need the storm, the whirlwind, and the earthquake.... the conscience of the nation must be roused...the hypocrisy of the nation must be exposed.[11]

The need for expertise (N3); creating a unified sense of purpose on board (N6)

Frederick Douglass was very clear about the destination: the abolition of slavery and equal rights for all American citizens, including the rights for freedom, education, and equal pay, as well as the right to vote. Douglass was not only determined to build a flourishing and sustainable society with no place for slavery; he also had a unique skill—a clear understanding of how to get there—and this helped the abolitionists win their cause.

Plato's navigator possesses strong expertise, and this applies to Douglass. As a former slave, he went through all the hardship of the institution. Though there were many good speakers in the antislavery movement at that time, only Douglass was a former slave who could speak about the ugliness of slavery first hand: 'abolition leaders needed a credible, moving account of slavery to win new converts, and no one... had such experience.'[12]

But Douglass' expertise did not just arise from his experience. Among other things was his extraordinary skill as a communicator. Because of his efforts (among others') the anti-slavery topic became the centrepiece of societal discussions. It moved to the front pages of newspapers, street discussions, and elsewhere:

As soon as the Civil War broke out, Douglass worked to define the conflict as one to eradicate slavery. Using his newspaper, the lecture circuit, and his political connections, he continued to push this perspective to the center of national debate.[13]

Not only did he help make the topic centre-stage, he was also a great rhetorician, and he used his skill to great effect to steer the ship in the right direction. Due to his unquenchable thirst for learning, his determination to change the things for the better, and his relentless persistence, Douglass learned how to read and write mostly on his own and by asking other 'free' kids to give him lessons they learned at school; and he became an eloquent and powerful speaker, which was very unusual for slaves at the time. In his childhood, Douglass was inspired by orators' books, which helped him achieve his ambition to become a public speaker.

Now, it might seem as if our case study is being blown off-course. Surely, it will be objected, Plato contrasts the true leader with the orators (the sailors) who use rhetoric to get themselves appointed captain by the shipowner. But this is to misunderstand Plato's approach to rhetoric. When Plato is critical of rhetoric, as in the *Gorgias*, he has a specific target in mind: not rhetoric in itself, but the use of it to flatter the demos or kowtow to public opinion. He is only opposed to the misuse of rhetoric.[14] Later on, in the *Phaedrus*, perhaps written shortly after the *Republic*, he revisits the topic and lays out the principles of the art of rhetoric, presenting it as a form of expertise, to be used for good ends. What exactly is the true orator skilled in? Aside from the basic tenets of speech construction, the orator needs a grasp of the audience's psychology (270a–272b). But, crucially, they also need to understand the subject matter about which they're speaking (259e–260d and 272d–273e). So, when the topic is justice, they need to understand justice—and so on. True rhetoric is not opposed to ethical understanding; the two are continuous. Good rhetoric arises when someone with genuine understanding seeks to communicate with others, not only appealing to their intellects, but their emotions as well. It is this kind of expertise that is crucial to the role of captain—a leader who needs to inspire unity and common purpose on board ship. They use their knowledge of the 'stars', i.e. the fundamental principles of morality and law, to do just this.

To return to Frederick Douglass. What he did was to deploy his rhetoric in a particularly skilful way, one that Plato would have recognized.[15] In some of his speeches and writings he took the core principles and values that his audience already espoused, and then showed that these values demanded an end to slavery. First there was the Constitution. In Douglass' time, common thinking had it that the US Constitution supported slavery and, as a result, many law-abiding citizens tolerated the institution. However, it was Douglass who, among few other great thinkers of that time, went against the main-stream opinion and argued that actually the US Constitution was not pro-slavery, but on the contrary, it was anti-slavery. He argued that it was the Southern states that had to abolish slavery to comply with the US Constitution.

> Perhaps, Douglass reasoned, the Constitution was not a fundamentally pro-slavery document. . . . Perhaps, Douglass theorized, by not mention-ing slavery—which the founding fathers understood was at odds with the principles of the republic—the authors of the Constitution intended to create what Douglass called a 'permanent liberty document'. It was, he determined after considerable reflection, ultimately antislavery. . . . Once he had decided that the Constitution was an antislavery document, several things became clear. One was that the fight to end slavery had to unfold within the *existing* political system as governed by that found-ing document. . . . The black reformer, like virtually all effective leaders, nurtured a pragmatic streak. . . . the black abolitionist reasoned the Northern states had no need to secede from the Union. . . .[16]

> 'The only intelligible principle on which popular sovereignty is founded,' Douglass told an audience in 1854, is contained in the Declaration of Independence: 'We hold these truths to be self-evident, that all men are created equal and are endowed by their Creator with the right of life, liberty and the pursuit of happiness.'[17]

Second, and more generally (i.e. moving beyond the actual Constitution), Douglass argued that slavery hurt not only blacks, but that it also killed the good inside white people, and deprived the whole nation of the great future it might otherwise achieve:

> The existence of slavery in this country brands your republicanism as a sham, your humanity as a base pretense, and your Christianity as a lie. It destroys your moral power abroad; it corrupts your politicians at home. . . . It fetters your progress; it is the enemy of improvement; the deadly foe of education. . . .[18]

> The lesson of all the ages on this point is, that a wrong done to one man, is a wrong done to all men. It may not be felt at the moment, and

the evil day may be long delayed, but so sure as there is a moral government of the universe, so sure will the harvest of evil come....[19]

Here, Douglass is looking to the 'stars', the values and principles on which society was meant to be based, and interpreting them in such a way that helped lead the ship to its destination—the abolition of slavery. This shows knowledge both of the principles themselves and of what will resonate with his audience—the two key components of what Plato took to be the expertise involved in true rhetoric. It is this expertise that Douglass used on board the ship of state.[20]

All in all, Douglass was both a navigator and a captain. As navigator, he charted the course: the complete abolition of slavery. This knowledge of the destination was based on his own direct experience of slavery and—more abstractly—on his deep understanding of what was entailed by really following his society's basic principles (constitutional, moral, and religious). As a captain, he managed to create unity and purpose among the crew by the use of rhetoric informed (again) by his understanding of their own principles.

The leader is not self-interested, but concerned with the well-being of the followers (N2).

Like Plato's navigator, Douglass truly cared for other people, the passengers on board the ship; he was fighting not only for his freedom but also for liberating each and every slave in the country. Having officially become a free man in 1846, he didn't stop but continued fighting to liberate all the enslaved men, women, and children. Also, he not only wrote about the need to liberate enslaved people in his speeches, newspaper articles, and books, but he actively helped fugitive slaves to get to safe places, get accommodated, find jobs, and start new lives.

This commitment can be linked to a wider attitude about power and oppression:

War, slavery, injustice and oppression, and the idea that might makes right have been uppermost in all such governments, and the weak, for

whose protection governments are ostensibly created, have had practically no rights which the strong have felt bound to respect.[21]

This rejection of the 'might-is-right' philosophy echoes Plato's position
in Book 1 of the *Republic*, the very place where he uses the comparison
with the sea-captain to refute Thrasymachus' claim that leaders should
oppress and exploit their people out of self-interest. Douglass would have
agreed strongly with Plato that the leader is concerned solely with the
well-being of their followers, whoever they may be.

The navigator is not afraid to stand apart from the crowd (N5)

To be an abolition agitator is simply to be one who dares to think for
himself, who goes beyond the mass of mankind in promoting the cause of
righteousness, who honestly and earnestly speaks out his soul's conviction,
regardless of the smiles or frowns of men, leaving the pure flame of truth
to burn up whatever hay, wood and stubble it may find in its way. To be
such an one is the deepest and sincerest wish of my heart . . . .[22]

Douglass faced the problem of persuasion: his appeals to put an end to
slavery and grant equal rights to all Americans were at first badly
received—not only in the South, but also by many in the North. His
ideas were revolutionary at that time, especially for the country that had
witnessed slavery for over two hundred years and where huge amounts of
wealth were generated through the suppression of minorities.

A postscript: the *North Star*

In 1847, Douglass set up his own anti-slavery newspaper and called it the
North Star. At the time, the most obvious point of the title was that slaves
escaping from the South would use the north star as a guide for making
their way to the Northern States or to Canada. But there was also a more
philosophical significance to the title: it suggests the existence of moral

principles, as enunciated by the paper, acting as a guiding light through turbulent times. And, in one of the 1848 editions (8 September), Douglass included a poem entitled 'The North Star', by George G. Abbott. It begins 'Lo! the Northern Star is beaming/ With a new and glorious light', and its third stanza reads:

> How the mariner, 'mid the surging
> Of the stormy waves and dark,
> Hails the Northern Star emerging
> From the clouds above his bark.
> 'Tis the trust that faileth never,
> And the light that never dies—
> 'Tis his beacon-star forever,
> Beaming in the Arctic skies.

To judge from his work as editor, we can be confident that Douglass would think the navigator a very appropriate model of leadership.

Arch McGill and navigating the choppy waters at AT&T

Like Plato's ship of state, the ship of the corporation faces dangers from competitors, uncertainty, its own stakeholders' varied interests, and a lack of leadership. Indeed, often the conflicts among members of an executive leadership team are the most difficult to resolve. Unlike Plato's ideal ship there are often many 'leaders' who disagree, making a navigator's job very difficult. Corporate navigators or captains must have a special expertise to steer through these troubled and dangerous waters even as boards of directors and top management teams may lose their will to adapt to a changing environment, especially when such change may lead to a lessening of profits, a cutting of the dividend, or questioning from Wall Street and other business pundits. The need to keep an external focus may well wilt under the pressure of seemingly competing short-term goals. Corporate leaders must also inspire discipline and loyalty, made more difficult under the conditions where there is a faltering lack of commitment to the destination. Arch McGill was one such navigator who was ultimately thrown overboard.

Charting a new course (N1); the need for expertise (N3)

In the 1970s the writing was on the wall. AT&T, and the entire telecommunications industry, had to change, and there was wide agreement that the change needed to be extensive. The problem was that there was a great deal of disagreement on the best route to change, the speed of the change, and whether the current employees could be retrained to manage the change. As the world was moving towards more digital integration, the differences between computing technology and telephony were disappearing. While the computer industry was fiercely competitive, the telephone industry consisted mostly of monopolies. To complete their voyage from a monopoly mindset to one that was more appropriate to a competitive business, AT&T's Board of Directors and senior executives hired Archie McGill, who had become the youngest Vice President ever at IBM, to lead the change. While the senior management and board of AT&T knew they needed to change, they had little idea about what the change would actually involve or how difficult it would be.

McGill's job was going to be very tough and in fact he faced enormous resistance from day one. His style was a brash and open dialogue that was very much contrary to the even-keeled and bureaucratic Bell culture of the time. His marketing expertise, honed at IBM, then recognized as one of the top marketing companies in the world, consisted of very different skills from those that existed at AT&T. In a monopoly, marketing was virtually non-existent. The emphasis was on making sure that the network of telephony worked and was affordable. Equipment and copper wire to tie it together often depreciated over a forty-year time span, making 'universal service' affordable to all, and virtually ignoring any specific needs and desires of real customers and other stakeholders. This was especially relevant to large business customers. With the advent of technological change, computer companies could install switching equipment that was virtually identical to telephone switches, and they could customize the equipment with software tailored to specific customer needs. IBM, McGill's career training ground, was especially adept at understanding customer needs and desires. IBM's sales process was adept at handling different sets of customer needs especially for business customers, and McGill was needed to bring this expertise to AT&T.

To some followers, the leader's expertise may seem ill suited to the task (N4).

Business pundits Alan Wilkins and Nigel Bristow have argued that long-time AT&T employees found it difficult to accept McGill's approach and expertise, which was based in marketing rather than engineering and manufacturing. The result was a struggle for control of the company:[23]

> McGill was seen by many as the antithesis of a 'Bell-shaped man' because of his 'combative, adversarial style'. Moreover, he was known as an innovator.
>
> A little over three years later, *The Wall Street Journal* reported strong evidence that marketing executives and manufacturing veterans were locked in a power struggle for control of the company, and that manufacturers had gained the upper hand. Manufacturers, not marketers, moved into the corporation's pivotal jobs under a top-level reorganization in December 1983, consolidating their hold on strategy, new product introductions, and day-to-day operations. Three of AT&T's senior marketing executives left the company during the previous six months, along with several other marketing managers.

While being outward-facing, the leader must be also be inward-facing and create a unified sense of purpose on board (N6).

McGill had a number of external stakeholders to take on the voyage to a more competitive marketplace, chief among them, customers. Additionally, there were substantial regulatory barriers to AT&T that other competitors did not experience. During almost the entirety of McGill's time at AT&T, the company was constantly negotiating with Federal and State regulators to both relax requirements on AT&T and to subject other competitors to similar regulations. McGill knew that the competitive vision for AT&T required massive investment in both people (who needed a new set of skills) and equipment (both manufacturing and research and development). However, AT&T was seen as a safe dividend stock, so that shareholders continued to expect a steady flow of good returns that was incompatible with the need for large strategic investments. What was necessary was a focus on external stakeholders. What actually happened was an internal power struggle among the senior management team.

Ultimately, McGill may have been a great navigator, but he failed as a captain to instil the right degree of unity and discipline on board ship. Rather than inspiring internal discipline to overcome the substantial obstacles facing AT&T and McGill, his personal style, perhaps honed at IBM, created the opposite and fractured the strong culture that existed at AT&T. Employees defined themselves as either pro-McGill, or deeply sceptical of his enterprise. The resulting power struggle handicapped the ability of the ship to sail on its necessary course. Perhaps if McGill had been completely in charge of AT&T he would have had more success, but he was unable to inspire others to follow his course, especially others outside his direct organization.

Once AT&T had agreed to break up the company in 1982, divesting the local Bell Companies, perhaps McGill would have an easier time navigating the necessary changes, as his resulting organization focused on equipment sales to large customers. However, the cooperation required across the company, as well as a number of competing internal organizations that had similar functions, all served to make persuading stakeholders to follow McGill's path extremely difficult. And he ultimately resigned after being passed over for what he saw was a key position to bring conflicting parts of the company together.

While McGill's tenure of ten years was controversial, he accomplished a great deal in terms of changing the culture at AT&T. A great number of people became fiercely loyal to him, though he also engendered at least an equal number of detractors who were appalled at his leadership approach. Finally after ten years, McGill's job was eliminated and he decided to leave, all while the Chairman, Charles Marshall, insisted that he wanted McGill to stay. Many concluded that he would be replaced by a more traditional AT&T executive and that the culture change McGill began would not last. Others opined that McGill had just run out of steam with the executive team.

'There is a time for a dynamic leader to shake people up, but there is a time for that dynamic leader to step aside,' said one former American Bell official, who asked not to be named. 'If the revolution doesn't end after a while, the rhetoric becomes meaningless.'[24]

Like Plato's navigator McGill was focused on how to get AT&T where it knew it needed to be. His methods for getting the company to change to a more competitive culture were controversial and somewhat unpopular. Eventually the 'demos' prevailed. McGill was unable to solve Plato's problem of persuasion, except for the loyal team that he had built. The inability to lead the large-scale change necessary to meet the shifting landscape haunted AT&T for decades and the company no longer exists as anything but a brand, bought and used, ironically, by one of its former subsidiaries.

Notes

1. The navigator model underlies the etymology of our word 'governor', which comes from the Latin *gubernator*. This was originally a naval term meaning 'steersman', but then became used for political leadership. In turn, the Latin is related to the Greek *kubernētēs*, which had the same double meaning.
2. Skemp (1987) 204 n. 1 refers back to the Greek poet Alcaeus (600 BCE), and Hunter (2012) 70–80 gives a detailed account of the ship of state image in Greek literature before Plato's time.
3. The concern the captain shows for his passengers is also mentioned in a later work, the *Statesman* (296e), which we discuss in Chapter 8.
4. Keyt (2006) 91–2.
5. We shall refine this point in Appendix 1.
6. Hence the reference to the use of drugs, a metaphor already used by the orator Gorgias when boasting about the power of rhetoric to manipulate the emotions of the audience. See Gorgias, *Encomium of Helen* 14, with Keyt (2006) 196.
7. Keyt (2006) 192. In English, this star is sometimes called the 'lodestar', 'lode' being the Middle English for 'course', and related to our word 'lead'. According to the Merriam-Webster dictionary, the lodestar is the 'star that leads'.
8. On Douglass' influence on Lincoln, see Koehn (2017) 169–70.
9. Koehn (2017) 256.
10. Koehn (2017) 257–8.
11. Koehn (2017) 253.
12. Koehn (2017) 238.

13. Koehn (2017) 276.
14. At 517a he briefly acknowledges the possibility of good rhetoric, although his focus in the work is on its bad form.
15. In the *Republic* itself he is prepared to use words to arouse people's shame or even fear into living more ethical lives (e.g. Book 9 588b–592b), just as we see Douglass doing below ('The existence of slavery in this country...'). The same applies even more in his last work, the *Laws*. See Scott (2020) 56 and 232–7.
16. Koehn (2017) 251.
17. Koehn (2017) 256–7.
18. Foner (1945) 51–2.
19. Foner (1945) 86.
20. On Douglass as a philosopher, see Sundstrom (2017).
21. Foner (1945) 88.
22. Foner (1945) 54.
23. Wilkins and Bristow (1987) 221.
24. Pollack (1983).

4

The Artist

Plato

Overview

One of the most famous speeches of the twentieth century contains the words 'I have a dream'. The speaker, of course, was Martin Luther King, Jr, one of the century's greatest leaders: not one who wielded political power in the regular sense, but someone who led a movement that profoundly changed his society, and also led directly to his own death. Perhaps we have another model of leadership here: the dreamer. A couple of things would stand out in this model. First, this is someone who tries to mould the world to fit their values—the complete opposite of the demagogue. Those were people who take their values from what the world already believes; everything they do is meant to conform to society's pre-existent expectations. By contrast, the dreamer turns this around: society must now fit their dream—whatever it takes.

The model of the dreamer also suggests a degree of detachment. We sometimes think of the dreamer as unrealistic—a romantic, with their head in the clouds. But detachment can be an advantage for the leader: they detach themselves from the pressure to conform, to compromise their ideals to fit so-called realities. This detachment allows the leader to question whether these 'realities' are indeed unchangeable facts of political life. This in turn opens up the possibility of realizing their dream.

Plato never actually talks of the leader as a dreamer, but he does offer us something quite close: the leader as artist. This model comes fairly soon after the ship of state, at *Republic* Book 6, 500c–501c, when Socrates returns to describing the true leader, not the debased version found in contemporary Athens. The true leader, he says, is like an artist looking to a model—a model of justice, order, and harmony. First, he tries to impose this on himself, and only then on society. He treats the state like a tablet (we would say a slate or a canvas) and looks to his model as he tries to create an image of it in the characters of his citizens and in the institutions of the state.

Like the model of the dreamer, this could not be further away from the demagogue. There the leader looks only to what the demos believes; here the artist looks to something beyond, a vision, and takes that as the starting point for political leadership.

The model of the artist also epitomizes detachment. Plato's artist looks beyond his actual surroundings to find his model. (Here we are reminded of the navigator who is mocked for being a star-gazer.) What he seeks to realize in political life is something possibly quite remote from it, just as the great reformers sought to create something quite unlike the political realities of their time.[1] Like the dreamer, the ability to detach oneself from social convention, not to be pressured by what others just accept as inevitable social reality, is essential if one is truly to change society. Plato also characterizes the artist as a somewhat lonely figure. Although in the ideal state there will be a group of guardians, here the leader is presented as working on his own. This reinforces the notion of detachment (which is also part of the dreamer model: a dream is essentially something you have on your own). You cannot always rely on the solidarity of friends to help you pursue your vision.

The artist's model

If the leader is like an artist, what is his model? Plato talks of him looking towards 'natural justice' and trying to replicate in the state (501b). In Plato's time it was common to make a distinction between two kinds of justice: natural and conventional.[2] Conventional justice is a term to cover conceptions of justice formed by society, where certain norms have taken root for historical reasons, especially when certain interest groups have managed to instil those norms and create an ideology that suits their interests.[3]

The artist stands aside from whatever conventions have been established by society and transcends them. What sort of justice did Plato think this might involve? In the same passage he talks of the artist looking to a model that typifies order (*kosmos*, 500c)—something we encountered with the doctor model. On Plato's view of justice, the citizens live in ordered relations among each other: each contributing their share to the common pool and taking from it according to their need. Their contribution is determined by what talents or abilities they have. There is a balance here, and achieving it brings about relations of friendship in society. It is not equality exactly, but does involve a kind of fairness. This, he believes, will create unity and a common sense of purpose among the citizens.[4]

As ever, we have to think how this model can be transferred beyond its Platonic context, and indeed beyond politics. We shall of course be doing this when we turn to the case studies, but it is worth pausing to see in general terms how this can be done. Obviously, it is not necessary to use Plato's own account of natural justice. But what is essential to the model is the adoption of some ideal that transcends what many people currently take to be inescapable. It involves breaking away, an effort of imagination or 'vision' (hence the connection with the dreamer). It may be a personal vision. Put like this, the model is easily applicable to other political leaders (such as King); it has obvious relevance to the charity sector: the leader of the organization has adopted a specific goal, typically something that contrasts with the current state of play. Their vision may stand in stark contrast to the impoverished state of the world that they seek to change. But the vision does not have to be a moral one: it could be cultural or technological (as our two case studies below will demonstrate). The important thing is that the leader tries to reshape their world, be it political, cultural, moral, or industrial, in a way that breaks away from the constraints by which conventional wisdom thinks us bound.

There is another point to mention, which is fundamental to Plato's conception of the artist, and it concerns personal integrity. Before the artist has even thought of becoming engaged in politics, he makes it a priority to impose the order (*kosmos*) of his model on himself. We saw in the case of the doctor that balance and harmony can exist both in the individual psyche and in a state more widely. Here, Plato goes out of his way to stress how the artist looks at his model and straightaway tries to make his own character resemble it as far as he can (500c–d). Then, if he is compelled for some reason to play a political role, he will do the same for the state and its citizens. This is a strong account of personal integrity: literally a 'wholeness'—a unity between inner and outer. By contrast, a leader who imposes a set of values on others, while secretly flouting them in their own life, is just a hypocrite. This kind of gap simply cannot exist where the leader is like an artist in Plato's sense: if they impose austerity on others, they themselves live like a monk; if they force others to work long hours, they are themselves workaholics, and so on. In fact, they only expect others to follow the ideal because they live it so thoroughly themselves; hypocrisy could never come into play in the first place.

Wiping the tablet clean

So far, Plato's model sounds admirable: the political artist wishes to realize an ideal of harmony, justice, and friendship in the state. But now look more closely at the way he describes the activity of the artist-leaders in relation to their citizens:

> They will begin by taking the state and the characters of the people within it, like a tablet. First, they will wipe it clean. This is no easy task. But whether easy or not, this will be the difference between them and every other legislator: they will have nothing to do either with individual or state, and not inscribe any laws, until they have either found, or themselves made, a clean surface.[5]

There is something chilling about this. What is the political analogue for wiping the tablet (or slate) clean? To answer this question, we need to look more closely at the 'ideal' state, as described in the *Republic*.

Plato's state is all about harmony and unity among its citizens. He goes to extraordinary lengths to ensure this. For one thing, he expects a very high degree of fellow-feeling from all the citizens, especially the auxiliaries and the guardians (Book 5, 462a–d). The desire to pursue the common good is paramount. This lies behind some of his most extreme political proposals. To prevent the rulers misusing their power in order to amass wealth, he bans them from owning private property: they will live austere lives, with only so much as they need (Book 3, 416d–Book 4, 417b). In an even more radical move, he abolishes the family, at least for guardians and auxiliaries. They will have children, but their children will be put into a public creche at birth, and the parents will not know who their children are. The objective is to avoid the 'privatization of feelings', and spread the sense of family among the state at large. If close-knit families and clans were allowed to develop among these classes, they would become rivals to each other, disrupting the unity and harmony of the state (Book 5, 457c–561e).

In pursuit of the same ends, Plato is also radical about education. The roots of disharmony and disunity in a state lie in greed and excessive self-assertion among its citizens. Any such tendencies need to be checked from an early age. Particularly important is the type of culture in which the citizens are raised. Stories and myths provide children with role models. In Greek culture these included heroes (such as Achilles) indulging their appetites and their emotions (e.g. fear, or anger in petty disputes); such stories even represented gods doing the same. Once imbibed by children, these stories played a pivotal role in shaping their characters. Plato decided the only solution was radical censorship of the arts, or rather, popular culture—and not just the content of the stories and myths promulgated, but even the music to which they were set. In their place he was prepared to create new myths that he thought would be beneficial to the citizens, even if, in some cases, these myths were what he called 'noble lies' (Book 3, 414b–415d).

So the ideal state would have been a truly radical—and unsettling—vision. If it was ever to come into existence, many citizens of prior states, used to their own ways of living, would find it wholly unpalatable. Hence they might have to be barred from it. Plato admits as much when he says, quite casually, that the best way to set up his state would be to expel everyone over the age of 10 and 'send them out into the fields' (Book 7, 540e–541a). Furthermore, upbringing aside, some people might be morally incapable of living, let alone flourishing, in the ideal state. The extraordinary level of public-spiritedness, altruism, and self-sacrifice would strain their nature too far. It is to meet this problem that Plato devises his very extreme programme of education. But there will surely be some people who will never be able to reach this level. They will also have to be 'rubbed out'.

All of this is connected to the artist image. Plato's artist has a vision in which he has total faith. He imposes it on his materials, erasing what was there before, wiping the slate clean. But, translated into political terms, this suggests a compete ruthlessness in regard to the pre-existent beliefs and values of his subjects. If they do not kowtow, they will be removed.

Karl Popper, Plato, and totalitarianism

As you might expect, Plato has been widely attacked for this aspect of his thought; some have even accused him of totalitarianism. His most famous critic was Karl Popper, who published *The Open Society and Its Enemies* in the late 1940s. It was set against the experience of totalitarian regimes in the mid-twentieth century, both fascist and communist, and it sent out a stark message: not only were thinkers like Plato deeply authoritarian, they provided actual regimes with the intellectual authority to go about their totalitarian business.[6] It was time, so Popper argues, for the likes of Plato to face the intellectual auditors.

Popper was unremitting in his attack. He saw the decades before Plato's birth as an extraordinary period of creativity, free-thinking, and innovation. (We mentioned some of the achievements of ancient Athens in Chapter 1.) As a free-thinking intellectual, Socrates was a hero in this story. But reflecting on the disasters that had befallen Athens, Plato— according to Popper—tried to turn the clock back to an older aristocratic era, which required deference to a strict code of values and a resistance to innovation. The *Republic* is in effect just a recreation of this older order. Popper objects especially to the stratification of the class system in Plato's state, the absolute power vested in its guardians, the extraordinarily repressive censorship of the arts, and the assault on the individual: the state is seen as some kind of super-person, an entity with interests that transcend the interests and rights of any one person. The leaders are therefore permitted, even obliged, to restrict, regulate, and punish individuals and steamroll their liberties. All the good work of Athenian democracy was to be undone.

The image of the artist who wipes the slate clean in the interests of imposing his vision on the state is grist to Popper's mill.[7] The ruthlessness with which the leader will expunge any hint of opposition in pursuit of the realization of his goal seems of a piece with the image. And in the light of the worst examples of totalitarian states, Popper did strike a chord. Whether they were fascists or communists, what was chilling was the way they pursued their political vision with utter indifference to the interests and rights of individuals, even their lives.

Popper's work certainly caused a spike of interest in the *Republic*. (You can literally see it on Google Ngram.) He also generated his fair share of hostility. Many thought it outrageous to lump Plato together with the totalitarians of the twentieth century, and in one sense they had a point. Before one makes such comparisons, one should see what kind of ideal a leader is trying to realize. Maybe you can call Plato a totalitarian, but since his ideal was all about social harmony, justice, and civic friendship, he must stand at the very opposite end of the spectrum from a twentieth-century dictator. Another line of defence, which tries to circumvent this problem altogether, is to claim that he never intended his ideal state as a blueprint to be realized in practice; it is merely an ideal to which we might approximate in some respects, but not others.[8] Such approaches find favour in some quarters, though not all, and many readers will remain concerned about the charge of totalitarianism.

A compromise: the leader as architect

If the artist model raises awkward questions when applied to political leadership, the problems may be much less acute when we move from politics to other arenas. In business, it is acceptable to make people redundant if they do not fit the new vision: no one has a human right to a particular job, and employment law is used to ensure employees have the right redundancy arrangements in place.[9] Nonetheless, it can be imprudent for the leader of a company or other kinds of organization to wipe the slate clean: they might need to retain talented or experienced employees. So a balance needs to be struck. When a business leader tries to 'wipe the slate clean' disaster is the usual outcome, as the remaining employees are usually frightened, experience survivor's guilt, and are not really committed to the new vision.

So let's end with a variation on the model. As we have just said, some scholars think Plato never actually intended to wipe the slate clean; he was merely offering an ideal from which we might select some features to imitate. Taking a cue from this approach, think of the leader as an architect. Good architects are artists: they may have an aesthetic vision that they seek to instantiate in certain materials. But there is a lot more for them to take into account than if they were painters or sculptors, working on their own. There are the practical requirements of the customer, which intrude far more into the work of the architect than any other artist. The materials, and the effects of the environment on them, have to be taken into account. Costs will affect the project, often in ways that could not have been predicted at the start, and may force a change of plan and design. In any modern context, there are planning considerations to be taken into account, requiring negotiations with all the relevant authorities and stakeholders. In short, here is an art form that has to compromise: something will remain of the original vision, but much else is the result of accommodation. This seems a more apt way of using the artist model in most contexts. In business the idea of the architect is important as the architect has a vision, but realizes that the elements of that vision must be found in the way the company actually can change, and that includes many of the current stakeholder relationships.

The artist. Key principles:

A1. The leader is a bit like a dreamer with a vision, trying to transcend what is currently thought to be possible.

A2. The leader epitomizes detachment.

A3. The model requires authenticity or integrity, as opposed to hypocrisy.

A4. The leader may have to 'wipe the slate clean'. (Compromise: the leader as architect)

Case studies

There are many examples of Plato's idea of the leader as artist, since vision is such an important element of leadership. We will consider two: Elon Musk, CEO of Tesla Motors, and, in the political realm, Ataturk, the father of modern Turkey. Each illustrates some of the strengths and weaknesses of the model.

Elon Musk, visionary CEO

Elon Musk has been called 'a genius', 'evil', 'quirky', and many other names throughout his career. While Plato's artist is a moral visionary, Musk is a technological one, though with profound moral consequences. He was a co-founder of a successful and innovative Internet payments company, PayPal, founder of SpaceX, a company devoted to space exploration, and CEO of Tesla Motors, a leading electric vehicle and solar battery company.

Musk the dreamer and visionary (A1)

Throughout, he has been driven by his vision of a better world. In particular, he has long been convinced that we must shoot for the stars to survive as a species. He said:

> I read a lot of Science Fiction as a kid and tried to think about the future and the problems that needed to be solved to make it a bright future, and I tried to get involved in that. I don't create companies for the sake of creating companies, but to get things done.[10]

Musk created his first company when he was 10 years old, a computer game called Blastar, which he offered for sale.[11] He sold his first major company, Zip@ for $307 million in cash and $34 million in stock options. Long an unconventional thinker, Musk has proposed inventing technological marvels that would put a human colony on Mars. He has used his company Space-X to begin to privatize space travel in preparation for such a colony. He has proposed a series of deep tunnels as a new method of transcontinental travel and has begun on a smaller scale in California. His satellite company, Starlink, has begun the process of putting thousands of small satellites into orbit that can serve as a worldwide Internet provider and connecter. And his automobile company, Tesla, has pioneered electric vehicles in terms of design and performance, putting the efforts of traditional automobile companies to shame. As a part of Tesla

Motors, he has begun to reinvent batteries so that the charge for electric cars lasts far longer than currently, acquiring SolarCity Corp. The scope of these 'visions' is breath-taking, and yet, as you can imagine, Musk has been far from a welcomed figure in many arenas.

His current vision for the electric car industry is comprehensive and wide ranging according to author K. Connors:

1. Create stunning solar roofs with seamlessly integrated battery storage.
2. Expand the electric vehicle product line to address all major segments.
3. Develop a self-driving capability that is ten times safer than manual via massive fleet learning.
4. Enable your car to make money for you when you aren't using it.

Detachment (A2); authenticity (A3)

Musk has long relied on his ability to craft a vision and to think logically, if grandly,[12] about the problems he believes we need to solve. He is not wedded to traditional problem formulation or thinking. He believes that, if we use our intellect and our creativity, there are not many problems that will be intractable:

> I don't believe in process. In fact, when I interview a potential employee and he or she says that 'it's all about the process', I see that as a bad sign. The problem is that at a lot of big companies process becomes a substitute for thinking. You're encouraged to behave like a little gear in a complex machine. Frankly, it allows you to keep people who aren't that smart, who aren't that creative.[13]

Indeed, he has said many times that he hopes to die on Mars, as he delivers his vision for humanity to become a multi-planet species. While Musk's vision demands a lot from his employees, he also works just as hard or harder than they do. Former employees have said that Tesla is a great place to learn, but that eventually you get burned out, the hours are so long and the pressure is so great. Musk has often complained that he just doesn't have enough time in each day, as he brings this conglomeration of visions to fruition. However, unlike many leaders in business Musk clearly inhabits the vision with all of himself, exactly in the way that Plato suggested artists do.

Musk's iconoclastic view has often gotten him into trouble as it has set him at odds with more conventional thinkers, including some of his Wall Street investors and regulators. When he is certain that he is correct he doesn't let rules, conventional thinking, or regulations stand in the way. Musk got into trouble with the SEC for tweeting about whether Tesla should be publicly traded or not:

> I don't create trouble just for the hell of it. . . . I think there are important things in the world that need to get done. Some people don't like change, but you need to embrace change if the alternative is disaster.[14]

Central to Musk's success has been the idea of feedback, not for the sake of accommodating himself to other people's opinions, but to improve the artist's vision and figure out how to realize it in a better way. He says:

> I think it's very important to have a feedback loop, where you're constantly thinking about what you've done and how you could be doing it better. I think that's the single best piece of advice: constantly think about how you could be doing things better and questioning yourself.[15]

The leader as architect (A4)?

Musk has not 'wiped the slate clean' in Plato's sense, so perhaps he is more like an architect. But he does resemble the artist in being adept at unconventional thinking about traditional problems in the automobile industry, and in taking completely new approaches to issues such as transportation by digging massive tunnels. When the artist is called by his vision, it doesn't matter that the chances for success may well be very small. As Musk says, 'When something is important enough, you do it even if the odds are not in your favor'.[16]

Ataturk and Modern Turkey

In the political arena, a great example of the leader as artist is Ataturk (1881–1938), founder of the contemporary Turkish state. After the defeat of the Ottoman empire in the First World War, he led the movement for the independence of Turkey and, once in power, dramatically reformed the country. In 1934, due to his achievements, the Turkish Parliament granted him the name Ataturk, 'Father of the Turks' (his original name was Mustafa Kemal).

Transcending what is currently thought to be inescapable: Turkification (A1)

Like an artist who wipes the slate clean, Ataturk ruthlessly wiped out the old beliefs and traditions of the Ottoman empire in order to build a completely new country. He had a clear vision of a more modern Turkey, and he pushed that vision forward regardless of the opposition. He said:

> Greatness means that you won't try and please anyone, that you won't deceive anyone, that you will discern the true ideal for the country, that you will strive for it, that everyone will turn against you and will try to make you change your course. You will have no means to resist. They will pile up endless obstacles in your path and you will surmount them, knowing all the time that you are not great, but little, weak, resourceless, a mere nothing, and that no one will come to your aid. And if after that they call you great, you'll laugh at them.[17]

Ataturk eliminated the previous state order, where power in the country belonged to the Sultan. He inaugurated the Turkish republic, a secular state where religion became separated from both the educational system and political governance. He made primary education compulsory and free, and opened thousands of new schools all over the country. He reformed the state criminal and civil codes to be more in line with European standards. He replaced the Arabic with the Latin alphabet, and purged the Turkish language of a number of words with Arabic or

Persian roots. He radically changed the way the Turkish people dressed by encouraging them to try more European styles. He granted voting rights to women, far ahead of many Western countries. He eliminated feudal titles and introduced last names. His role was critical in the creation of national banks and industrial production. The list of Ataturk's radical reforms can go on and on. All this paved the path to the creation of modern Turkey—one of the most developed countries in the Middle East.

Like Plato's leadership model of the artist, Ataturk was a person with a clear vision. Even as a student, he shared anti-monarchical views that caused him to be arrested right after graduation. After his release a few months later, he devoted his life to fighting for Turkey's independence and making Turkish society embrace more democratic, progressive changes. He saw that the Ottoman empire was built on old traditions that were very often not applicable to the modern world and prevented the country from making much needed progress.

Detachment (A2); wiping the slate clean (A4)

With such a strong vision of the artist we expect some aloofness or detachment from social conventions. Ataturk experienced such detachment from an early age:

> Since my childhood I have always preferred to be alone and independent, and that is how I have always lived. I have another trait: I have never had any patience with any advice or admonition which my mother—my father died very early—my sister or any of my closest relatives pressed on me according to their lights. People who live in the midst of their families know well that they are never short of innocent and sincere warnings from left and right. There are only two ways of dealing with them. You either obey or you ignore all these warnings and admonitions. I believe that neither way is right. How could you obey? To take heed of the warnings of a mother, twenty or twenty-five years my senior, wouldn't that have meant retreating into the past? But to rebel would have upset the heart and mind of a mother of whose virtue, good faith and superior womanly qualities I was convinced. That wasn't right either.[18]

Yet there were also some negative side effects of Ataturk's wiping the slate clean. During his leadership, an unconditional priority was given to ethnic Turks, and all other minorities, such as Kurds, Jews, Greeks, and Armenians, were suppressed. The minorities were not allowed to speak their own language, occupy state positions, or serve in the army. All protests against 'turkification'—Ataturk's initiative to create a homogeneous nation—were ruthlessly repressed. Turkey today suffers from the fragmentation of ethnic minorities and the independence movements that have inevitably arisen.

So, wiping the slate clean has its darker side, particularly in the enormous amount of oppression that has been carried out in the name of 'visionary leadership'. While Plato may have assumed that the artist-leaders in the *Republic* had a common moral core and set of values, unfortunately, the modern world has shown us in a graphic way that this is not always the case. Also, it should be pointed out that Ataturk's reforms in Turkey have produced a schizoid republic, with President Erdogan being able to gain power on the strength of his promises to overturn much of Ataturk's secularizing legacy. Still, Turkey is far more secularized and Europeanized than many of its neighbours; so it is true that some of Ataturk's legacy has endured.

Integrity (A3)

When setting out Plato's model of the artist, we stressed the importance of the personal qualities of the leader. In Ataturk's case, this is an important theme. First, there is evidence of his integrity. When he was a junior officer posted to Damascus, Ataturk witnessed other officers corruptly enriching themselves at the expense of the local Druze in Hawran. He refused to share in the spoils, and urged his friend and fellow junior officer Mürfit Özdeş to report the episode, asking him:

'Do you want to be today's man or tomorrow's?' 'Tomorrow's, of course', replied Mürfit. 'Then you can't take the gold. I too haven't taken it, nor can I ever.'[19]

Similarly, it is related that, when his commanding officer proposed to falsify a report to the Sultan (Abdülhamit), Ataturk upbraided him, saying 'I'll have no part in a fraud'.[20]

Even during periods of flux demanding considerable politicking, such as in 1918 (after the Ottoman empire signed its armistice with the Allies), Ataturk always kept his artist's vision at the front of his mind. In an interview in November 1918, he opined that:

> A nation [i.e. the Turkish nation] must be strong in spirit, knowledge, science and morals. Military strength comes last...today it is not enough to have arms in hand in order to take one's place in the world as a human being.

In the interpretation of Andrew Mango, Ataturk's biographer: 'Always present in Ataturk's mind was the ultimate objective of securing Turkey's place in the community of civilized nations.'[21] Another historian, Patrick Kinross, cites further evidence of his detachment and singlemindedness:

> Once, when a friend proposed a gesture to public opinion, he [Ataturk] flashed back at him scornfully, 'I don't act for public opinion. I act for the nation and for my own satisfaction'.[22]

Again, on the darker side, it is worth noting that, like so many other visionaries, Ataturk often domineered people into submitting to his vision and his authority. One such fellow Turkish nationalist who was subject to Ataturk's wilfulness commented afterwards that 'Mustafa Kemal Paşa's [Ataturk's] domineering character had been obvious all along'.[23]

Notes

1. It is no coincidence that the artist is presented as someone detached from his state. In the passage from Book 7 where he sets out the image of the artist, 500a–501c, Plato is defending his proposal for philosopher-rulers, which we mentioned in the previous chapter. He is aware that most people will think the

proposal absurd, not least because of the other-worldly image that philosophers have: how could they possibly be effective rulers? Here he takes the bull by the horns and argues that the very feature for which we mock the philosopher, detachment, is actually a qualification for leadership. We discuss the idea of philosophers as rulers in Appendix 1. See also Appendix 2.

2. The distinction is discussed by Lane (2014) 41–52.

3. This idea has already appeared in *Republic* Book 1, 338c–339a, when Thrasymachus proposes that justice is simply the 'interest of the stronger'. What he means is that whoever is in power will make laws to suit their interests. For instance, in a society dominated by the wealthy (in Plato's terms, an 'oligarchy') the rulers establish laws requiring a high property qualification for holding public office, claiming such laws are just. But this 'justice' is merely conventional, lacking any foundation in nature; it has no authority over and above what a particular interest group happens to want or believe. Natural justice, by contrast, would have this kind of independence: like scientific laws, the norms of natural justice would hold whatever human beings happen to believe to be true.

4. Plato has another way of characterizing the artist's model, in terms of his more esoteric 'theory of forms': the artist looks to the essence or archetype of justice, rather as a geometer might look to the perfect circle as opposed to the imperfect approximations manifested in the physical world. We discuss this theory in Appendix 2.

5. 501a, trans. Jowett (1871) II, modified.

6. Volume 1 was devoted entirely to Plato; the second discussed Hegel and Marx.

7. Popper discusses the artist passage in this context in (1962) I 165–8. More recent discussions of his critique can be found in Pappas (1995) 201–11 and Taylor (1999).

8. On this kind of approach, see Blackburn (2006) 54–8.

9. This is related to a more general point we made in the Introduction: not only are many of Plato's claims in the *Republic* applicable outside of politics, sometimes they are actually more plausible in non-political contexts, especially business.

10. Butcher (2012).

11. Connors (2018).

12. Plato expects a true leader to have grandness of vision at *Rep.* Book 6, 486a.

13. Anderson (2012).

14. Stern (2011).

15. Ulanoff (2012).

16. Pelley (2012).

17. Mango (2004) 74.

18. Mango (2004) 35–6.

19. Mango (2004) 58. This story is narrated by Ataturk's adoptive daughter Afet, and so might be apocryphal.
20. Mango (2004) 59. Again, the narrator is someone sympathetic to Ataturk.
21. Mango (2004) 219.
22. Kinross (2001) xvii.
23. Mango (2004) 254.

5

The Teacher

Plato

Overview

When Barack Obama was called 'Professor in Chief', it was not intended as a compliment. Probably the main point of the sneer was that he lacked the backbone to be an effective leader. He is no commander, his critics wanted to say.[1] But, aside from that, many would raise an eyebrow at the idea of a leader as professor, teacher, or educator. Applied to politicians, the model might even sound ridiculous: what have that motley crew of individuals got to teach us? If anything, it ought to be the other way around. But once you put the polemics to one side, and think about leadership not just in politics but beyond, the idea should attract less hostility. A teacher is supposed to have some sort of expertise, which we surely expect in a leader; and it seems right that they should find a way of communicating their expertise to others. Also, there is something positive in the model when it comes to the relation between the leader and the people they lead. Admittedly, it can seem patronizing to think of the rest of us as pupils awaiting the instruction of the leader. But a lot depends on how you understand the nature of teaching or education. Don't think of it as simple-minded instruction or rote learning; think instead of one person who has some expertise trying to bring others towards a similar level of understanding. Great teachers treat their students with intellectual respect. They do not patronize them, but seek to provide good reasons for accepting the conclusions they themselves believe. They are open to question and interrogation from the student; they are honest and intellectually generous. Above all, they do not indoctrinate or manipulate their students into believing anything irrationally.

So it is possible to present the model of leader as educator in a better light, even if it begins to sound a bit idealistic. Not every aspect of leadership can be captured in this way, but at least it shows what a leader ought to be doing in certain contexts. It puts the emphasis on the right kind of communication.[2] This point has acquired urgency in the current pandemic. Consider the question of what model of leadership is most required just now. Of course we want doctors in the literal sense but, in terms of leadership, perhaps the navigator would be a more obvious candidate: someone who can take us where we need to be, while keeping everyone united in the sacrifices that have to be made. But as well as the navigator, some would say we want a teacher. Many have stressed the need for politicians to communicate more openly with the citizens on whom they seek to impose restrictions. Here, for example, is an extract from an article written in *The Times*, entitled 'Lack of clarity over coronavirus lockdown exit strategy treats public "like children": senior Tories angry at cabinet silence on exit plan':

> Tobias Ellwood, chairman of the defence select committee, said: 'Communication is critical in keeping people on board. You need to educate the nation about what to expect in the next phase. That is the conversation we can start to have now.' ... Tom Tugendhat, chairman of the foreign affairs committee, said: 'Trusting people is about helping everyone plan for the future. The uncertainty we're seeing needs to be limited as much as possible and I hope the government will trust our citizens and open up the conversation.'[3]

The allegory of the cave

But let us now turn to Plato and examine how he applies the model of the teacher to leadership. To do this we have to start by asking what he thinks education actually involves, and one of the most famous places to look is a passage in the *Republic* that uses an allegory to describe the nature of education: the allegory of the cave (Book 7, 514a–517b).

Here Plato asks us to imagine a group of people sitting in a row at the bottom of a cave. They are facing a wall and, although they do not realize it, they are prisoners chained to their seats, unable to move; they cannot stand up or even turn their heads around. Behind them is a fire, and behind the fire is a steep path rising up to the mouth of the cave. Between the backs of the prisoners and the fire, puppeteers are moving objects along a wall—imitations of animals and other artefacts. The puppets cast shadows on the wall in front of the prisoners, who spend their time trying to predict what will happen next. As they have no idea of what is behind them, they think the shadow play is reality, not a dim reflection of something else.

Now imagine that one of the prisoners is unexpectedly freed: his bonds are released and he turns around. Initially, forced to look at the light of the fire, he is blinded; when asked to look at the puppets and say what each of them is, he is unable to reply, but would much rather turn back to where he sat before and look at the shadows on the wall. Next, someone drags him up the steep and rugged path towards the mouth of the cave. Outside, he is initially unable to see anything because of the brightness of the light. But gradually he becomes able to see a little more: he looks at reflections of objects in pools of water (trees, animals, and the like); he can then make out the moon and the stars. But only after a long time is he able to see objects directly in the sunlight.

Then we are to imagine him returning to the cave. At first, he is blinded by the darkness and can see nothing. When he addresses the other prisoners, he tries to tell them what it is like outside. But seeing him stumbling around in the dark, they just laugh, saying that the journey has ruined his sight. If he (or anyone else) attempts to lead them out of the cave, they grow angry with him and even threaten to kill him.

Having presented us with this allegory at the beginning of *Republic* Book 7, Plato does not go on to give a detailed account of how to cash it out. He does give a few indications, but otherwise leaves it to the reader to decide how it applies to education. In this chapter we shall give our own take on the allegory, focusing on what it has to tell us about leadership.

Before we do so, a word about the possible background to the allegory. In thinking up the image, Plato may have been influenced by a certain practice not uncommon in his own day. Cities like Athens would frequently send out a few of their citizens as ambassadors to another state, even as far away as Persia, to learn about their customs and practices, typically by visiting a religious festival. Sometimes individuals would do this on their own rather than on a state-sponsored visit. Upon their return to their native city, they would often be met with as much hostility as curiosity, because their new perspective alienated them from their fellow citizens.[4] In the allegory of the cave, Plato may have been creating his own highly elaborate variation on this theme: the learner undertakes a journey, which gives them an entirely new take on the world; they then make a return journey back home, where they view their old ways through an entirely different lens. In doing so they find themselves completely alienated from their erstwhile companions.

Plato's cave allegory develops this idea as a vehicle to explain his own distinctive theory of education. The details of his theory have intrigued his readers over the years, and huge amount of scholarly ink has been spilled on the matter. For readers who want to know more, we shall discuss this a little further in Appendix 2. But for our purposes, it is important not to lose sight of the wood for the trees: encapsulated in the allegory is a core set of ideas about education, which can be applied to many different contexts, practical as well as academic.

One of these ideas is that of a 'perspective gap'. As we have just said, the person who turns around from their seat and exits the cave goes on a journey. In doing so, they are disorientated, encountering something that gives them a radically different perspective on what they thought before. Central to the allegory is the person's attempt to match the new perspective with the old one: the journey ends when they return to where they began, but understood from a very different viewpoint.[5]

As we have just said, Plato offers us the cave allegory as a way of presenting his own distinctive account of education. For him, the crucial move is from the particular to the abstract. Take the example of justice: most people have views about who or what counts as just or unjust—everyday life is full of arguments on the topic, many of them quite heated. For Plato, we need to move up to a level of abstract definition, and then return to apply this understanding to the particular level. He thinks most people find highly abstract reasoning difficult and disorientating. It is the task of philosophy to drag us up to this level.

But we can detach the allegory from its original Platonic setting, and apply the basic idea behind it wherever there is a 'perspective gap'. Consider, for instance, the way modern physics revises the way we perceive things, and presents us with an utterly different account of the world.[6] This account of reality is radically different from anything Plato ever thought, but what both have in common is an almost shocking gap between the way we subjectively perceive the world and the way it is as revealed by scientific or philosophical inquiry.

Beyond academia, you can imagine perspective gaps opening up in practical contexts. Take someone who has been used to working at a relatively low level in an organization, who then gets promoted into a more strategic role, forcing them to understand quite different parts and functions of the organization, involving travel to different parts of the world. This would in itself give them an entirely different perspective on the relatively limited arena in which they used to operate. Again, Plato's allegory of the cave has application here. Sitting at the bottom of the cave, most of us live in our own comfort zone. We are used to understanding the world in a certain way, and can only be forced to give this up with great reluctance. As we proceed out of the cave towards the light outside, what is happening is a perspective shift, which turns our sense of reality inside out.

Leadership within the cave

The allegory is about education. So why are we using it as a model of leadership? At one point, Plato talks of the prisoners at the bottom of the cave arguing about justice in the law courts and elsewhere (517d). This suggests that they stand for people in Athens who took part in public life, in juries and assemblies, with strong views about ethics and politics. The released prisoner is challenging them to overhaul their views, with all the practical implications that would entail, both in private and public. He wants to drag them all out of the cave so that they can gain the true perspective. Such a figure is some kind of social reformer and public intellectual. Obviously, we are meant to think of Socrates and the way in which he challenged his fellow citizens in the public sphere, for which he was first ridiculed and eventually sentenced to death.[7] The allegory is continuous with Socrates' self-image as a public intellectual, mentioned in Chapter 1: like a gadfly that won't let a horse enjoy its slumbers, he refused to let the Athenians stay in their comfort zone, pursuing the values of empire and wealth.[8]

So although the allegory is initially billed as being about education, it makes us imagine a teacher who aspires to be a political reformer and leader. We say 'aspires', because the teacher's attempts at leadership fail even before they have barely begun. But that doesn't stop the allegory telling us about what leadership could involve at its best. After all, the true navigator as described through the ship of state image in *Republic* Book 6 never gets to put his hand on the steering oar: the point of the image is to show us whom we ought to choose as a leader. So too with the doctor in the *Gorgias*: this is a model for political leadership, but is rarely instantiated because of public opposition. But again, this doesn't stop it being a useful model of leadership.

If this is a model of leadership, what are its core components? The first point is about the challenge the leader faces: the state of the followers. It is essential to the allegory that they are trapped in a certain way of seeing the world and acting within it. Some of our models can be differentiated from each other by the way they portray the initial challenge: the leader as doctor is needed because of an institutional disease (specifically an imbalance, where some goal or group tends to the excess); the navigator and captain because setting a new direction creates uncertainty and discord about the means to get there. In this case, it is all about leading a group of people trapped in a mindset that will ultimately harm the organization.

The second component is that the followers cannot simply be left in their comfort zone and somehow managed within that perspective. They have to be shifted away from it, to take the same journey that the leader took. This may sound obvious, given the first point but, in principle, the followers could be left in their comfort zone while the leader operates outside of it. But on the teacher model, this is not an option: the followers need to take the same road as their leader.

How does the leader do this? Here we come to the third point. The process must involve a direct appeal to reason. This doesn't require the leader to be a 'professor in chief', giving lectures, seminars, and tutorials. But at a minimum, they must avoid manipulating their followers or restricting the flow of information; they openly share evidence, and encourage questioning to stimulate debate. But how far can they go in this? For Plato, the teacher aspires to raise the student to the same cognitive level as themselves. This is clear in the allegory, where the role of the educator appears twice: initially, when the person turns around from the wall of the cave, there is someone who forces him to look at the fire and then drags him out of the cave; but then the released prisoner himself is seen as an educator when we imagine him attempting to do the other prisoners what his educator did for him. The student has become the teacher.

It may be unrealistic to expect that leaders will break down the barriers between themselves and others completely; they would no longer be leaders. To be sure, you try and educate others to take another perspective and leave their comfort zone, but there are limits to how far this can be done. But at least one can say that the barriers that all too often exist between leaders and others in the organization start to become porous.

The fourth and final point is about the risks of leadership. By taking on the role of teacher in the specific sense implied by the cave allegory, the leader pits himself against others, at least initially. In the cave allegory, the released prisoner is a solitary figure, stumbling out of the cave, with some help from his guide but otherwise on his own. The same applies when he returns: the contrast is between him and everyone else, the prisoners still chained to their seats, ridiculing him and threatening him with death. As we have seen, this is because Plato is thinking of him as a public intellectual and social reformer, with all the danger and antagonism that involves. In this way, the model of the educator in the cave allegory highlights the problem of persuasion discussed in previous chapters: recall the doctor who, by dint of his expertise, may have to prescribe a remedy that he is unable to persuade his patient to take; or the true navigator, who is written off as an irrelevance and a stargazer. But in a less dramatic way, there are risks for any leader who attempts to move people out of their comfort zones, in whatever type of organization.

Part of what makes the task difficult is that, although the journey out of the cave qualifies the released prisoner in one sense (by giving him a certain expertise that the others lack), the perspective he gains can also disqualify him from effective communication with his fellows; it creates a gulf between the leader and their followers. And this in turn contributes to the hazards of this kind of leadership.

The teacher. Key principles:

T1. The leader as teacher is confronted with followers who are prisoners of their own comfort zone.

T2. Having left this comfort zone, the leader tries to do the same for their followers.

T3. The leader appeals directly to the rationality of their followers. They are open to question and interrogation from those they lead.

T4. Leaders who try to move people out of their comfort zones can expect to encounter hostility and resistance.

Case studies

Mikhail Gorbachev

An excellent example of leading people out of the cave is Mikhail Gorbachev's Perestroika and the breakup of the Soviet Union.

Gorbachev was born in the agricultural region of the Soviet Union; his father was Russian and his mother Ukrainian. Both of his grandfathers were repressed by the Soviet system in the mid-1930s and then rehabilitated several years later. His father fought in the Second World War against Nazi Germany and upon returning continued working in the agriculture sector. The hardship of Gorbachev's childhood years shaped his views that something should be changed in the Soviet system. He was a self-made individual who graduated with distinction from high school in a far-flung region of Russia and was admitted to the top law school in Moscow from where he graduated with distinction as well. He had no support from his family as he climbed to the very top of the complex Soviet hierarchical system.

Confronting people in their comfort zone (T1); leading them out of it (T2)

As he climbed the party hierarchy, Gorbachev became convinced that the Soviet Union was badly in need of change. Once he became the General Secretary of the USSR (the top position in the country), he started educating people by a process of reform, a considerable change from the previous seventy years of Soviet history. However, several of his initial programmes, such as focusing on getting citizens to drink much less, were failures. Gorbachev had to reach out with a different and more open method. One of the turning points for him was the disaster at the nuclear power plant in Chernobyl. Nuclear power had long been a high priority in Soviet Union, but Gorbachev could easily see that even this area of Soviet life was unworkable and far from 'world-class'. It was emblematic of what he needed to change. He realized that 'the old system had exhausted its possibilities'.[9]

> Russia had more than enough capable people. They could have accom-plished a great deal had they been given freedom and rights, but they were paralyzed by the dictates of the party, by the narrow and rigid framework of party directives, by the rules of the system of command from above. Decades of existence under conditions of totalitarianism and the personality cult inevitably resulted in apathy, anemia, loss of initiative, and the extinguishing of social energy in our country.[10]

He combined all his reforming initiatives under the umbrella name 'Perestroika' ('restructuring'). The main idea of Perestroika—its 'philosophy', to use Gorbachev's own term[11]—was not only to change the way of life in the USSR, but, more importantly, to get people's buy-in to make the changes themselves. Gorbachev's Perestroika made people understand that there is another way to look at things, both within the country and outside.

The leader appeals directly to the rationality of their followers (T3)

Openness (in Russian, *Glasnost*) was required if there was to be progress and Gorbachev allowed freedom of speech in all areas of national life (press, TV, public places) and democratized elections by allowing the creation of other parties apart from the Communist Party.

What makes Gorbachev different from many other leaders is that he used a teaching style to accompany his reforms. According to Plato's model, the teacher must get people out of their comfort zone, and get them engaged in creating a better life. Likewise, the teacher should expect that this will be difficult and that many people will resist. Consistent with treating others with respect, the teacher has to be open to questioning from their students and must patiently explain the necessity of change again and again. And this was surely Mikhail Gorbachev's approach. Whenever he was speaking in public, he did not just say how things should be (as many authoritarian leaders do), but was always eager to explain why the previous way of life was not sustainable and why the country needed reform.

In part due to Gorbachev's teaching approach, every year more and more people in the Soviet Union came to accept his ideas. It is important to note that, when the first attempts simply didn't work, Gorbachev changed his approach to be more comprehensive, and he constantly learned from his experience and from pushback by his allies and critics. He says:

> Of course, learning from the experience of others is something we have been doing and will continue to do.[12]

> I keep repeating that with the end of confrontation differences can be made a source of healthy competition, an important factor for progress. This is an incentive to study each other, to engage in exchanges, a prerequisite for the growth of mutual trust. For knowledge and trust are the foundations of a new world order. Hence the necessity, in my view, to learn to forecast the course of events in various regions of the globe, by pooling the efforts of scientists, philosophers and humanitarian thinkers within the UN framework.[13]

Unlike previous leaders of USSR, whose authority relied on the strength of the KGB and the Soviet Army to stay in power, Gorbachev's authority relied on persuading people to voluntarily accept his ideas. Appealing to their reason as well as their hearts, Gorbachev consistently, from one meeting to another, from one public speech to another, educated them about a new horizon that could be open to the country. He was what Howard Gardner would call a 'leader by choice'.[14] People needed to choose to follow him rather than relying on positional authority.

> Perestroika's greatest achievement was to awaken and liberate the mind. People were freed to think without the constraint of fear—of the authorities or of nuclear war. For the first time, they had the right to choose. The effect of that is long term, and not yet over.[15]

Leaders who try to move people out of their comfort zones can expect to encounter hostility and resistance (T4)

Ultimately, this was the undoing of Gorbachev's Perestroika, as a group of hard-liners led a coup against him in August 1991. The coup failed, eventually resulting in the break-up of the Soviet Union. His unwillingness to rely on the KGB and military force caused Gorbachev to lose his position of the General Secretary of the USSR in 1991, when it devolved into fifteen independent countries. However, because of his teaching, the people in each of the new independent countries had the opportunity to become freer and more integrated into the rest of the world.

Indra Nooyi: Perestroika and Pepsi

> I've tried to be a lifelong student. That's especially important given the age we're living in.... I'm constantly trying to consume as much information as I can from as many sources as I can. I can't afford to stop learning. None of us can. CEOs need to be students for life, and all our employees do, too.[16]

Indra Nooyi was born in India, where she lived the first twenty-three years of her life, receiving a bachelor's degree in Physics, Chemistry, and Mathematics, and working as a product manager for Johnson & Johnson and Mettur Beardsell. Afterwards, she moved to the United States, where she received a master's degree in Public and Private Management at Yale School of Management (1980). After that she worked for consulting firms Booz Allen Hamilton and Boston Consulting Group, and then held strategy roles at Motorola and Asea Brown Boveri. She joined PepsiCo in 1994, became its CFO in 2001, and its President and CEO in 2006.

The leader as teacher is confronted with followers who are prisoners of their own comfort zone (T1)

When she took over as CEO at PepsiCo she found an industry that had been sheltered by its own set of beliefs. It was in its own cave. As in Plato's cave, many habits and beliefs of those inside the industry as well as the customer masses were wrong, or based on faulty understandings of how the world works. The consumption of so-called 'junk foods' in developed countries was high. High sugar-concentrated soft drinks, such as some of those sold by PepsiCo, were one of the best-selling categories in any typical retail store, restaurant, cinema, or basically in any public place. Potato chips and other salty, fatty snacks were advertised and consumed everywhere, including schools and kindergartens. Obesity had become one of the biggest challenges faced by many around the world, especially in the West.

Having left this comfort zone, the leader tries to do the same for their followers (T2)

As the company began to deal with these issues it became apparent to Nooyi that she needed to teach the company how to behave differently, and she had to do this in a way that was both financially viable, intellectually acceptable, and respectable to the PepsiCo employees. Like Plato's teacher, she needed to be a reformer of actual practice. She said:

> When I came on as CEO, I didn't want to completely change the direction of the company. But I also believed we needed to bring a

new sense of meaning to the work we did every day. We called it, 'Performance with Purpose'.... It was a philosophy that also pointed to a larger idea that's fundamental to how I see the world—the idea that companies don't exist in a vacuum. We should be responsive to the needs of the world around us. Performance with Purpose is our way of doing that.[17]

Nooyi classified the company's product portfolio into three categories: 'fun for you', such as regular soda drinks and potato chips, 'better for you', such as low-fat or diet versions of the first category, and 'good for you', standing for healthy foods. Nooyi managed to reallocate a large part of corporate resources from junk foods to healthier products. It was important not to make what people had been doing wrong, but to reorient them towards a better way of satisfying customers, one that was good for both PepsiCo and its customers. It was unthinkable, prior to Indra Nooyi's stepping up as CEO, that a worldwide leader in soda beverages like PepsiCo could begin to admit that there are healthier drinks than soda and begin to move corporate spending toward healthier products.

Nooyi took the lead in dramatically increasing the share of healthy products in the corporate product portfolio by acquiring a number of companies, including Tropicana, Quaker, and KeVita, and adding such brands as Quaker Oats, Naked Juices, Izze, and others. Nooyi was also a strong believer that customers should not pay more for healthy products than for their less-healthy alternatives and healthy products should be ubiquitously available in stores.[18] Apart from focusing on promoting healthy products, Nooyi also initiated a major restructuring of the legacy products from 'fun for you' and 'better for you' categories to reduce the amount of unhealthy ingredients in them. In fall 2016, PepsiCo announced 'a plan to cut the sugar content and calories of drinks it sells around the globe' by at least two-thirds within the next eight years.[19] As a result of Nooyi's focus on healthier products, PepsiCo turned into a more diversified business compared to its closest rival, The Coca-Cola Company.

We don't want to exaggerate. Though Indra Nooyi is a good example of Plato's teacher-reformer from many perspectives, you might object that what makes Nooyi different is that she started from a base of a financially viable company. Since Nooyi did not stop selling traditional, popular lines of drinks and snacks from the 'fun for you' category, she didn't have to confront the cave dwellers who had never been outside the cave. As Nooyi herself mentions, 'When you're a CEO, you can't break too many stereotypical expectations'.[20] Indeed, it would have been a radical change for PepsiCo if its new CEO completely abandoned sugared soda and salty, fatty snacks from the very start. In large organization it may require quite some time to fully change the mindset and teach the company to do completely new things. There is a complex system at many organizations that must be approached carefully as many things have to be considered: changing production processes, retraining employees, finding new trustworthy suppliers, informing customers about new products, etc.

The leader appeals directly to the rationality of their followers: they are open to question and interrogation from those they lead (T3)

To lead this change Nooyi had to educate PepsiCo employees and other stakeholders as well. She said:

> If the CEO doesn't feel the change, as opposed to just talking about the change, people will see right through it. So the first thing I had to do was make sure that whenever I talked to employees about it, *I shared experiences, observations, data*. I talked about water shortages in parts of the world. I would show them examples of plastic waste, the lack of recycling programs and what that could do to the environment. And I would talk about people's consumption of fat, sugar and salt.[21]

In all this, Nooyi operated by means of persuasion, not coercion. Nooyi's goal was to make PepsiCo's product portfolio healthier, and within a decade she considerably reduced the share of junk food in PepsiCo's sales. However, she was not going to persuade people to stop buying fun-but-unhealthy products. She knew she had to leave the choice to people themselves to decide which products to buy. She could do everything in her power to educate her stakeholders, but ultimately the choice was up to them. Unlike the artist, the teacher does make efforts to educate people, so that by gaining knowledge they can make better decisions.

Leaders who try to move people out of their comfort zones can expect to encounter hostility and resistance (T4)

Nooyi had a number of critics who thought she was leading the company down a path that was inappropriate:

> We are trying to . . . reduce the salt, sugar, and fat. I didn't create Pepsi Cola. I didn't create Doritos or Fritos or Cheetos. I'm trying to take the products and make them healthier. And guess what they tell me? 'Don't be Mother Teresa. Your job is to sell soda and chips.' . . . We are trying to take a historical eating and drinking habit that has been exported to the rest of the world and make [it] more permissible.[22]

Many market analysts criticized Nooyi for stepping away from traditional products, but Nooyi's vision proved to work. In the words of one business pundit:

> Just a few years ago, it wasn't clear whether Indra Nooyi would survive as PepsiCo's CEO. Many investors saw Pepsi as a bloated giant whose top brands were losing market share. And they were critical of Nooyi's shift toward a more health-oriented overall product line. Prominent activist investor Nelson Peltz fought hard to split the company in two. These days Nooyi, 59, exudes confidence. The company has enjoyed steady revenue growth during her nine years in the top job, and Pepsi's stock price is rising again after several flat years.[23]

Nooyi attributes her ability to lead the change and manage resistance, against all the odds, to her upbringing. As she recollects:

> Every night at the dinner table, my mother would ask us to write a speech about what we would do if we were president, chief minister, or

prime minister—every day would be a different world leader she'd ask us to play.... At the end of dinner, we had to give the speech, and she had to decide who she was going to vote for. The winner of the debate then signed a piece of paper that stated they had become whatever the world leader of the day was. The girls and their mom would laugh and have fun with it, but Nooyi said she and her sister came to appreciate it.... '...she [Nooyi's mother] gave us that confidence to be whatever we wanted to be. That was an incredibly formative experience in my youth.'[24]

Notes

1. A claim made by Sarah Palin, among others. See Stripling (2010).
2. The teacher differs from the other models in not being a metaphor: this kind of leader really does teach their followers, in some sense. What they do is unlikely to be exactly like a professional teacher, but there is a strong similarity: rational communication, openness to question, and a willingness to explain when things are unclear.
3. *The Times*, Saturday, 18 April 2020. https://www.thetimes.co.uk/article/lack-of-clarity-over-coronavirus-lockdown-exit-strategy-treats-public-like-children-2d0rp3snl.
4. See Nightingale (2004). She describes the cultural practice in ch. 1 and links it to Plato's cave allegory in ch. 3. See pp. 44, 48, and 65 on the hostility such travellers might encounter upon their return.
5. Compare T. S. Eliot, *The Four Quartets, Little Gidding*: 'We shall not cease from exploration/ And the end of all our exploring/ Will be to arrive where we started/ And know the place for the first time.'
6. See Reichenbach (1938) 219–20: '...we see the world in the scale of our sense capacities: we see houses, trees, men, tools, tables, solids, liquids, waves, fields, woods, and the whole covered by the vault of the heavens. This perspective, however, is not only one-sided; it is false, in a certain sense. Even the concreta, the things which we believe we see as they are, are objectively of shapes other than we see them. We see the polished surface of our table as a smooth plane; but we know that it is a network of atoms with interstices much larger than the mass particles, and the microscope already shows not the atoms but the fact that the apparent smoothness is not better than the "smoothness" of the peel of a shriveled apple.... We do not see the things, not even the concreta, as they

objectively are but in a distorted form; we see a substitute world—not the world as it is, objectively speaking.'

7. The comic poet Aristophanes wrote an entire play ridiculing him, appropriately entitled *The Clouds*.

8. According to Plato, the historical Socrates denied that he was a teacher (*Apology* 33a). By this he meant that he did not have the knowledge, and hence the authority, that he thought a true teacher should have. But he was still a teacher in the sense of an intellectual mentor (to those who were prepared to listen).

9. Taubman (2017) 242.

10. Gorbachev (2000) 31.

11. Gorbachev (2006)14.

12. Gorbachev (2006) 13.

13. Gorbachev (2006) 24.

14. Gardner (2011) 12–13.

15. Gorbachev (2006) 125.

16. Nooyi (2017).

17. Nooyi (2017).

18. Safian (2017) 78–9.

19. Aubrey (2016).

20. Ignatius (2015).

21. Nooyi and Gelles (2019), emphasis added.

22. Safian (2017) 78.

23. Ignatius (2015).

24. Feloni (2015).

6

Doctors and Teachers

Plato

Plato's *Laws*

This chapter is a direct sequel to the previous one. We shall look at the way Plato used the teacher model of leadership in his last work, the *Laws*, where he combines it with the model of the doctor, discussed in Chapter 2. The best leaders are those who address an ailment in society, but who also try to give their patients a rational explanation of what the illness is and how it needs to be treated; they don't just impose the cure.

Plato was in the final stages of writing the *Laws* when he died, around the age of 80. It is roughly as long as the *Republic* and, as its title suggests, is about political philosophy. He imagines writing the constitution for a new colony, and the main purpose of the work is to set out the laws that will govern the state, although the work also contains more general reflection about the nature and purpose of legislation.

Given its subject matter, the question arises of how it relates to the *Republic*, written probably three decades before. The main difference is that the *Laws* is not attempting to establish an ideal state; its starting point is the need to be realistic, and so it treats human beings more as they are than as they might be. Making allowances for human fallibility leads Plato towards a less radical constitution than in the *Republic*. There are no philosopher rulers with absolute control, and there are even some concessions towards democracy: all the citizens have a role in public affairs, either by voting for public officials or by actually taking on such positions themselves. The *Laws* is also a great deal more specific than the *Republic*. Although it begins in a very general way when it discusses the nature and purpose of law, as it goes on, it gets down to the nitty-gritty of law-making. There are detailed laws about all manner of topics—e.g. homicide, retail trade, property ownership, and religion.

The legislator as teacher and doctor

The passage in which we are interested comes during a discussion of the best way to present laws to the citizens. By their nature, laws coerce: once a law is established, you have no choice but to obey it, on pain of punishment. But Plato is uneasy about relying merely on compulsion. It would be better if the citizens were persuaded to act in accordance with a law on the grounds that it has been justly instituted. So the people who write the laws need to bear this in mind when they legislate. It is at this point that he starts to appeal to models of leadership, comparing the legislator to a doctor who is at the same time a teacher. To describe the model, he begins by explaining how he thinks the best kind of doctor should practise. Some doctors just

> … rush about on flying visits or wait to be consulted in their surgeries. This kind of doctor never gives any account of the particular illness of the individual slave, or is prepared to listen to one; he simply prescribes what he thinks best in the light of experience, as if he had precise knowledge, and with the self–confidence of a dictator.   (Book 4, 720c)[1]

The best kind of doctor takes a very different attitude:

> His method is to construct a case-history scientifically, by consulting the invalid and his friends; in this way he himself learns something from the sick and at the same time he teaches the individual patient as much as he can. He gives no prescription until he has somehow persuaded; then, making him gentle by such persuasion, he tries to complete his restoration to health.   (Book 4, 720d–e)

Later on, in a back-reference to this passage, Plato adds:

This doctor would be acting almost like a philosopher, engaging in a discussion that ranged over the source of the disease and pushed the inquiry back into the whole nature of the body.   (Book 9, 857d)

Plato wants to apply this model to the legislator, the political leader. Such a person can introduce a measure either by force, persuasion, or both. In the end, Plato thinks they should do both; and the reason for medical comparison is to illustrate why it is unsatisfactory to get citizens to obey merely by compulsion.

Before we look at how the teacher-doctor model applies to political leadership, let us look at the medical side of the comparison in a little more detail. The doctor aims to reach a scientific understanding of the disease, but to do so gains information about the patient's malady by learning from the patient himself and from others who know him. On the basis of the information gathered, he then explains to the patient what needs to be done and why. Presumably, what he is communicating here is precisely what he himself has learnt in the course of his inquiries. His persuasion is not rhetorical trickery or manipulation, but genuine teaching: he attempts, in so far as he can, to impart a scientific understanding to the patient. He wants the patient to accept his remedies on rational grounds and, like any good teacher, treats his student with intellectual respect.[2] This in turn will make his patient open to being persuaded and will generate trust.

The role of listening is very important here. The doctor spends a great deal of time listening, both to the patient and those who know him well. This was not something we found highlighted when we discussed the teacher in the *Republic*, but it is part of what facilitates communication between doctor and patient here. Not only does it provide the doctor with important information about the disease; the fact that the doctor has actually listened to the patient creates a bond of trust between them.

So, all in all, this passage is important because of its approach to communication. Applied to medicine, what we have is a notion of informed consent: the doctor tries to get the patient to accept the treatment by informing him in the appropriate way.

How does this apply to political leaders and legislators? Ultimately, all citizens will be compelled to obey the laws, but they should also have been persuaded to do so. What Plato has in mind is the idea that the legislator will attempt to educate the citizens about the need and rationale for each and every law in the state. Like the doctor, the political leader will communicate with the citizens to explain the benefits of the legislation. If we take the reference to teaching literally, they will not do so by manipulating their subjects, lying, using rhetorical tricks, or in any way infantilizing them. They will explain the point of each law rationally, appealing to the cognitive capacities of their citizens. And, if we take the reference to listening seriously, the political leader will include listening to the citizens as part of the process of communication.

This turns out to be crucial to the way the rest of the *Laws* is written. As Plato now embarks on detailed legislation, he announces his intention to preface each law with a 'prelude' or 'preamble', which is designed precisely to explain the benefit or rationale of the law, in just the same way as the doctor tried to justify his treatment to the patient. As we read through the rest of the work, we encounter numerous preambles, some quite short, but others remarkable long and complex, which are meant to fulfil the role of educating the citizens.

So in the *Laws*, Plato selects two of the models we examined in previous chapters, the doctor and the teacher, synthesizes them, and so anticipates our notion of informed consent.

Plato's ambivalence about the teacher model

Plato was well aware that this model of leadership might raise a few eyebrows. As we saw, later on in the work he makes a back-reference to the doctor-teacher model and describes the doctor as 'almost philosophizing' with his patient, engaging in a discussion about the origins of the disease and pushing 'the inquiry back into the whole nature of the body', i.e. into a systematic discussion of medicine (Book 9, 857d). He then imagines a critic who thinks the whole comparison ridiculous. Even as an account of what doctors do, it seems wrong: Plato's doctor is more interested in turning the patient into another doctor than curing him. In other words, the critic accuses him of conflating the distinction between medical patient and medical student. (Note how this point picks up a feature of teaching and learning that we identified in Chapter 5: the teacher ultimately aims to put the learner on the same level as themselves.) On this objection, Plato may be right about the relation between teacher and student, but is wrong to find a similar relationship in the political arena: leaders should not try to elevate citizens to their own level. What is interesting is that Plato makes no attempt at all to defend himself from this objection; he shrugs it off as if he thinks it entirely appropriate to treat citizens with such rational respect.

And yet, when one looks at the *Laws* more closely, we find that Plato himself is ambivalent about the model. Although the doctor passages from Books 4 and 8 do present the leader as someone who leads by educating in a rationalistic sense, other passages in the work suggest a different picture. When it comes to the actual examples of preambles given in the work, some of the arguments Plato offers are not of the kind that treats the interlocutor with much intellectual respect. Rather, he is prepared to use mere rhetoric and even some manipulation to bring the citizens round, apparently bypassing their rational faculties.

How should we deal with this? The best thing is to say that, by combining the teacher and the doctor, the *Laws* gives us a model to which we can easily relate (especially if we have with the notion of informed consent at the forefront of our minds). On the other hand, circumstances may often force the leader to adopt less rationalistic means. They need to be wary, just like doctors who simply can't explain to their patients all the science involved their disease and treatment. So Plato remains ambivalent about the teacher model, just as he was in the *Republic*, and the same practical message we drew in the last chapter applies: the leader should be prepared to adopt the teacher approach, with all its advantages, but also be discriminating about what cognitive abilities to expect of people at different levels of the organization.[3]

Case studies

To find good illustrations of the connection of these two leadership models we need look no further than Roy Vagelos at Merck and Indra Nooyi at Pepsi, who featured as case studies in Chapters 2 and 5 respectively.

Roy Vagelos

As Merck's development of a drug to alleviate river blindness progressed, Vagelos originally thought that simply solving the scientific problem would be sufficient. After all, this was a terrible disease, and if the scientific problem could be solved then surely someone, some organization, some government would step forward and implement it. Of course, this didn't happen. And there may be many reasons that no one wanted to help a rich American drug company alleviate the symptoms of a dreadful disease half a world away. Vagelos went to President Ronald Reagan and others in his administration and suggested that the US government should be involved in getting Mectizan to the people suffering from river blindness. It would be a hallmark programme depending on the ingenuity of American capitalism, cooperating with government, that should appeal to a broad swatch of the Reaganites. As Vagelos tells the story, he was turned down due to 'lack of budget'.

He understood that he and Merck had to become teachers, in a number of senses. First of all they had to get key participants knowledgeable about the disease. They also had to educate the victims and potential victims about Western medicine so that they would accept help. And perhaps most importantly, they had to teach governments and health care workers in the affected countries how to administer the drug: to be teachers themselves. After years of efforts on their own, going it alone, Merck has been able to secure help from organizations all over the world.

Vagelos began to understand that he had to go on a journey that allowed him to move from the vantage point of his scientific and medical expertise to being a leader of people both inside and outside of Merck. As he realized, the challenge was one of boldly leading and garnering support from multiple stakeholder groups. And, that task could only be completed by educating them, all in addition to solving a very substantial scientific problem.

Vagelos' leadership depended on being able to inspire his employees, so that they could use their expertise to solve problems like river blindness. However, he also had to develop the skills of a business leader and combine them with his own values. This is how he describes his journey:

I would have to learn how to do an entirely different job at Merck. I would have to become a business leader and would have to rearrange my priorities: I would have to become a corporate leader first, a medical scientist promoting innovation second, and a physician concerned about healing third.[4]

As I now understood, one important role of a leader is to convince people, before the fact, that they should change.[5]

Indra Nooyi

In Chapter 5, we showed how Indra Nooyi embarked on a transformation at PepsiCo where she had to teach the company about good health and healthy products. But she also acted as a doctor in the metaphorical sense—a corporate doctor. When we discussed the model in Chapter 2, one of the key points we highlighted was that such a leader confronts an organization's tendency to favour short-term goals (D3). This was exactly what Nooyi had to do in reforming PepsiCo. It is very easy for big corporations to follow the temptation of pursuing short-term profits in order to please Wall Street. However, that is not the path that Nooyi chose. As soon as she became CEO of PepsiCo, everyone expected her to immediately improve the business that had struggled for years by launching cost-cutting and improving marketing initiatives, and imitating The Coca-Cola Company. Nooyi decided that she had to act differently:

I had a choice. I could have gone pedal to the metal, stripped out costs, delivered strong profit for a few years, and then said adios. But that wouldn't have yielded long-term success. So I articulated a strategy to the board focusing on the portfolio we needed to build, the muscles we needed to strengthen, the capabilities to develop. The board said, 'We know there will be hiccups along the way, but you have our support, so go make it happen'. We started to implement that strategy...strengthening the company for the long term.[6]

There is another respect in which the doctor-teacher model is relevant to Nooyi's case. In the *Laws*, Plato talks of the doctor-teacher as someone who listens to their patients; carried over to leadership, this makes the crucial point that the leader should also be open to what their followers are saying. As a leader, this is exactly what Nooyi did. She had to have the right kind of communication both inside and outside of PepsiCo. She had to remain open to questions, while still communicating the need for the change in a meaningful way. She said:

> There's a reason we have two ears and one mouth. We should do more listening than talking. We should lead as CEOs. But we should also learn to follow, if needed. We should listen to the wisdom all around us.[7]

Vagelos' ability to see his own leadership model of a scientist as in need of reform was one of the key factors in Merck's success for his years as Chairman and CEO; Nooyi's ability to listen to her followers and stakeholders hastened the transformation of PepsiCo. Like Plato, both of these highly successful business leaders knew that building trust with those actually doing the work was a necessity.

Notes

1. Translations from the *Laws* are by Saunders (1975), with slight modifications. In this passage, Plato is describing the kind of medical treatment given to slaves in his time.
2. Some scholars have doubted this somewhat optimistic or rationalistic interpretation; we will return to this below.
3. See Chapter 5 and Appendix 2.
4. Vagelos and Galambos (2006) 3.
5. Vagelos and Galambos (2006) 22.
6. Ignatius (2015).
7. Nooyi (2017).

7

The Shepherd

Plato

Whose interest?

The leader as shepherd is perhaps the oldest model of leadership there is, traceable to the Hebrew scriptures,[1] the ancient Egyptians, and the Mesopotamians, who had the proverb, 'Soldiers without a king are sheep without their shepherd'.[2] As well as being very familiar, the model is also comforting, with connotations of protectiveness and care. The shepherd looks out for his flock, guarding and tending the sheep. Because it sounds continuous with the doctor and the navigator in the way it stresses the notion of care, you might expect the shepherd to have appealed to Plato. It does indeed feature in some of his dialogues, but in one of them he actually reveals problems for the model and in another rejects it altogether.

The shepherd's most conspicuous appearance in Plato comes towards the beginning of the *Republic*. The opening book of the work is mainly taken up with an argument between Socrates and Thrasymachus, which we have already mentioned elsewhere in this book.[3] Much of the time, they focus on the relation between leadership and self-interest. Thrasymachus has asserted that rulers, by whom he means good rulers, always rule for their own benefit. They make decisions and laws, which they call 'just', but only if they suit their own advantage. Socrates objects to this. For him, rulers rule, leaders lead, purely for the benefit of their followers. He argues for the point at 341c–342e, using a number of parallels, including doctors and sea captains, who serve the interests of their patients and crew respectively. It is the role of each type of leader to do this and nothing else.[4]

Faced with Socrates' argument, Thrasymachus refuses to accept defeat, but bounces back with a counter-example: the shepherd (343a). Socrates, he claims, would have us say that the shepherd tends the sheep for their own good and not his own. But Thrasymachus claims the opposite: the shepherd is working for himself; he fattens the sheep only to kill them (343a and 345c).[5]

In response, Socrates argues that this is to misunderstand the true nature of the shepherd. In so far as someone is a shepherd, he cares only for the good of his sheep. If a shepherd then takes them to market for slaughter, he is acting not as a shepherd, but as a money-maker, which is a different job altogether. The underlying point is that you need to distinguish between a profession and the ability to monetize it; but, in so far as someone is a shepherd, they look to nothing other than the good of their sheep. For Thrasymachus, by contrast, there is only one profession, which begins with protection and ends in slaughter.

Is Socrates making a valid distinction here, or is he just indulging in sophistry? Is it really true that you can separate out one role—protecting the flock—and restrict the term 'shepherding' to it, while treating other, less salubrious activities as belonging to a quite different profession? We leave it to the reader to decide who has the stronger position. But, without resolving the dispute, we can see that there is a stand-off between two very different views of the shepherd, resulting in two opposite conceptions of leadership. For Socrates, the shepherd illustrates the same duty of care he had illustrated with the models of the doctor and the navigator. For Thrasymachus, the leader as shepherd exploits his followers for his own interests. Taken to an extreme, this gives us the figure of the tyrant, whom Thrasymachus treats as his ideal very soon after using the example of the shepherd to refute Socrates (344a–b).

This debate has obvious contemporary relevance. Rachel Barney, a scholar in ancient Greek philosophy, makes a very interesting application to current debates about the professions, in particular journalism and medicine:

Is the good newspaper the one which maximizes its own financial health, or the one which serves some disinterested end distinctive to journalism, such as making the public better informed about important political and social questions? Most journalists hold the latter, Socratic view; but proprietors, publishers, and the investors increasingly take the Thrasymachean one. Medicine too is now in practice a contested field, with doctors and profit-orientated healthcare companies often dividing along Socratic and Thrasymachean lines.[6]

Perhaps this is a little too generous toward journalists, but Barney is certainly right about the relevance of the debate between Socrates and Thrasymachus to contemporary professions.

The shepherd withdraws

After Book 1, there is no reference to the leader as shepherd in the *Republic*, apart from one point in Book 4 where Socrates briefly compares the three classes in his ideal state—guardians, auxiliaries, and producers—to shepherds, dogs, and sheep respectively (440d; cf. 416a). This shows that he still believes what he said about the true shepherd in Book 1, so that it remains appropriate for him to liken his rulers to shepherds wholly devoted to their flock. But, beyond this, he has no further use for the model.[7]

Why might this be? One problem with the model is that it makes the leader a different species from their followers; followers are likened to dumb animals, reduced to the status of being wholly irrational.[8] Plato might have thought this a difficulty with the model, even if he thinks Socrates has refuted Thrasymachus about the nature of the true shepherd in Book 1. Of course, critics of Plato's political philosophy, such as Karl Popper, might say that he ought to welcome the shepherd model, since he treats the subject citizens as uneducated masses, 'proles' (to use Orwell's term): manipulated, sometimes deceived, and never treated as rational agents—in a word, sheep.[9] But when we discussed the model of the teacher, whether on its own or combined with the doctor, we saw that this is not Plato's view: he expected there to be rational engagement between leaders and followers where possible.[10] To this extent, he ought to be cautious about using the shepherd model; and it should come as no surprise that later on in his career, when he wrote the

Statesman, he makes just this point: we should be wary of comparing the political leader to a herdsman of any kind, because doing so creates too big a gulf between leaders and followers. The shepherd model would be apt if the statesman were a divine being put in charge of humans (274e–275c); so he would have no quarrel with the Psalmist who calls the Lord his shepherd (cf. n. 1 above). But a human leader is too close in nature to his subjects for the comparison to a shepherd to be appropriate.[11]

If Socrates' model of the good shepherd does not play a big role in Plato's thinking about leadership, what about Thrasymachus' model of the shepherd, the bad shepherd? This is not explicitly mentioned in the rest of the *Republic* at all. But the underlying model still manages to haunt the work much later on. As we saw, Thrasymachus uses it to introduce the notion of the tyrant, who exploits his subjects, enslaving or even killing them, to further his own interests. Later in the work, Plato returns to the figure of the tyrant for a much more detailed examination.[12] One of the questions he asks is how tyrants come to power: why do people allow them to take control when they turn out to wreak so much havoc? In Plato's view, tyranny evolves most naturally out of democracy (Book 8, 565c–569c). In a democracy, especially the more extreme form with which he was familiar, leaders are chosen by the will of the people, due to their success in persuading the citizens that they are right for the job. Plato then describes the rise of a certain kind of demagogue, who manages to convince the majority that he is their protector and saviour, but is under threat from his political rivals. He therefore convinces them to provide him with a personal bodyguard (566b), which he then uses to accrue more power, still with the consent of the majority. Eventually he acquires so much power that he is able to turn on them and subject them to slavery or worse.

In this somewhat chilling description of the way democracy can slide into tyranny, Plato is effectively giving us the model of Thrasymachus' shepherd all over again. A crucial feature was the way the shepherd appeared to be one thing, but was actually another: an exploiter masquerading as protector.

You might think that Plato's concerns about the shepherd in the *Statesman* also apply to the Thrasymachean version. If the model is problematic because leaders and followers are not members of different species, even a tyrant cannot be modelled on a shepherd. But this is not quite true. At one point in his description of tyranny, Plato mentions those who praise the tyrant for being on a par with the gods (Book 8, 568b; cf. Book 2, 360c). Whatever its deficiencies for understanding true leadership, the shepherd is more apt in this case: the tyrant sets himself up above the human level. Also, he treats his subjects as resources—mere things to further his own interests. From his point of view there *is* a yawning gap between leader and led. So, in a way, the shepherd captures something about the nature of the tyrant that it misses when applied to true leadership.

Finally, there is a further historical parallel we can make at the level of inter-state relations. Recall the way the Athenians built up their empire, which we mentioned in Chapter 1. Several Greek states, under threat from the Persians, agreed to pool their resources into a defensive alliance, the Delian League, which would provide a fighting force against future invasion. The Athenians set themselves up as leaders of the alliance—shepherds, if you like, of the Greeks. They persuaded the others to provide tribute to the fund, which they would control and use to build their own fighting force. Athens started by appearing to be the protector, but, just like Plato's tyrant in *Republic* Book 8, gradually revealed its true colours as an imperial overlord, subjugating the previously free states and punishing them at will, if they ever tried to leave or withhold their taxes. For Plato, therefore, the model of the bad shepherd is enormously important for understanding the origins of tyranny, both individual and collective.

The shepherd. Summary:

Although previous societies had compared leaders to shepherds, Plato finds the model problematic. It could be used to make the same point as the doctor and the captain: leaders are concerned solely for the well-being of their followers. But it could also be used to make the opposite point: leaders *seem* to care for their followers, but their underlying aim is exploitation. Another problem is that, by comparing leaders to members of a higher species, the model makes them too remote from their followers. Plato is therefore more reticent about using the shepherd than the other models.

Case study

Travis Kalanick and the Thrasymachean shepherd

Travis Kalanick was born in Los Angeles in 1976. He enrolled in the Engineering program at UCLA, but dropped out to form his own start-up. During the next decade, his first start-up went bankrupt, while the second one was more successful and he sold it for $19 million. After moving to San Francisco, he started providing Uber service in the city in 2010. Over the next seven years, his start-up grew into a global giant, offering its services in seventy-six countries and having market capitalization of about $70 billion.

There is an important component in Uber corporate strategy that makes its leadership style resemble the Thrasymachean model of the shepherd. Trying to be attractive to its drivers, Uber claimed that it opened up great opportunities for them: they could work flexible hours, plan their routes, use different app features that would make their work-life balance easier, and make more money than their other alternatives.[13] However, this reminds us of the case of the shepherd who diligently takes care of his sheep for the time present, but only till it is time to put them to death. Kalanick seemed to care about his employees only to the point that he needed them to make profit. Once that became irrelevant, he did not hesitate to get rid of them. Kalanick admitted publicly that the company strategy was to switch to self-driving cars, so the company could save on the costs of the drivers.[14]

> Uber CEO Travis Kalanick said he loves the idea of autonomous vehicles... and would happily replace his human drivers with a self-driving fleet. 'The reason Uber could be expensive is you're paying for the other dude in the car,' Kalanick said.... 'When there is no other dude in the car, the cost of taking an Uber anywhere is cheaper. Even on a road trip.'

Kalanick's leadership style reveals the elements of self-interest and exploitation present in Thrasymachus' model of the shepherd. As of

2017, Uber has already launched self-driving cars in Pittsburgh and Arizona as a pilot test.[15] In the future, this may entail a loss of jobs for some Uber drivers during the period that the company is executing its strategy of providing self-driving services.

To better understand the hypocrisy surrounding Kalanick's leadership style, we need to look closer at the overall story of the Uber development. Like the shepherd who takes care of others, Kalanick positioned Uber as 'good guys' that wanted to make the travel experience for many people in cities more convenient by easier-to-arrange, faster, cheaper, and more reliable rides. Kalanick would refer to any opposition to his undertaking, be it traditional taxi companies, local regulators, reporters, competitors, or anyone else, as 'a collective asshole'. To people who talked to Kalanick, he would seem to be someone who 'would make the world more efficient if only obstructionists would let him. "He's a fighter. He is against institutional structures."'[16] Despite all the turmoil around Uber's 'creative disruption' of the global taxi industry, the company expanded extremely fast both in the United States and abroad, and Uber became the world's fastest-growing start-up and most valuable venture-backed company, as well as an iconic story for many entrepreneurs.

However, whatever its success from an economic point of view, Uber continues to suffer from ethical problems. From the very beginning, Kalanick's Uber could hardly be considered a responsible company. The whole story of Uber's development has been filled to the brim with numerous scandals. Uber has denied any responsibility for the misconduct of its drivers in admittedly rare cases of alleged assault, rape, kidnapping, and harming others in car accidents. The company developed software tools that trespassed customers' privacy or discriminated against certain clients. Its 'God View' software secretly tracked users and 'Greyball' aimed to avoid providing company service in the locations where municipal authorities were located. Uber has been also criticized for raising its prices to exploit others. For example, when President Trump proposed a ban on immigrants from seven countries, many people in New York volunteered to go to the airport to help international travellers who got stuck there; but Uber immediately raised prices for the rides to the airport. This attitude of making extra money from volunteers, who were hurrying to help those in need, outraged many people in the United States and caused hundreds of thousands of customers to close their Uber accounts following the #deleteUber campaign.

The apogee of Uber's ethical lapses came from within the company itself. The unhealthy company culture, built by Kalanick, was exposed in Susan Fowler's blog that brought to the surface the issues of sexual harassment, discrimination, retaliation, unhealthy internal competition, mismanagement, and chaos. As a response, Uber hired a law firm, led by former US Attorney General Eric Holder, to conduct an internal investigation about the company's overall culture. At the same time, the problems for Uber were multiplying. An Uber driver revealed a video in which Kalanick was blaming him (the driver) for Kalanick's own hardship at Uber. Google issued a trade-secrets lawsuit accusing Uber's leadership of organizing the theft of its fourteen thousand documents on the technology development for self-driving cars. Finally, after the Holder report, in 2017, Kalanick resigned, and a new CEO was appointed.

Notes

1. 'The Lord is my shepherd; I shall not want. He makes me lie down in green pastures. He leads me beside still waters. He restores my soul' (Psalm 23:1–3).
2. Collins (1996) 21–3 and Adair (2013) 21–2.
3. See Chapter 1, Chapter 2, and Chapter 3.
4. For an analysis of the argument, see Barney (2006) esp. 49–52 and, in the context of contemporary leadership debates, Angier (2015) 28–32.
5. In another context, the philosopher Bertrand Russell (2001) 35 used the example of a farmer who comes each day to feed his chickens, and then one day wrings their necks. The chickens look forward to his daily visits but, tragically, their expectations are eventually dashed.
6. Barney (2006) 51.
7. In Chapter 2 we noted that the doctor is also mentioned only once after Book 1 of the *Republic*. However, the doctor remains important to the *Republic* because the analogy between health and justice is central to the work. There is no equivalent analogy to keep the shepherd in play, apart from the point that shepherds protect their flock, as leaders work for the interests of their followers.

But this point is already well made by the doctor and the navigator. So there is no distinctive role for the shepherd to perform.

8. According to Collins (1996) 21–2, this feature was built into the model long before Plato's time; it can be found in Homer's depiction of the leader as shepherd who just barks orders at his men (p. 28).

9. We discussed Popper's view of Plato in Chapter 4.

10. See Chapter 5, Chapter 6, and Appendix 2.

11. This is not to deny that the comparison between leaders and shepherds can help illuminate a particular feature of leadership. Plato uses it even after the *Statesman*, in the *Laws* (Book 5, 735b), not as a fully fledged model, but merely as an analogy for one task that his political leader has to perform: excluding the wrong kind of people from joining a state ('culling the flock'). But this is different from elevating the comparison to the status of a model: in our sense, a model incorporates several components, or key principles, into an integrated whole.

12. Plato's critique of the tyrant is the culmination of a long analysis of morally degenerate character types. There are four in total: the tyrant, the democratic character (someone obsessed with freedom), the oligarch (obsessed with the acquisition of wealth), and the timocrat (obsessed with honour and reputation). So, all in all, if one includes the just character already analysed in *Rep.* Book 4, there are five basic character types in the work. Bauman (2018) 260–9 uses this five-fold typology to throw light on issues in contemporary business leadership, including modern case studies for each character type, and cites the former CEO of BP, John Browne, as an example of the tyrant (pp. 268–9). A note of caution: whether all these characters are presented as leadership types has been disputed. See Ferrari (2005) 49–50.

13. Bhuiyan (2017).

14. Newman (2014).

15. Siegel and Silverman (2017).

16. Steinmetz and Vella (2017).

8

The Weaver

Plato

The function of the weaver

In this chapter we turn to a model of leadership found in one of Plato's later works, the *Statesman*, written at some point between the *Republic* and the *Laws*. As its title suggests, the work is very much focused on political leadership, even more so than the *Republic*. As well as statesmanship, Plato also deals with a number of closely associated topics, including political authority: to what extent should the statesman coerce his subjects, and should he ever be above the law (292a–300e)? At a more abstract level, Plato has become even more explicit about the right methods to use in philosophy, and here he is especially keen about using models: trying to define something relatively problematic (in this instance, political leadership) by comparing it to something more concrete and perceptible (277a–279a). In the *Statesman* he chooses an entirely new paradigm for the task: the statesman as weaver (279b–311e).[1]

Before embarking on his analysis of the statesman as a metaphorical weaver, Plato takes a great deal of care to describe what literal weaving involves (279b–283b). He is particularly concerned to distinguish weaving itself from all the other skills and crafts involved in the making of garments (e.g. those that help produce the strands that will be woven together), just as he will later on be concerned to distinguish the political leader from other functionaries in the state (287b–290e). But for our purposes, the most important point comes when he distinguishes the two kinds of thread that the weaver has to combine: the warp and the woof, the former being the firmer strands of the fabric, the latter the more supple. In essence, a weaver is someone who successfully intertwines the warp and the woof into a durable fabric (283a–b).

In adopting the weaver as his favoured model for political leadership, Plato assumes a corresponding model of the state. Earlier in this book, we've already encountered the 'body politic' and the 'ship of state' (Chapters 2 and 3); now we have the 'social fabric'. The point of the model is that the state (or, for that matter, any organization led by someone modelled on a weaver) is composed of very diverse kinds of people, and the job of the leader is to bring them together in such a way that they can jointly realize their common goals.

What sort of diversity did Plato have in mind? He could have used the model to make the rather general point that any state (or any organization) consists of people with myriad talents and temperaments; the job of the leader is to weave them together to make a successful enterprise. This is already an important point to make about team leadership and organizational leadership.[2] But when he actually comes to describing the weaver-statesman (305e–311e), he has something more specific in mind. Taking up his earlier interest in the distinction between warp and woof, he focuses on one particular difference among the citizens. Broadly speaking, he thinks, people divide into (what we now call) doves and hawks. Some citizens are distinguished by 'quiet' or amenable qualities, others by fierceness or vigour. In Plato's time, these were sometimes labelled as two different virtues: temperance (or 'moderation') and courage. This is to conceive the different qualities in a good light, but (as he points out) the same underlying tendencies could be manifested as feebleness and excessive aggression respectively. He claims that the temperate character 'is very careful, just, and safe, but lacks thoroughness and go'. By contrast, 'the character of the courageous … falls short of the former in justice and caution, but has the power of action in a remarkable degree'. He then adds: 'where either of these two qualities is lacking, cities cannot altogether prosper either in their public or private life.'[3]

The leader's task is to weave together these qualities into one fabric. How does he do this? Plato describes different ways. For instance, he insists that neither type of character should be allowed to become too extreme: the hawks must not become too aggressive, or the doves too pliant. So we need to keep a close watch on the education and upbringing of the citizens in order to prevent this happening. But this is still not to homogenize the two groups. They differ by nature and, although we can prevent them lurching towards the extremes, we can never eliminate their underlying character, nor should we even try.

So one important requirement of the model is that the leader tolerates difference. Plato accepts that the quality of moderation will characterize one group of the citizens, and courage the other. Ideally, of course, these qualities would be combined in the same person. This was clearly Plato's view of the guardians in the *Republic*, who possessed all the virtues: their being courageous in no way prevented them from also being moderate. Applying this to the *Statesman*, we would expect him to say that the leader does manage to combine qualities such as caution and fairness with those of vigour and effectiveness, a very rare phenomenon. In fact, he does explicitly require that anyone holding one of the higher offices must combine both sets of qualities (311a); if so, the same must surely apply to the person who holds the very highest office. Nonetheless, this remains the ideal. When he has the great majority of people in mind, he treats them as having rougher versions of these qualities: when a hawk has 'courage', it is only an approximation to true courage, which would be a quality sufficiently refined as to be able to co-exist with true moderation.

We should see the toleration of difference as a strength of Plato's position: any actual organization, and certainly a political state, will be composed of radically different types of people, and the last thing a leader should be doing is trying to homogenize their followers. If this sounds obvious, it is worth pointing out that certainly not all leaders find it so. So it is already a useful moral to take away from the *Statesman*.

Unity through shared values

But the question remains: how does a leader enable both kinds to work together? Plato's answer is that there will be co-operation and unity only if the different groups of people, despite their contrasting characters, espouse the same conception of what is just and beneficial (309c). More broadly, the most effective way to weave together the different characters and personalities in an organization is to have them espouse the same values. This is striking—and plausible. If accepted, it makes ethics absolutely central to an organization. It is all too common, especially in business, to think of values or ethics as an add-on, something that is superfluous to the economic functioning of the company, bolted on for PR purposes. But Plato forces us to challenge this: any organization that did not have values at its core, that did not ensure that its members shared the same set of values, whatever their temperaments, roles, or abilities, would fail to meet its objectives adequately; in the worst case, it would simply fall apart. The values are what hold the fabric together.

Ruthlessness

The next point to highlight is more critical. In the case of the artist and the shepherd, we saw how a model of leadership can initially appear positive, even comforting. But if one thinks through the logic of the model more carefully, it might seem more sinister. In the case of the artist, the political leader often wipes the canvas clean before imposing his vision upon it. As we argued in our chapter on the artist, this could lead us straight to totalitarianism. Unfortunately, something similar can be said about the web of state and its weaver.[4] In preparation for his work, the weaver needs to discard certain strands of wool if they are unsuitable. Plato has no qualms about translating this into political terms: some citizens fall at the extremes of the two character types, and do so by nature. No amount of education or training can ever improve them. They will therefore be enslaved, banished, or executed (308e–309a). Like the artist model, this smacks of authoritarianism, or worse.

When faced with these sorts of criticism, there is one response worth making. Much of what Plato has to say about the political state is undeniably authoritarian. But consider (as with the previous models) what happens when you use his writings not as prescriptions for a political state, but for some other kind of organization—for example, a company. Here there is nothing in principle wrong about discarding unnecessary or unworkable materials. The reason is that banishing a person from their state is typically a violation of a human right, whereas excluding them from other, more limited kinds of association is not: firing someone from a company is a matter of regret for the employee, but it need not infringe any human rights, as long as it is done in the right way, e.g. with the appropriate compensation. So perhaps the most obvious criticisms of the weaver model can be avoided when we are applying it to entities other than the state.

How does the weaver relate Plato's to other models of leadership?

In the Introduction to this book, we discussed whether or not one should attempt to take a 'one-size-fits-all' approach to leadership: is the task to find a single all-encompassing definition? One advantage of studying Plato's views on the subject is that he tends not to force a single definition on his readers. Instead, he offers us a variety of models, from which he can select the most appropriate according to the circumstances.

However, the *Statesman* seems different in this respect. Its purpose is to find *the* definition of the political leader. Plato does this by selecting the appropriate model (or 'paradigm', as he calls it at 277d), but the status of this model, the weaver, seems rather different from what we have seen in some of the other cases. The navigator and the artist, as presented in the *Republic*, are used as pedagogical or rhetorical devices— analogies to help readers who may be struggling with Plato's thought. As such, they are useful tools with which to think. But in the *Statesman*, he is much more self-conscious about the use of models or paradigms (277a–279a), and is intent on finding exactly that model which captures the essence of statesmanship (305e). So here he does seem to follow the 'one-size-fits-all' approach.

What, then, would he have to say about his other models? Are they now to be discarded? We have already argued that he discards the shepherd in the *Statesman* 274e–275c (see Chapter 7). But the other models can easily be kept in play. Indeed, two of them are implicit in the description of the weaver's activity, as if deliberately incorporated: the teacher and the doctor. When talking of the way in which the weaver will bind everyone together with a common set of values, Plato stresses the need for education

(308d–310a): the weaver can only do his job if he supervises the education of the citizens. As for the doctor, it is easy to see how the model could be incorporated into the weaver: his task is to keep two different tendencies in balance, without letting either one become the defining characteristic of the state. This is the sort of balancing act we made central to the doctor in Chapter 2. If it is not achieved, the state or organization is beset with conflict and disunity (even war, as we saw in our Monnet case study). Interestingly enough, Plato refers to the conflict that the weaver tries to avoid as a 'disease', the worst that could affect a state (307d).[5]

The model of the artist, though not mentioned in the *Statesman*, is nonetheless consistent with its requirement that the weaver unites all the citizens around a single vision of what is just and beneficial. The point of the ship's captain is also relevant when you think of the way the captain needs to keep the crew united: Plato is now saying that the key point here is to ensure that their different temperaments can be woven together to preserve common purpose.[6]

So the *Statesman* keeps most of the models in play; it does not turn its back on them. At the same time, it gives the weaver a special status as capturing the essence of political leadership. However, this did not appear to have become entrenched in Plato's thought. The *Laws*, a much longer political work written after the *Statesman*, mostly ignores the model of the weaver when talking about the legislator, and instead reverts to the doctor and the teacher.[7]

There is one final point to make about how the weaver differs from the other models. The moment we reintroduce the doctor or the teacher, we once again highlight the centrality of expertise. Taken in isolation, the weaver does not actually put the same kind of stress on expertise (although elsewhere in the *Statesman*, Plato does insist that the political leader is an expert). True, the political weaver has a skill: blending people together but, unlike political doctors, navigators, or teachers, they do not bring in a perspective 'from the outside'; they do not come down from the mountain with tablets of stone, as it were, something that can cause friction with their followers. So, there is something much less remote about this kind of leader than these other models—the doctor with his unpalatable remedy, the navigator gazing in an entirely different direction, or the teacher returning from an alien world. That not all the models stress the importance of expertise in the same way fits with our general approach in this book: they pick out different strands of leadership, no one of which has to run through all examples of the phenomenon.[8]

The weaver. Key principles:

1. The leader weaves together different sorts of people, in particular doves and hawks.
2. There will only be co-operation and unity if the different groups of people espouse the same values.
3. The leader needs to be prepared to discard certain strands that do not fit into the pattern of their woven cloth.
4. A good leader manages to weave the virtues of both courage and moderation into their own character.

Case studies

Nelson Mandela

While Nelson Mandela fits a number of Plato's leadership models at different times in his long career, the weaver is particularly apt for someone who did so much to bring unity to a fractured nation. This is very clear when he was thrust into the limelight after his release from prison in 1990, but it is also evident in his role as a political activist from the 1940s onwards.

Mandela lived in a country with a legal and social framework that, since the 1950s, had divided citizens into four racial groups: Bantu, Coloured, Asian, and White. Inequality and disparity were formally codified to perpetuate these social divisions within a system known as apartheid (which translates as 'apartness'). In the 1940s and 1950s Mandela was active in the ANC (African National Congress), an organization dedicated to overthrowing the apartheid regime. From the 1960s onwards, he spent twenty-seven years in prison for his role in the ANC. From 1990 to 1994, after his release from prison, he worked with the government of South Africa and other stakeholders to negotiate an end to apartheid. When he became resident of the country in 1994, he exercised his leadership to bring together a country long torn apart by racial division. We see an exemplar of his weaving ability when he endorsed a new type of restorative justice process the world hadn't really seen before, the Truth and Reconciliation Commission (TRC), in one of his first acts as President. Just as importantly, he had to craft a coalition in his own ANC party that consisted of exiles, communists, revolutionaries, militants, and others; and he had to do so on a worldwide stage without appearing to 'sell out'.

Weaving together hawks and doves (W1)

We can see this principle evident in different stages of Mandela's career, both before and after apartheid was dismantled. From early on, he tried to strike a balance between radicals and accommodationists within the ANC. Although he was opposed to the aggressive tendencies of the more militant Pan-Africanist Congress (PAC), he nonetheless recognized the value and the inevitability, given black resentment against the apartheid regime, of armed struggle. In the late 1940s, he helped to shift the ANC towards direct action (strikes and boycotts): he relates that he and his allies 'guided the ANC to a more radical and revolutionary path'.[9] This is an example of Mandela changing the attitudes of doves within the ANC via the power of persuasion. Likewise, in the early 1960s he persuaded dovish factions within the ANC, including its then leader, Albert Luthuli, to support the formation of the uMkhonto weSizwe (MK), the wing of the ANC that would attack South African infrastructure and military targets.[10] But its focus on sabotage, which avoided any guerrilla warfare against civilian targets, helped to appease dovish members of the liberation movement; Mandela also foresightedly argued that it would be more likely than other forms of struggle to be consistent with post-apartheid racial reconciliation in South Africa. In adopting a limited form of armed resistance, Mandela maintained the trust and the goodwill of both hawks and doves within the ANC.

In the post-apartheid era, the TRC provides a good example of a mechanism that Mandela set up to help constrain the more extreme tendencies of both hawks and doves. It heard complaints against both the apartheid state and its supporters, and against revolutionary anti-apartheid organizations. Predictably, the prescription was hard to sell on all sides. To take an example of restraining the hawks: the family of the murdered anti-apartheid activist Steve Biko castigated the TRC as a 'vehicle for political expediency', and brought a legal challenge against the Commission on constitutional grounds. Supporters of Biko's family wanted Biko's killers to be punished for their actions; Mandela felt that this kind of retribution against former apartheid state employees would present too great an obstacle to future national reconciliation. But Mandela also ensured that concessions to doves by the TRC were not too extreme. In the end, it only granted 849 out of 7,111 amnesty applications made.[11] (Applicants for amnesty had to prove that their human rights violations were politically motivated, and that they told the Commission the full truth.) By contrast, moderate Afrikaners like F. W. de Klerk (the state President who dismantled apartheid) had hoped for a blanket amnesty, and for an equal number of pro-apartheid and anti-apartheid members on the Commission.[12]

So the TRC was an institutional framework for which Mandela managed to solicit reasonably widespread support. Once in place, it could function to moderate both radicals (hawks) and accommodationists (doves) within the ANC and the wider liberation movement. Empirical studies suggest that a large majority of both white and black South Africans regarded the TRC as effective at uncovering the truth, and that black South Africans thought it effective at bringing about national reconciliation.[13]

Promoting a common set of values (W2)

Mandela saw the importance of a clear set of shared values early on. In 1955, the Congress Alliance (comprised of the ANC, the South African Indian Congress, the Coloured People's Congress, the South African Congress of Trade Unions, and the white-led Congress of Democrats) adopted the Freedom Charter, a statement of values that Mandela described as 'an inspiration to the people of South Africa'.[14] The Freedom Charter was something that brought together liberationists of all stripes—radicals and accommodationists.

Mandela also recognized that a unifying vision of a future South Africa (the 'rainbow nation') could help to gain support for the shared values that he believed would be necessary in order to arrive there:

> We can build a society grounded on friendship and our common humanity—a society founded on tolerance. That is the only road open to us. It is a road to a glorious future in this beautiful country of ours. Let us join hands and march into the future.[15]

Discarding people who are too hawkish or too dovish (W3)

As President, and with much more power to realize his goals of reconciling a divided nation, Mandela appeared to shy away from ruthlessness. However, he did not hesitate to drop ideas and the people committed to them when he found a better way. For instance, the Communist Party had long favoured nationalizing many industries in order to address the economic inequality in South Africa. Mandela stayed loyal to the Party even as de Klerk and others urged him to abandon it. However, after attending a World Economic Forum and talking with business and political leaders from around the globe, he decided that nationalization was not a very robust strategy, and he abandoned the communist doctrine.

And there are more specific examples. In the late 1940s, when he led the ANC Youth League, Mandela moved against ANC President Xuma, who refused to countenance greater action against the apartheid regime, such as strikes, boycotts, and large public protests. Here we see Mandela moving to eliminate a dove. Xuma was removed as president by a vote of no-confidence, replaced by James Moroka, who was more willing to countenance direct action.[16] On the other hand, Mandela opposed the Africanist (Black-nationalist), highly militant wing of the ANC, and was happy to see the Africanists leave in 1959 to form their own

Pan-Africanist Congress (PAC). Mandela commented that the ANC was better off without them, describing their hawkish, pugnacious stance as 'immature' and 'naïve'.[17]

Another example of Mandela moving to marginalize an excessively hawkish member of the ANC came in 1995, when he sacked his fire-brand estranged wife Winnie from the South African cabinet. Winnie was particularly militant (having been convicted of kidnapping in 1991), and during her time in government had 'criticiz[ed] the pace of government reforms... and def[ied] the president by leaving on a state visit to West Africa against his orders'. At the time she was also being investigated by the police for corruption.[18]

The leader weaves courage and temperance into their own character (W4).

Mandela represented the middle ground within the liberation movement: willing to countenance limited armed resistance against the apartheid state, but unwilling to embrace the more violent Afro-nationalism of groups like the Pan-Africanist Congress (PAC).

He certainly had a hawkish side, but he was also prepared to moderate it when the circumstances required. After his release from prison, when he was negotiating with the white South African government, he supported and helped to organize mass protest marches and strikes. After the September 1992 Bisho massacre (twenty-eight protestors were shot dead during a protest march), however, Mandela realized that his hawkish tactics were counterproductive: he called off ANC mass action and recommenced his (previously suspended) negotiations with the government.[19]

The following quote from Mandela illustrates how he worked to moderate his hawkish side and develop his temperate side:

Our emotions said: the white minority is our enemy, we must never talk to them. But our brains said: if you don't talk to these men, your country will go up in flames, and, for many years to come, this country will be engulfed in rivers of blood. So we had to reconcile that conflict, and our talking to the enemy was the result of the domination of the brain over emotion.[20]

The other models

As we said at the outset, Mandela can also be seen as embodying many of the other models of leadership. Particularly striking is his approach to education. We saw that Plato incorporates the model of the teacher into the work of the political weaver, and so it is appropriate here to mention the educational dimension of Mandela's leadership. No matter his circumstances, he prioritized educating others: this was true of his time in prison as well as after his release, always believing it was the most effective way to help people of different backgrounds see what unites them with others, rather than what divides them:

> No country can really develop unless its citizens are educated. Any nation that is progressive is led by people who have had the privilege of studying. I knew we could improve our lives even in jail. We could come out as different men, and we could even come out with two degrees. Educating ourselves was a way to give ourselves the most powerful weapon for freedom.[21]

Educating others to strengthen the fabric around him was always of critical importance for Mandela, even while a prisoner. His efforts to educate his fellow prisoners led to the notoriously harsh prison on Robben Island being dubbed 'the University of the Struggle' against apartheid South Africa. These efforts helped him to strengthen the fabric around him, even while imprisoned, as he assiduously attempted to weave together a lasting reconciliation of disparate groups within his deeply divided apartheid South Africa.

As well as the teacher, the doctor is highly applicable to Mandela. In promoting the TRC, he was applying the right remedy at the right time, like a prescription. It sought a balance: there was the need to see justice done against human rights abusers, whilst restraining the victims' anger in order to avoid a reactionary backlash against Afrikaners and other white South Africans.[22]

Finally, Mandela himself briefly makes a comparison between one facet of leadership and a shepherd: 'A leader... is like a shepherd. He stays behind the flock, letting the most nimble go out ahead, whereupon the others follow, not realizing that all along they are being directed from behind.'[23]

Jim Kutsch: blind weaver

Jim Kutsch was born in 1950 in West Virginia, where he attended a local public elementary school and, then, a private military academy.[24] When he was 16, he completely lost his eyesight and right-hand fingers due to an experiment with pyrotechnics and explosives in his backyard. However, he didn't despair or give up, but continued his studies at school. With the help of a fellow-student at school and of his parents, who read his school assignments to him and transcribed his answers, he graduated from school and enrolled at university. He obtained a bachelor's degree in Psychology, a masters in Computer Science at West Virginia University (WVU), and PhD in Computer Science at the University of Illinois. From his own experience of what it means to study when you are blind, Kutsch managed to develop the first talking computer for the blind while working on his PhD. At the same time, he also invented one of the first screen readers to help the blind. After completing his PhD program, he returned to WVU to teach computer science. After several years, he left the academic world and joined business. He worked for AT&T and Convergys where, over the years, where he reached the position of Vice President of Technology. In 1990, he joined the company The Seeing Eye, which specializes in breeding and training dogs for helping the blind. In 2006, he became the first blind president of the company.

Weaving together hawks and doves (W1)

When we introduced the notion of diversity in Plato's model of the weaver, we said that there are two ways it could be understood. Taking a very broad view, one could point to the existence of very different talents and temperaments in an organization and say that the leader's job is to knit them together, so that everyone is co-operating in the same enterprise. Kutsch clearly believed in the importance of diversity in this sense:[25]

> Diversity is essential as you work with other people. If all of your friends are exactly like you, then you have a lot of spare people in your life. There are plenty of chances to use different talents of different people. You need to focus on the abilities, not the limitations or the disabilities, of others.

But our focus here is on weaving in the narrower sense—achieving the co-operation between hawks and doves in an organization. Kutsch devoted much of his life to integrating disabled people into regular work environments and making employees with different health conditions work together as one team. He empowered his team members, trusted them, and expected everyone in his team to do the same.[26] According to one of Kutsch's co-workers:

> Kutsch had a knack for resolving interpersonal conflict and a natural ability to present a reasoned approach to potential antagonists and build consensus. He was proactive in solving conflicts among people. For example, site leaders...were empowered to take whatever action was necessary [during crisis situations]. At times other people would become involved and they would want to run the incident. [He] was very good at pulling that particular person aside and saying, 'This person is already empowered to do this, trust them to do their job.' He was supporting the site leader or incident commander—and at the same time, dealing with the interpersonal reasons—so [the outside manager] understood the reasons why.

Kutsch empowered particular (sorts of) people to do particular jobs, and then made sure that others didn't interfere. He was very careful to restrain any hawks who were liable to jump into things that fell under another person's purview. On the other hand, like a good weaver, he also empowered and encouraged potentially dovish employees, first by letting them know that, if they did not act, nobody else was going to step in to help, and second by ensuring that they had what they needed to do the job:

> When employees here come to him with 'But I'm blind,' he doesn't accept that as an excuse for not performing. That's where his caring and compassion come in. He asks them, 'What are the accommodations you need? Let's make it happen. You can be successful regardless of who you are.'

As this shows, Kutsch was very keen that people (especially doves) take responsibility: 'I see him in his leadership role at The Seeing Eye—and he holds people to task. I always think of the phrase "No Excuses". That sums him up.' He set high standards both for himself and for the team. By not allowing any excuses, even for the disabled, he made everyone feel that they were part of a team of equal individuals working together toward a common goal.

Promoting a common set of values (W2)

What is also distinctive about Kutsch's leadership style is his moral character, as one of his co-workers testified:

> She had witnessed first-hand his [Kutsch's] commitment to earning rather than expecting respect; the high standards to which he continued to hold himself and everyone around him; his rational, considered, decisive action; his generosity of spirit; and his unwavering commitment to doing the right thing regardless of external circumstances.

Kutsch cared about his people and expected others to have the same attitude toward their teams. He promoted a common set of values in so far as he applied his own high standards to 'everyone around him'. Whenever anyone from his team needed help, he acted immediately, without any delay:

[He] was acting as unified commander for North America and India. If we had a situation that would impact multiple sites, he would pull people from each site into a telecom bridge. He was the first one to say, 'How can we take care of our people?' For example, we had hurricanes coming up the coast of Florida that were impacting sites. He had supplies delivered [to our sites], like diapers and water, making sure they were up with generators, so they could not only make a wage but also take care of their families...he's extremely magnanimous. He's always very quick to give credit to others...if he were being rewarded for some action that he took, he was always quick to recognize the team.

It is easy to show that Kutsch illustrates key principle W2 (the need for shared values) in the case of a non-profit like Seeing Eye. There is ample evidence to be had of his own firm commitment to these values. He says that all the whilst building his professional career 'I [was] still looking for practical ways to develop technology for people with disabilities. I designed software that would...depict graphic data [with sound], including stock market readers based on sound so [blind] people could track the stock market....I never made any money from them but was certainly willing to share them.' From the late 1980s he served a seven-year stint on the President's Committee on Employment of People with Disabilities.

As for principle W4 (a good leader weaves the qualities of dove and hawk into their own character), Kutsch managed to combine dove-like care or justice for others with his hawkish 'no excuses' approach towards employees of the company.

Notes

1. On the analysis of political leadership in this work, see Lane (2012) and (2006) 180–4. Klein (1988) uses Plato's weaver to look at business leadership, taking a broad historical view of American corporate culture.
2. As one of the anonymous readers for this book commented: 'the cloth is made better by allowing its elements to shine brightly with their individual virtues, as long as these are appropriately placed within the fabric. The point would be that leaders will find that they cultivate teams that are successful by enabling the individuals within them to flourish or excel in their distinctive ways.'

3. 311a–b, trans. Jowett (1871) modified.
4. Popper (1962) I 166.
5. It should not be surprising that Plato keeps the doctor and the teacher in play, as he will later go on to give them joint prominence in the *Laws*. See Chapter 6.
6. There are various nautical parallels in the *Statesman*. At 292a–300c, Plato uses the parallel of the navigator or captain (alongside the doctor) to think about political expertise. At 292d, he seems to be alluding to the ship of state in *Rep.* Book 6, when he criticizes demagogues in actual states who claim to be navigators or helmsmen. For the point that a captain focuses on the well-being of his passengers (as opposed to his own), see 296e.
7. Plato does refer briefly to the weaving analogy in the *Laws* (Book 5, 735a), but in a different way from the *Statesman*. The rulers are assimilated to the firm warp-like strands, the subjects to the woof-like ones. In the *Statesman*, the rulers incorporate both kinds of strand; similarly, both kinds can be found among the rest of the citizens.
8. The idea that corporate weaving isn't really about expertise has been voiced by Lynn Good, CEO of Duke Energy. See Parker (2018): 'It is interesting to note that Good doesn't see expertise in a single subject matter to be the single most important characteristic for people in senior leadership positions at corporations. Instead, she believes that to be the ability to manage a diverse group of people, which makes sense because senior leaders are meant to, well, lead rather than do everything on their own.'
9. Mandela (1994) 165.
10. https://www.sahistory.org.za/article/umkhonto-wesizwe-mk.
11. https://www.law.cornell.edu/wex/south_african_truth_commission; and https://www.usip.org/publications/1995/12/truth-commission-south-africa.
12. Allen (2006) 362–3.
13. Vora and Vora (2004).
14. Meredith (2010) 134.
15. Mandela (2011) 116.
16. Meredith (2010) 78–9.
17. Meredith (2010) 167–8.
18. Drogin (1995).
19. Meredith (2010) 467–71.
20. From Nelson Mandela on Oprah—see https://www.youtube.com/watch?v=0i-BH3HXT24.
21. https://www.oprah.com/world/oprah-interviews-nelson-mandela/5.
22. See Mandela's own words in his inauguration speech: 'The time for the healing of the wounds has come' (https://speakola.com/political/nelson-mandela-inauguration-1994). There are plenty of references to healing by other commentators, e.g. Miliband (2013): 'It was President Mandela who helped heal the wounds of the past with his combination of tough determination as well as compassion and

generosity to those who jailed him and oppressed his people.' (Note the combination of 'tough determination' and 'compassion', which recalls principle W4.)
23. Mandela (2011) 146.
24. James and Oliver (2009).
25. Kutsch (2012).
26. What follows is based on James and Oliver (2009). The quotations used also derive from this source.

9

The Sower

Plato

Overview

Most of the leadership models we have considered so far were initially conceived by Plato to apply to politics. But our last model is about thought leadership, the kind of leadership Plato himself exercised. It can be found in his dialogue, the *Phaedrus*.

Written sometime after the *Republic*, the *Phaedrus* is often described as being about rhetoric. Although Plato had been highly critical of orators in his earlier works, especially the *Gorgias*, here he reveals a more positive attitude. As we saw in previous chapters, he had been worrying about how you persuade people of something they are reluctant to accept. So, in and of itself, rhetoric might actually help, provided that it is not misused by demagogues and the like. This is the position of the *Phaedrus*, which tries to characterize the art of rhetoric in such a way that it can actually benefit its audience.

But to say the *Phaedrus* is about rhetoric is too narrow; it is really about the power of words more generally. Rhetoric is one manifestation of this power, but words can be written as well as spoken. So, although most of the dialogue is taken up one way or another with the spoken word, the last section looks at writing: how effective is it at spreading one's ideas and influencing others (274b–277b)?

Although we can only speculate, it is likely that this question had a deep resonance for Plato at this point in his career. He had already authored several books, including masterpieces like the *Gorgias* and the *Republic*. But, as we shall suggest, he was beginning to worry about the effectiveness of writing as a medium to make a genuinely profound influence on his successors. In our terms, he was probably having legacy issues.

You might think that the whole point of writing is to leave something behind when you are no longer there to spread your ideas in person. But in the *Phaedrus*, he argues that writing is in fact a very poor tool for the job. When it comes to spreading your ideas and leaving behind a real legacy, some other solution needs to be found.

The writing paradox

In order to focus our minds on the nature and limitations of writing, Plato uses an interesting pedagogical device. Writing is all around us, more so now than in his day, but even then it was still a phenomenon that people took for granted. So, to make us think of it afresh, he imagines the point in history when it was first invented (274c–275b). He tells a story of an inventor called Theuth, who visits the king of Egypt, Thamus, to boast of his latest ideas, writing being among them. The king looks through them all, approving of some, but objecting to others, especially the invention of writing.

His fear is that it will make us lazy and lead to false pretensions of wisdom. Instead of holding all your knowledge in your own head, you can effectively create an external storage facility and save yourself the trouble of having to remember it. (Compare modern concerns that digitization is reducing our mental capacities by allowing us to 'outsource' our memories.) Worse, if you pick up a piece of writing and learn it, you can *appear* to understand it, when all you're really doing is regurgitating it. Plato makes a comparison to the religious festival of Adonis, when people used to decorate their houses with pots of flowers that were planted to bloom in a week, but wouldn't have lasted very long (276b). This is a good analogy for the kind of display that writing facilitates. When most people memorize a written text, they don't necessarily understand it or, as we say, 'internalize' it. So, when questioned and asked to defend or explain it for themselves, they won't be able to respond effectively; all they'll really be able to do is to repeat back what they've memorized. Their 'wisdom', like the flowers of Adonis, wilts under interrogation.

And there's even worse to come when you consider the author's perspective. If you send a written text out into the world, not only can you never ensure that anyone really understands it, they may actively misunderstand it. Written texts can fall into the wrong hands, and an author has no ultimate control as to how their writing is received. The dangers of misunderstanding, misinterpretation, and slander may be insurmountable.

As we suggested above, Plato had reached a stage where he had already written a large number of dialogues and was beginning to worry about his intellectual legacy. He foresaw, or thought he foresaw, the dangers of merely leaving behind a collection of manuscripts for anyone to do with what they wished.

So what is the solution? Writing can't be uninvented; in fact, it has its place. According to the *Phaedrus*, if you already understand something, writing can be a useful *aide memoire*, especially as you get older and more forgetful; but all it can really do is to remind you of something you already know. There's no substitute for actual, living dialogue between two people: patient cross-questioning, on both sides, ultimately leading to genuine understanding, fully internalized. Plato calls this 'writing on the mind': instead of using pen and paper (or the Greek equivalent), the teacher uses dialogue to influence the mind of the student directly.

All this applies as well to the problem of authors and their legacies. You can't secure your legacy just by leaving behind written texts. You have to leave behind real people, who have internalized your ideas. In their turn, they can do the same with the next generation. In principle, the process could continue indefinitely. Plato compares the original idea to a seed that is planted in the correct soil (not like the flowers of Adonis) and grows into a flower, which in turn produces the same seeds again. The idea acquires a kind of immortality (277a).

Plato's critique of writing has generated a great deal of attention.[1] For one thing, it is very easy to dispute. To be sure, some people treat the written word uncritically, but not everyone does. An individual could pick up a book, mentally question it, and form their own views on the subject. Even if they eventually agree with the author, they might have done so autonomously. In fact, as the reader of the *Phaedrus* ponders such objections, they may have a sense of paradox: Plato writes all this down. So how much credence are we meant to give it? And if we ourselves are arguing with the text and interrogating it, doesn't that undermine the very point he is making? Writing has more value than just as an *aide memoire*, especially if it can be crafted in such a way as to provoke an internal dialogue in the reader, as Plato's own works tend to do.[2]

But our main interest is in Plato's solution to the problem of writing, his model of what true thought leadership involves: 'writing on the mind.' He sees it as a kind of farming or husbandry: a matter of finding the right seed, planting it in the right soil, nurturing the plant that subsequently grows, and then allowing its seeds to create the next generation of plants. On this model, success requires that the leader is a pioneer, with ideas big enough to create a legacy in the first place. Also, it is built into the nature of the model that the leader steps back and lets others take over for themselves. But it is not enough to step back (a negative point), leaders must positively empower those they entrust with their ideas; only if this happens can the process continue. A thought leader who just indoctrinates—who does not create a genuine dialogue with others—is no leader at all.

Tolerating mutation

We can gain more insight into the sower if we step outside the *Phaedrus* and look at what Plato actually did as a thought leader, historically speaking. The moral of the *Phaedrus* is that you can't lead people just by writing books; you have to engage with their minds more directly. How did Plato himself do this? His mentor Socrates did so as a public intellectual. He never wrote any of his philosophy down, but went around having dialogues with different individuals, often quite eminent citizens. Plato also made dialogue the centre-piece of his work, but in a more institutionalized way.[3] What he did was to found his own school, known as the Academy, a privately funded institute of higher education and research. Its members studied philosophy in our sense. But it was not merely a philosophy institute: he actively supported the study of geometry,[4] and his interests ranged over many other fields, including astronomy, cosmology, history, language, law, music, and religion. Given this breadth of interests, it is quite appropriate to see the Academy as an embryonic university. It survived for centuries after his death and became a model for other schools to follow.[5]

The Academy would have had a library, which of course included Plato's own works. But, as we would expect from the *Phaedrus*, students were required to do far more than immerse themselves in books. A central component of their education was 'dialectic', a term with more technical connotations than our word 'dialogue'. For Plato, philosophy did need to involve dialogue or conversation, but what is required is something very challenging, where one party interrogates another and forces them to defend their views.[6] In promoting 'dialectic', what he seems to have done is to create a more formal training procedure, creating something analogous to gymnastics, which would empower his students in hard-nosed philosophical argument. Making this a core component of education in the Academy may have been his way of institutionalizing the process of 'writing on the mind' described in the *Phaedrus*.[7]

What sort of legacy did Plato's Academy produce—or, what was it meant to produce? It is very unlikely he wanted to promote dogmatic adherence to a fixed set of beliefs. If that was his objective, encouraging dialectic would have been a risky business: students might end up rejecting his views rather than believing them. Dialectic empowered them to think for themselves and develop their own philosophies. It is more likely that he wanted to point his successors in the direction of certain ideas, without forcing them into compliance. The strength of the ideas would be enough to ensure they survived in some form, but empowering his students with dialectic would mean, inevitably, that those ideas would undergo mutation and cross-fertilization with other ideas that might emerge over time.[8]

In the event, whatever Plato's original intentions, this is certainly what happened. The institution of the Academy allowed for the development of a certain brand of philosophy, 'Platonism': a set of ideas, constantly changing over time, but recognizably similar to some of the views we that find defended in his works and that he would have discussed in the Academy. These ideas range over many areas of philosophy, and in this book we have already encountered several of them, particularly those to do with politics, ethics, and education. After his death, these ideas got mutated over the centuries: philosophers and other thought leaders often professed to be inspired by Plato, but their own work was typically a variation of what he had once thought. In terms of the *Phaedrus* image, the seeds that grew from his plants mutated, adapting themselves to environments he could never have anticipated.[9]

It is obviously impossible to do justice to the breadth of his philosophical legacy in a few sentences. But perhaps the general idea underlying
'Platonism' is the need, in various contexts, to look beyond the material
world. It was this that inspired some of his followers to focus their
energies on seeking out the mathematical order that lies behind observ-
able phenomena. In moral and political contexts, his anti-materialism (or,
as we might say, anti-consumerism) criticizes the obsession with maximizing material possessions rather than focusing on mental or spiritual
well-being and building social cohesion. In the realm of education, he
emphasized the importance of 'learning from within': external inputs,
especially sense perceptions of the material world, are only catalysts to
make us draw upon our own internal resources. (Plato was a believer in
the theory of innate knowledge.) The twentieth-century philosopher
A. N. Whitehead was famously impressed by Plato's legacy: 'The safest
general characterization of the European philosophical tradition is that it
consists of a series of footnotes to Plato.'[10]

Of course, many philosophers have taken issue with these kinds of
views. But over and above his philosophical legacy, the specific ideas he
helped to perpetuate, there is his institutional legacy. In founding the
Academy, not only did he create an institution that would last for
centuries, he also inspired others to do likewise and establish their
own philosophical schools. This started with his own student Aristotle
founding a school (the Lycaeum), whose theories developed often in
direct opposition to Plato's, with a strong emphasis on empirical observation and the collection of data. After Aristotle two further schools
emerged, the Stoics and the Epicureans, who went on to be very
influential in the Roman empire (the former claiming the emperor
Marcus Aurelius among their adherents). So within a couple of generations after Plato's death there was an enormously vigorous intellectual
scene in Athens.

How did Plato manage this? There may have been many factors: sheer
good luck, friends in high places, and money.[11] But again, a key factor
may have been the way he developed dialectic as a technical tool,
empowering his students (like Aristotle) to argue with him and each
other. Another factor was the sheer breadth of the curriculum in the
Academy, which allowed for extensive cross-fertilization between different fields.[12] We said in the Introduction that the Academy might be seen

as the fore-runner of the modern university: much smaller in scale, but containing the seeds for what was to follow. This is no exaggeration.

Conclusion

We are now ready to turn to our case studies. But before we do so, we should raise a question that may already be in the reader's mind: how does the model of the sower differs from the teacher? The *Phaedrus* presents the sower as someone concerned with the best way to teach their students, and the emphasis is on distinguishing true from false forms of education. Plato's own example suggests that as a teacher he was also a sower. This question is a good one: of all the models we have considered, these are closest to each other. So are they really distinct? We shall argue that they are, but shall defer the issue until the next chapter. In outline, our point is that a sower is concerned with perpetuating an idea or set of ideas among successive generations of followers; according to the model of the teacher, the leader focuses on their immediate followers, adopting a policy of rational communication. But it is true that a particular leader might exemplify both models at once. Even so, it can be useful to distinguish the two aspects of their leadership. In our case studies we shall encounter three individuals who have had an enduring legacy. The first worked in the natural sciences, the second in education, and the third in economics and business. Each of them might have been included as case studies in Chapter 5, and the reader will see occasional references to their teaching activities. But this does not undermine their claim to be great examples of the sower.

The sower. Key principles:

S1. Originate ideas big enough to create a legacy.

S2. Step back: allow others to take up your ideas, initiatives, etc.

S3. Empower those you lead.

S4. Tolerate mutation: allow people to change your ideas into something else (as circumstances demand).

Case studies

Marie Skłodowska Curie

Originate ideas big enough to create a legacy (S1)

Marie Skłodowska Curie (or, in short, Marie Curie) was a Polish-French physicist and chemist who made vast contributions to advancing human knowledge and took an active citizen position. She was born in 1867 in Poland in the part of the country that was then under the Russian empire and she received her initial scientific training in Warsaw. At the age of 24, she moved to Paris where she studied, researched, and taught at the Sorbonne.

Curie is a clear example of a thought leader along the lines of Plato's sower. She was responsible for some major scientific breakthroughs: e.g. the theory of radioactivity and the discovery of polonium and radium. Her research also contributed to the development of the X-ray in medicine. She went on to found two research institutes, one in Paris, the other in Warsaw. Apart from her intellectual leadership in science, Curie was deeply dissatisfied with the school system in France and shared ideas on how to reform it. Along with a group of scientists, artists, and academics, she organized The Teaching Cooperative to teach their own children. Compare the way Plato not only generated a plethora of ideas, he also saw the need to create an educational vehicle to disseminate them, the Academy.

Empowering those you lead (S3)

Curie was not only a great scientist, but she put a lot of effort in making others around her learn from her and achieve high accomplishments. Her role was crucial in creating the family legacy of winning Nobel Prizes: five members of her family were awarded Nobel Prizes (there has been no other family that would have more than two members receiving Nobel Prizes). Curie shared her first Nobel Prize with her husband, Pierre Curie (though it was she who originated the research). Their daughter, Irène Joliot-Curie, received the Nobel Prize for

Chemistry in 1935 (a year after Marie Curie's death), together with her husband Frédéric Joliot-Curie. Marie Curie put a lot of effort into Irène's scientific education, and was at least partially responsible for her success. Furthermore, Curie's second daughter's husband, Henry Labouisse, was awarded the Nobel Peace Prize in 1965 when heading Unicef, the UN Children's Fund.[13] Marguerite Perey, one of Curie's students, discovered the element Francium and became the first woman elected as a member of the French Academy of Sciences. As Curie said, 'You cannot hope to build a better world without improving the individuals. To that end each of us must work for his own improvement, and at the same time share a general responsibility for all humanity, our particular duty being to aid those to whom we think we can be most useful.'[14]

Marie Curie contributed to society not only through her research, but also through active citizenship. This enabled her to build trust from others, which was extremely important for her work as a sower to be successful. She also empowered people to apply and extend her ideas by making an effort to teach them. For instance, 'During World War One, Curie helped to equip ambulances with X-ray equipment, which she herself drove to the front lines. The International Red Cross made her head of its radiological service and she held training courses for medical orderlies and doctors in the new techniques.'[15]

Stepping back and tolerating mutation (S2 and S4)

The following extract from Curie's biography of her husband Pierre testifies to the generosity with which both of them allowed their work to be disseminated:

> Our investigations had started a general scientific movement, and similar work was being undertaken in other countries. Towards these efforts, Pierre Curie maintained a most disinterested and liberal atti-tude. With my agreement he refused to draw any material profit from our discovery. We took no copy-right, and published without reserve all the results of our research, as well as the processes of the preparation of radium. In addition, we gave to those interested whatever

information they asked of us. This was of great benefit to the radium industry, which could thus develop in full freedom, first in France, then in foreign countries, and furnish to scientists and to physicians the products which they needed.[16]

In a nutshell, Curie's humility, selflessness, and concern to get others involved was a hallmark of her leadership. We may not normally think of the scientist as leader, but Plato understood that those who sow ideas and create a tradition of inquiry in a new field would make an indelible contribution to humanity, as he himself did.

Maria Montessori

Maria Montessori (1870–1952) was born into a well-educated family, the only child of an Italian civil servant father and a mother who strongly valued education. At a young age she attended a technical school rather than pursuing classical studies, which was the norm for girls at that time. This nonconformist spirit continued into higher education, when—against the wishes of her father—she chose to study medicine at the University of Rome, a field that was considered taboo for women at the time. She went on to become the first woman in Italy to receive a degree in surgery and medicine in 1896.[17]

In her first position after graduation, Montessori pursued her true passion, pedagogy, when she investigated how to best teach intellectually disabled children at a University of Rome psychiatric clinic. Her success in this area helped her secure a lectureship in pedagogy (1900–7) and a chair in anthropology (1904–8) at her alma mater. In 1907, she pursued a new endeavour that would ultimately help launch her onto the world stage: in an impoverished neighbourhood in Rome, she founded her first school called the Casa dei Bambini ('Children's House').

Her observations and experiments as a teacher within this school for young children informed her landmark book, *The Montessori Method*, which she published in 1912.[18] In it, she argued that the current educational system was damaging children, their future, and—with it—humanity's future.

Originating ideas big enough to create a legacy (S1); empowering those you lead (S3)

Montessori argued that the educational system relied on an unscientific and false view of both childhood and human nature. She derided the standard pedagogical practices of her time as 'scholastic slavery'.[19] Her concern was that the teacher's relationship with the children and the classroom environment were effectively designed to stifle and coerce them into submission by adults who fought to wrangle them into acting as they thought society dictated. The prevailing pedagogical paradigm was antithetical to her belief that it was the individualism and independence of the child that mattered most. One could not properly educate a child without liberating them spiritually (mentally, psychologically) through a teaching paradigm which exhibited traits closely associated with monasticism. To be a successful and virtuous Montessorian teacher, it was imperative that one practise self-control and self-restraint like a monk, patiently and keenly observing while intervening only rarely, so as not to belittle the spirit of the child in her pursuit of the truth. As well as listening and observing more, the teacher must foster a spontaneous love of discovery. They should also put an absolute premium on the intrinsic rewards of learning and discovery; Montessori detested the use of extrinsic rewards (e.g. prizes) for students in education. As for punishments: 'the soul of the normal man grows perfect through expanding, and punishment as commonly understood is always a form of *repression*.'[20]

The early success of her first school in 1907 quickly attracted attention. As a result, she founded three more schools over the next few months in Italy, and in 1909 her ideas spread to Italian Switzerland.[21] The following years saw more Montessori schools opening in different European countries, and she made a tumultuous visit to the United States in 1913. As the years went by, she worked tirelessly—writing, lecturing, and giving teacher training courses. She visited India from 1939 to 1946 and helped found more schools there. For some time, she insisted on personally certifying every teacher of her method, a point to which we shall return in a moment.

To judge from the following quotes, she was very conscious about creating a legacy:

> Every great cause is born from repeated failures and from imperfect achievements.... But the St. Francis who so ingenuously carried the stones, and the great reformer who so miraculously led the people to a triumph of the spirit, are one and the same person in different stages of development. So we, who work toward one great end, are members of one and the same body; and those who come after us will reach the goal only because there were those who believed and laboured before them.[22]
>
> We cannot know the future of the progress of thought: here, for example, in the 'Children's Houses' the triumph of *discipline* through the conquest of liberty and independence marks the foundation of the progress which the future will see in the matter of pedagogical methods. To me it offers the greatest hope for human redemption through education.... This book of methods [*The Montessori Method*] compiled by one person alone, must be followed by many others. It is my hope that, starting from *the individual study of the child* educated with our method, other educators will set forth the results of their experiments. These are the pedagogical books which await us in the future.[23]

She would presumably be pleased that there are now many thousands of Montessori schools across the world, based on her underlying philosophy and using the techniques she devised, e.g. mixed age groups, a carefully controlled learning environment, and the use of specifically designed materials. It is a matter of debate how far mainstream her ideas have penetrated, but they are nonetheless discussed by scientists and educational theorists well beyond the confines of the Montessori schools themselves.[24]

Stepping back and tolerating mutation (S2 and S4)?

As Montessori's fame grew quickly, she travelled to the United States in 1913 to much fanfare. One of her biographers, Rita Kramer, describes the nearly religious experience and expectations for her followers who exuberantly welcomed her visit:

> Everywhere she went she was hailed as a prophet of pedagogy and a major force for wide social reforms, and by the time she sailed for home on Christmas Eve it seemed reasonable to suppose that American schools would never be the same again—at the very least, that Montessori would leave some lasting effect on education here.[25]

However, these lofty expectations of Montessori's prominence as a sower of social and educational reform in the United States turned out to be premature. Kramer goes on to note that Montessori and her attendant method were all but forgotten in the United States when she died forty years later (though she remained influential in Europe):

> At the time of her death in 1952 many readers of her obituaries either did not know who she was or were surprised that she had still been alive and active in the postwar years. She seemed to belong to another time.... With the perspective of time, her genius becomes clearer. She remains one of the true originals of educational theory and practice.[26]

Harold Solan provides one explanation for why the 'Montessori Method' flourished worldwide after her death but had not proliferated as much as one would have expected given her international fame ante-mortem:

> The Montessori Method of teaching ultimately was recognized internationally. However, her insistence upon certifying each new teacher personally did limit the growth of the Montessori Method in spite of her extensive writing and lecturing. It should be emphasized that much of what she conceptualized in the past century is now part and parcel of standard educational practice. Furthermore, her basic concepts of developmental vision and the role of intersensory development in learning still continue to influence optometric treatment of children diagnosed with learning related vision disorders.[27]

This highlights the dilemma for the leader as sower. The more you step back, the more your ideas might take root; but there is also a risk of contamination or distortion. This tension was already clear in Plato's *Phaedrus*, when he worries about the way an author's works may fall into the wrong hands—those who misunderstand their intent. So a balance has to be struck between nurturing your ideas and controlling them.

Mohammed Yunus and the Grameen Bank

Mohammed Yunus was a US-trained economist teaching at Chittagong University in his home nation of Bangladesh.[28] He noticed while walking to work every day that there was a woman who made beautiful rattan furniture, but he also observed that she was very poor and had a lot of trouble feeding her family. After some investigation he figured out that she had to borrow money from moneylenders who charged high interest and demanded that she sell her products to them at a cheap price, so that she could never 'get ahead'. Yunus sent his students out in the community to find out if there were others like this woman. They discovered that there were forty families who could become self-sufficient with a total investment for all of roughly 800 takas (= \$28). So Yunus inquired at a local bank about the loans, and he was laughed at because of course these very poor people had no collateral, and were 'not bankable'. This led Yunus to start a revolution which became known as 'microfinance'. His organization, the Grameen Bank, has lent money to the poorest of the poor, now over a billion dollars to millions of poor people. The mission of the Bank is that 'poverty belongs in a museum'. As he put it:

> Observing the failure of existing institutions to lift the terrible burdens of deprivation from the shoulders of the poor, I was moved, like many other people, to seek a better answer.... Thus began a lifelong involvement in efforts to alleviate social problems using innovative organizational structures—structures that, I hoped, might be more effective, flexible, and self-sustaining than the failed institutions of the past.[29]

Originate ideas big enough to have a legacy (S1); allow others to take up your ideas (S2)

Yunus is clearly a thought leader, and has been recognized with a Nobel Peace Prize in 2006. Hence he is a good example of Plato's sower model. He has established a legacy for himself in a number of areas. 'Microfinance' is the name given to the discipline that Yunus established in Bangladesh with his Grameen Bank, and it has grown to be practised in a number of ways around the world from very economically poor countries to the United States. In addition, he has been an advocate of 'social business': a way of thinking about investing in a business, getting your investment returned but eschewing profit. He worked with a number of existing companies such as Danone, the French yogurt maker, to start joint ventures that were social businesses and could help alleviate poverty in developing countries. Grameen also works with Whole Foods Market to make micro-loans in the communities of Whole Foods suppliers to build stronger local business communities.

Empower those you lead (S3)

In the early days of the bank, Yunus went village to village talking primarily with women in a culture where men and women simply did not mix very much outside the family. He believed that the only thing missing from the poor was money, or access to credit. He says:

> To me, the poor are like bonsai trees. When you plant the best seed of the tallest tree in a six-inch-deep flower pot, you get a perfect replica of the tallest tree, but it is only inches tall. There is nothing wrong with the seed you planted; only the soil-base you provided was inadequate. The poor are bonsai people. There is nothing wrong with their seeds. Only society never gave them a base to grow on. All that is required to get poor people out of poverty is for us to create an enabling environment for them. Once the poor are allowed to unleash their energy and creativity, poverty will quickly disappear.[30]

He taught others about how money works, and he built a cadre of other leaders who could teach others, thereby perpetuating his legacy. In turbulent political times Yunus steered the bank through some difficult issues with the Bangladesh government, and he never wavered from his vision of what the business could be or of its commitment to helping the poor to build a better society. Again in his own words:

> An ideal society should create an enabling environment around each individual so that all his or her creative energies can be unleashed to the very fullest. A maximum of personal freedom is vital to the creation of such an enabling environment.[31]

Recently he has been forced out of Grameen Bank due to political manoeuvrings in Bangladesh, but he had created a system of other leaders who could step in and continue his work. Yunus was also a direct leader in addition to being a thought leader, putting his ideas into practice. Like Marie Curie, he understood thought leadership's connection to actually doing things in the world. For him it wasn't in the lab, but in the field, building Grameen Bank village by village. Yunus engenders great trust by others. His simple honesty and straightforward manner gives him an authority so that others want to pay attention.

The seeds sown by Yunus and his followers at Grameen and companies around the world will yield positive results for generations. Once again Plato would recognize this sower of the seeds of knowledge.

Notes

1. For some discussion, see Nehamas and Woodruff (1995) xxxiv–vii and Blank (2012).
2. By writing dialogues instead of treatises, Plato brings to life views that challenge the arguments of his principal interlocutor Socrates. This has the effect of inviting readers to put themselves in the opposition's shoes. Sometimes a reader might actually come to see the strength in an opposing view, even if Plato presents Socrates as winning the argument. A good example is his use of Thrasymachus in the first book of the *Republic*: some readers find his critique of Socrates refreshing and in places quite convincing. For instance, his point

about the shepherd as exploiting the sheep (discussed in Chapter 7) certainly makes us sit up and think; it deters us from just accepting Socrates' position uncritically, even if we ultimately agree with it.

3. Recall Jean Monnet's claim that 'nothing is made without men; nothing lasts without institutions', cited in our case study in Chapter 2.

4. There was an inscription over the entrance to the Academy, which ran: 'let no one enter who is ignorant of geometry.'

5. On Plato's Academy, see Karamanolis (2012), Bonazzi (2013), and Adamson (2014) 309–14.

6. In the *Republic*, he talks of dialectic as being 'like a battle' (Book 7, 534b). The point is that, if someone just accepted one of his philosophical views and spouted it as the truth of the master, the student should always be challenged to justify it for himself.

7. Our evidence comes from Aristotle, Plato's top student in the Academy. See Smith (2020) 8.3.1, discussing 'gymnastic dialectic': 'there appears to have been a form of stylized argumentative exchange practiced in the Academy in Aristotle's time. The main evidence for this is simply Aristotle's *Topics*, especially Book VIII, which makes frequent reference to rule-governed procedures, apparently taking it for granted that the audience will understand them.'

8. Another possibility, much further along the scale, is that Plato's interest was not so much in any specific doctrines as in a way of doing philosophy, one that he inherited from Socrates. The basic principle here is that 'the unexamined life is not worth living' (Plato *Apology* 38a): human beings have a duty always to pursue open-minded inquiry, wherever that might lead. Perhaps this was the seed that Plato really wanted to sow. This approach can be found in Vogt (2013).

9. If asked whether he was the archetypical sower, Plato might have deflected the compliment towards Socrates, his mentor and inspiration: many Platonic ideas could be seen as developments and transformations of Socratic ideas (which may be why he uses Socrates as the main speaker in most of dialogues, including the *Phaedrus*). But if he meant us to see Socrates as the original sower of his ideas, he would surely endorse the principle that good sowers approve when others mutate their ideas.

10. Whitehead (1978) 39.

11. There is an interesting story about the funds used to purchase the land for the Academy, 'Plato's Garden'. The anecdote comes from the ancient biographer Diogenes Laertius, Book 3, 18–20. On his first visit to Syracuse, Plato got into an argument with the ruling tyrant, Dionysius I, insisting that a ruler should never prioritize his own self-interest. (The topic of argument is very similar to the debate between Socrates and Thrasymachus in *Republic* Book 1.) Things became heated: Dionysius accused Plato of blabbering like an old man; Plato accused him of being a tyrant. In his fury, Dionysius wanted to have Plato executed, but was

prevailed upon to exact a lesser penalty: to have him sold as a slave. Plato was shipped to another location for sale, but a man called Anniceris recognized him and paid the ransom so that he could be freed and sent back safely to Athens. Another of Plato's friends, Dion, offered to recompense Anniceris for the cost of the ransom, but Anniceris refused to take it for himself, saying that it was an honour to be able to help the great philosopher. Instead, he used the money to buy the site that became known as Plato's Garden.

12. On the importance of cross-fertilization to thought leadership, see Gardner (2011) 74–5, talking about 'intellectual leaders whose interests naturally spill across an ensemble of disciplines'. Plato definitely belonged to the class.

13. Pace (1987).

14. https://en.wikiquote.org/wiki/Marie_Curie.

15. http://www.bbc.co.uk/history/historic_figures/curie_marie.shtml.

16. Curie (1923) 53.

17. Jarvis et al. (2017).

18. Montessori (1912).

19. Montessori (1912) 367.

20. Montessori (1912) 24–6.

21. Montessori (1912) 43–4.

22. Montessori (1912) 6.

23. Montessori (1912) 374.

24. For a major scientific study, see Lillard (2005). In her review of Lillard, Gill (2007) 774 argues that, because Montessori promoted the autonomy of the child while at the same time designing a carefully controlled learning environment, her work can help negotiate between the extremes of freedom and regimentation that have long characterized education debates.

25. Kramer (1976) 16.

26. Kramer (1976) 16.

27. Solan (2007) 61. According to Haberman (1976) 189, in her later years Montessori persisted 'foolishly in trying to control the applications of her approach when she would have been better advised to let her ideas mature and leave "mammolina" with her blessing'.

28. This section is based on Yunus and Jolis (2003).

29. Yunus and Weber (2007) 43.

30. Yunus and Weber (2007) 54.

31. Yunus and Weber (2007) 211–12.

10

Teachers and Sowers

Differentiating the two models

In the previous chapter we raised the question of how the models of the teacher and the sower differ from one another. They can seem so close as to be indistinguishable: in the *Phaedrus*, the sower sows by teaching; conversely, the best teachers create students capable of teaching others, and so can extend their influence.

And yet the models are distinct. The demands of the sower are very high: the leader is the one who has the big idea, whereas a teacher could be teaching other people's ideas. So not all teachers are sowers (except as subordinate sowers, disseminating what was ultimately someone else's seed). Conversely, not all sowers are teachers: you could sow by creating a meme, e.g. in the arts or business, which you then inspire and enable others to imitate, but without actually teaching in any sense. This kind of enabling might include deliberately not hoarding your ideas or control-ling their reuse and availability (so not insisting on IP rights, for instance), but it need not be pedagogical. (We shall return this point in the next chapter when we discuss Howard Gardner's concept of thought leadership.)

This is enough to distinguish the models and to show that you could have a leader who exhibits one without the other. However, the fact is that they do often converge, and that should not be a surprise. In the Introduction to this book, we said that the point of the models is not to choose one to the exclusion of another. It is quite possible that a leader exemplifies two models at once.[1] Our case studies for the sower, Curie, Montessori, and Yunus, were all professors; so, as well as leaving legacies behind, they were also teachers. Even here, though, it is still useful to distinguish the two aspects when thinking about such cases. If the two models converge, they pick out different aspects of leadership. The teacher focuses on the relationship between the leader and their immediate followers, stressing the need for rational engagement and communication; the sower looks beyond the relationship between the leader and their immediate followers towards subsequent generations, and to the perpetuation of ideas. As a model, the sower is more 'idea-centric' than the teacher.

To illustrate the two models working in tandem, we now turn to examples of leaders who undoubtedly left great legacies, but also show quite specific similarities to the Platonic teacher: Florence Nightingale and Margaret Mead.

Case studies

Florence Nightingale

Considered the founder of modern nursing, Nightingale revolutionized health care in hospitals over 150 years ago in a way that saved countless lives. Her innovations continue to be utilized throughout the world today. This would be seen as remarkable accomplishment for anyone, but it is especially impressive given that she was a woman in an era dominated by men, where women were heavily restricted in their career options and not taken seriously either in the professions or in academia. Nightingale persevered through this adversity and always considered this perspective when teaching others, especially women, to provide quality care to their patients. Her patients gave her the nickname, 'The Lady with the Lamp', a term of endearment which spoke to her drive to care for them late into the night.[2]

Born in 1820 into a wealthy family, Nightingale lived for ninety years. Unusually for her time, she received a thorough education at home (her parents were highly progressive in this respect). She became an accomplished mathematician and also learned languages, including ancient Greek. One visitor to the house found her reading Plato when she was only in her teens.[3] Her interest in Plato remained with her throughout her life, a fact to which we shall return at the end.

Her family was not so supportive of her nursing ambitions, but she managed to pursue her training, working in various places, in France, Germany, as well as England. In 1854 she was working at a hospital in London, but was thinking of moving to King's College Hospital, in order to be able to train nurses.[4] Then history intervened. The Crimean war was in progress and reports were reaching England of the dire conditions facing wounded soldiers in army hospitals. Nightingale was a personal friend of Sidney Herbert, the Foreign Secretary, and they agreed that she should go with a team of nurses to help. Appalled at the conditions there, she battled with the army doctors and others to improve the treatment of the soldiers. To this end, she revolutionized the way they were cared for, and in doing so had a deep and long-lasting effect on nursing care. After the Crimean war, she returned to England in triumph, though also ill-health. She retreated to her sick-room for the rest of her life, but continued in her campaign to improve and reform her profession, writing and lobbying prolifically.

Nightingale as sower

Nightingale clearly satisfies the first principle of the sower model: creating an idea (or set of ideas) big enough to have a legacy. Throughout her career she developed a set of scientific ideas about nursing and it should differ from the medical practice of the time. For her, nursing needed to become a fully fledged profession, involving high levels of discipline and training, which promoted and sustained health by attending to all sorts of features in the environment—hygiene, ventilation, warmth, food, light, etc.[5] She also took a holistic approach to health. In addition, she was passionate about the use of statistics to help understand complex phenomena related to illness, death, and preventive measures to improve the welfare of her patients. In this way, she tried to convince others to look at issues in a new light, rather than speculate about the best ways to treat patients.[6] As well as her scientific views, she also had a seminal influence on the way people thought about the status of women in the professions. In true Platonic spirit, she saw no reason why tasks in medicine (or in society more generally) should be allocated according to gender. (She wrote about this vehemently in a pamphlet entitled *Cassandra*.)

Nightingale also satisfied two other key principles of the sower: stepping back to allow others to take up your ideas (S2), and empowering those you lead (S3). This will be clear as we go along, but let us put the sower to one side for a moment, and look at her leadership through the lens of the teacher.

Nightingale as teacher

Education was of fundamental importance to Nightingale. She once wrote: 'Let us never consider ourselves finished nurses.... We must be learning all our lives.'[7] We have already noted that, even before her time in Crimea, her objective was to become involved in nursing education.[8] Once in Crimea, an important aspect of her work was training her team of nurses. When she returned her pedagogical mission continued, though in different ways. Two achievements are particularly worth noting here. One is the founding of the School of Nursing at St. Thomas' Hospital in London, which had a knock-on effect on the profession world-wide. Another was her book, *Notes on Nursing: What It Is and What It Is Not*, which had an immediate and significant impact on the field:

> The booklet, an assemblage of her clinical observations while working with patients in London hospitals and the Crimean War, imparted instructional erudition and canons of nursing practice.... Additionally, Nightingale's letters, notes, and pamphlets would provide the language, knowledge, and subsequent standards of care that future nurses would utilize to inform their practice in London and abroad in the United States.[9]

Nightingale was also a teacher in the rather specific sense we discussed in connection with the cave allegory in Chapter 5. A key principle of the teacher model is that the leader is confronted by people who are prisoners of their own comfort zone (T1), and the challenge is to bring them out of that zone (T2). We mentioned that Plato was thinking of Socrates, who had compared himself to a gadfly, trying to wake his fellow Athenians out of their dogmatic slumbers. All this applies clearly to Nightingale's case. Her contemporaries, particularly the medical men in the British army, and the establishment back home, were comfortable where they were and saw no need to revise their views. In this connection, LeVasseur (1998) 282–3 makes a very interesting point:

> A striking parallel between Nightingale and Socrates lies in their conceptions of their relations to society. In the *Apology*, Socrates called Athens a great lazy horse and himself the gadfly that stings it to action .... God, he believed, put him in Athens for this service and 'no greater good has happened in the state than my service to God'.[10] Nightingale wrote in a letter to Sidney Herbert from the Crimea: 'Such a tempest has been brewed in this little pint-pot as you could have no idea of. But I, like the ass, have put on the lion's skin, & when once I have done that (poor me, who never affronted any one before), I can bray so loud that I shall be heard, I am afraid, as far as England.'[11] In these metaphors of the stinging gadfly and the braying ass, we have twin images of Socrates and Nightingale outside of society goading it toward reform.

But the state of the army and its medical officers in Crimea was not her only experience of confronting a comfort zone. In helping to found the nursing school at St. Thomas' Hospital, her view was that the state of nursing urgently needed to be professionalized. By complete contrast, the Senior Surgeon at the hospital, Mr South, took the view that things were fine as they were:

> He was 'not at all disposed to allow that the nursing establishments of our hospitals are inefficient, or that they are likely to be improved by any special institution for training.' He believed that the nursing at St. Thomas's was good (as indeed in many respects it was), and he did not perceive that what the Nightingale Fund had in view was to raise the general level, and to send out from St. Thomas's trained nurses, who in their turn would train other nurses elsewhere. Perhaps, if he had perceived this, he would have regarded it as superfluous. His point of view was that of the man who finds the world very well as it is.[12]

Nightingale had to confront people's views about how medicine and nursing should be practised. This is a scientific comfort zone. But, as we have already indicated, she also had to confront their social comfort zone, about the place of women in society. In *Notes on Nursing*, she cuts through stereotypes of the day to make sure her students conduct high quality care in the face of social stigma:

> You do not want the effect of your good things to be, 'How wonderful for a *woman*!' nor would you be deterred from good things, by hearing it said, 'Yes, but she ought not to have done this, because it is not suitable for a woman.' But you want to do the thing that is good, whether it is 'suitable for a woman' or not.... It does not make a thing good, that it is remarkable that a woman should have been able to do it. Neither does it make a thing bad, which would have been good had a man done it, that it has been done by a woman.[13]

Because Nightingale was attempting to lead people out of their comfort zones, she inevitably encountered hostility and resistance, another key principle of the teacher model (T4). The National Army Museum describes one instance of the resistance Nightingale and her nurses received from contemporary male doctors:

> At Scutari, near Constantinople, the conditions were dire. The dirty and vermin-ridden hospital lacked even basic equipment and provisions. The medical staff were swamped by the large number of soldiers being shipped across the Black Sea from the war in the Crimea. More of these patients were suffering from disease than from battle wounds. Despite these conditions, the male army doctors didn't want the help of Florence and her nurses. At first, they saw her opinions as an attack on their professionalism. But after fresh casualties arrived from the Battle of Inkerman in November 1854, the staff were soon fully stretched and accepted the nurses' aid. Florence and her nurses improved the medical and sanitary arrangements, set up food kitchens, washed linen and clothes, wrote home on behalf of the soldiers, and introduced reading rooms.[14]

Her biographer Edward Tyas Cook recounts another episode of resistance to her authority and reforms, along with her reaction:

There was a somewhat similar dispute about another transference of nurses in the Crimea made without Miss Nightingale's sanction; and some of the women, taking their cue from their superiors, were inclined to question and flout her authority. 'I don't know what she wants here,' said one, when the Lady Superintendent appeared on the scene. All this controversy raised Miss Nightingale's vexation to white heat. On January 7, 1856, she wrote an official letter to the War Office, complaining of the encroachment on her department by the Medical Officer. In semi-private letters to Mr. Sidney Herbert (Feb. 20, 21, 1856) she formulated her grievances. Dr. Hall was 'attempting to root her out of the Crimea'. Other officials were traducing her behind her back. The War Office was not adequately supporting her. 'It is profuse,' she said, 'in tinsel and empty praise which I do not want, and does not give me the real business-like efficient standing which I do want . . .'. The memory of the petty persecution to which she was subjected by hostile and jealous officials in the Crimea never faded from Miss Nightingale's mind.[15]

Back to the sower

All of this makes a strong case for seeing Nightingale through the lens of Plato's teacher. But it also shows, even more clearly than before, that she was a true sower. We mentioned above that she had an abundance of ideas big enough to create a legacy. As her career went on, she tended to move over more and more to the sower model. That is, she stepped back (if only out of ill-health) and empowered others to take up and implement her ideas. Commenting on the founding of St. Thomas' Nursing School, Cook said 'what the Nightingale Fund had in view was to raise the general level, and to send out from St. Thomas' trained nurses, who in their turn would train other nurses elsewhere'.[16] Quite generally, she moved from being a nurse herself and a trainer of nurses, to creating institutions to train the trainers.[17]

Postscript: Nightingale and Plato

As part of her education, Nightingale acquired expertise not just in mathematics (which enabled her to develop her passion for statistics), but also in ancient Greek. Her love of Plato never left her. Much later on, in the 1870s, she corresponded with the eminent Plato scholar Benjamin Jowett.[18] He translated the complete works of Plato and wrote extensive introductions, which Nightingale read in draft, providing long and often critical comments. She also wrote her own work on philosophy and theology, *Suggestions for Thought*, which she showed to the philosopher J. S. Mill.[19] It is difficult to say exactly which works or passages of Plato impressed her most, but there have been recent articles arguing for a quite general influence.[20]

In the *Republic*, Plato envisaged a group of philosopher-guardians, informed by their ethical knowledge (gained through exiting the cave) and driven by a sense of public duty to shape society in the image of the good. Nightingale, whose own philosophy may have merged Platonic and Christian themes, might well have seen herself along these lines. More specifically, the holistic approach she took to medicine, where bodily health has to be seen alongside psychological health, can be found in Plato.[21] Her love of statistics was not divorced from her moral and theological views: she saw statistics as a way of understanding the mind and the laws of God,[22] rather as Plato thought mathematics can lead us to grasp the beauty, goodness, and the order of the cosmos (*Republic* Book 7, 531c). We have already noticed the similarity between their views on the function of women in society. Finally, there is a possible link in their views on education. In the preface to *Notes on Nursing*, she sounds strikingly Platonic (or Socratic) in her approach to education:

> The following notes are by no means intended as a rule of thought by which nurses can teach themselves to nurse, still less as a manual to teach nurses to nurse. They are meant simply to give hints for thought to women who have personal charge of the health of others .... I do not pretend to teach her how, I ask her to teach herself, and for this purpose I venture to give her some hints.[23]

Margaret Mead

Few people in the United States were as famous as Margaret Mead was when she died in 1978 at the age of 76. She was seen as an influential public intellectual, not just a scholar of cultural anthropology who developed new concepts and analytical tools in her field.[24] She came into the public's consciousness with her first book, *Coming of Age in Samoa*, published in 1928. This started a fifty-year period of Mead sowing her thoughts into public discourse. As with so many of her writings, this book quickly stirred up fierce debate with its candid depictions of attitudes and behaviour around sex among Samoan youth. Mead also framed the findings from this ethnographic study to throw light on Western culture.

Mead as sower

Coming of Age started a long-lasting foray into writing on numerous social topics, ultimately for the general public. She believed that human behaviour was primarily influenced by culture. This made her a proponent of cultural determinism, which is primarily contrasted with genetic or biological determinism. She observed that cultures varied significantly across the globe and across time, and that these differences influenced human development. Her comparative studies of human development within cultures in Oceania highlighted significant cross-cultural variations and were published as books to great success. In *Sex and Temperament* and *Coming of Age in Samoa*, she used cross-cultural comparisons to explain that our own cultural norms and expectations are made by us and, as such, are malleable. She writes forcefully on these subjects in her books:

> Whether or not we envy other peoples one of their solutions, our attitude towards our own solutions must be greatly broadened and deepened by a consideration of the way in which other peoples have met the same problems. Realising that our own ways are not humanly inevitable nor God-ordained, but are the fruit of a long and turbulent

history, we may well examine in turn all of our institutions, thrown into strong relief against the history of other civilizations, and weighing them in the balance, be not afraid to find them wanting.[25]

Another of her books, *Growing Up in New Guinea*, also had a seminal influence:

> The Manus work, published as *Growing Up in New Guinea*, effectively refuted the notion that 'primitive' peoples are 'like children'. Different developmental stages, and the relationships between them, need to be studied in every culture. Mead was thus the first anthropologist to look at human development in a cross-cultural perspective.[26]

According to Howard Gardner, who used her as an example in his book *Leading Minds*, Mead preached a 'gospel of a varied but essentially unified human nature'.[27] This is how he characterizes her view a few pages later:

> a single human nature, whatever its limits, could nonetheless spawn a large variety of cultures. None has a monopoly on wisdom; none is inherently superior on all dimensions to all others. The result, Mead asserted optimistically, will be a world in which mutual understanding may help to reduce conflict.[28]

Much of her work focused on the family, adolescence, and sexuality. In Samoan culture, for instance, family relations were more diffused than in Western societies: there were no nuclear families, with all the angst that they generate; adolescence was a more relaxed phase of life, especially in terms of sexual experience. By describing Samoan culture in this way, Mead 'strongly urges her compatriots to draw lessons about alternative ways in which they might better rear their children and lead their own lives';[29] there is no one way to approach childhood and adolescence.

This attitude may be what drove her to tirelessly leverage many different channels and outlets in an effort to promulgate her ideas for social reform, including radio, TV (e.g. *The Tonight Show* with Johnny

Carson), magazines (e.g. *Redbook*), scholarly journals, governmental committees (e.g. the National Research Council), association leadership roles, and books. As she herself said:

> It's a little hard, you know, to judge what impact you've had on a field. Initially, I think the most important thing I did was to introduce anthropology to the general, literate public.[30]

Mead has had her share of controversies. For instance, the feminist thinker and activist Betty Friedan took her to task for double standards in *The Feminine Mystique* (1963), pointing to a disparity between some of the liberal attitudes she professed to encourage and her own conservative views on marriage and feminism. She accuses Mead of 'a glorification of women in the [traditional American] female role—as defined by their sexual biological function'.[31] More dramatically, in the 1980s the anthropologist Derek Freeman claimed that in her work on Samoa she had been hoaxed by two of her interviewees and that her research was therefore unreliable.[32] Anthropologists have since attempted to rebut Freeman, with some success, casting doubt on his own scholarship and methods.[33]

Despite all this, her influence is beyond dispute: she was a prolific sower of her ideas. Indeed, it is difficult to exaggerate the pervasiveness of her writings in the United States in the 1950s and 1960s and her influence during a rapidly changing social landscape, especially around such areas as the family, youth, the sexual revolution, and women's rights. There is an excellent statement of her cross-generational influence by Betty Friedan, who prefaces her stinging critique of Mead with the following tribute:

> The most powerful influence on modern women, in terms of both functionalism and the feminist protest, was Margaret Mead. Her work on culture and personality—book after book, study after study—has had a profound effect on the women of my generation, the one before it, and the generation now growing up. She has written millions of words in the thirty-odd years between *Coming of Age in Samoa* in 1928 and her last article on American women in the *New York Times*

Magazine or *Redbook*. She is studied in college classrooms by girls taking courses in anthropology, sociology, psychology, education, and marriage and family life; in graduate schools by those who will one day teach girls and counsel women; in medical schools by future pediatricians and psychiatrists; even in the theological schools by progressive young ministers. And she is read in the women's magazines and the Sunday supplements, where she publishes as readily as in the learned journals, by girls and women of all ages. Margaret Mead is her own best popularizer—and her influence has been felt in almost every layer of American thought.[34]

Three decades later Howard Gardner was able to write:

Many of the positions in debates about sex and lifestyle that are now taken for granted were first brought to the attention of nonacademicians by Mead and are now defended—or attacked—by individuals who have never heard her name.[35]

Finally, one of the components of the sower model was an ability to tolerate mutation of one's ideas (S4). There is reason to think that Mead did well on this score. A prolific writer on civil rights, race relations, and education reform, not all of her ideas gained traction in society (e.g. newlyweds purchasing 'marriage insurance' or paying students to attend college as if they were employed), but she kept pushing new ideas. She was always looking for ways to solve societal problems even if—or perhaps because—they went against popular conventions. She pushed ideas to shake up the status quo, engender debate, and let others continue the work of reform. But—and this is the point—as societal norms changed, she was willing to adapt (without abandoning her core principles, such as the importance of family). For example, she noted that her earlier idea of a formalized two-step marriage (i.e. one without children, then one with children) 'had been informally adopted and publicly accepted with young people living together openly and then getting married later'.[36] She did not insist on pressing her original idea.

Mead as teacher

Mead was obviously a teacher in the sense that she communicated her ideas as a public intellectual (over and above her academic teaching). She had a remarkable ability to translate complex ideas into terms non-experts could understand. In his biography of her, Robert Cassidy writes: 'Mead's special gift, apart from her capacity for field work, was her ability to assimilate complex information, organize it, and make it understandable to the layman.'[37] Based on his experience of interviewing her, he says: 'I had heard of her remarkable ability to stimulate others to perform at higher than normal levels; now I had seen firsthand how she did it.'[38] (This also evidences her ability as a sower to empower others: S3.) Shankman describes Mead's approach as a *Redbook* columnist: 'Attempting to reach a "reasonable" conclusion about an issue, Mead encouraged her readers to consider "new ways of thinking".'[39] And, as Deborah Gewertz observed from her own interactions with Mead: 'she knew how to convince people by not pushing them too hard, while nudging them toward the right conclusions.'[40]

That Mead led by teaching in a general sense is obvious. What we want to do here is to bring out a more specific connection with Plato's model of the teacher. When we discussed the model in Chapter 5, we saw that Plato has a very focused idea of what it involves, which he conveys through the cave allegory. The leader in this sense is someone who has left their comfort zone, travelled to 'another place', and then returned—with their perspective transformed—to inform and educate their fellows. When introducing the allegory, we suggested that Plato may have been inspired to use it by reflecting on a particular cultural practice at the time. States like Athens would send its citizens on 'embassies' to inspect another culture; sometimes individuals would make such trips as private individuals, and in either case they might have gone as far afield as Persia or Egypt. They would return with a knowledge of the other culture that might transform the way they look at their own, often antagonizing their fellow-citizens in the process. As we look at Mead from the perspective of Plato's teacher, this point has obvious application. She quite literally went to other cultures and came back with a new understanding of her own. She wrote: 'I have spent most of my life studying the lives of other peoples, far away peoples, so that Americans might better understand themselves.'[41]

The idea of self-knowledge is very important in the cave. Before their release, the prisoners have no real self-knowledge. Bound by their chains and prevented from moving their necks, they are unable to see themselves (515a); all they see are their shadows on the wall in front of them. So whatever else the freed prisoner learns from leaving the cave, he learns about himself—what he looks like, and what a narrow, cramped, and even pitiable life he lived before. So, the journey up and down is partly one of self-knowledge. This is exactly the point earlier Greeks had grasped when they visited other cultures, and it is obviously central to Mead's work.

That she spent so much of her life using her anthropological perspective of faraway peoples to educate her fellow citizens makes her an excellent example of Plato's teacher. And that her legacy has endured in some way or other (even if most people are unaware of the fact) makes her also a quintessential sower.

Conclusion

We end with a comment that is relevant to both this chapter and the previous one. It concerns the sower and the role of institutions in perpetuating ideas. The model allows for a leader to start in the absence of an institution; but, as their ideas become disseminated and the seeds grow into plants, they can create institutions to ensure the sustainability of their work. Nightingale is a good example, as is Montessori with the foundation of the Association Montessori Internationale. As a professional scientist, Curie did work within existing institutions, but also created scientific institutes of her own. Mead, however, operated outside of institutions, or at their fringes.[42] Of all our models, the sower is best suited for leaders, like women, who could not rely on pre-established institutions to welcome them into their ranks and rise up the hierarchy.

Notes

1. Among our case studies, there are clear opportunities for viewing a leader through the lens of different models, beyond the one we actually selected. For instance, although Jean Monnet makes an excellent case study for the doctor, he could also be understood in terms of the artist/architect. Writing in the *Washington Post*, Smith (1979) describes him as the person whose 'vision was of a Europe in which traditional prejudices and animosities were submerged in institutions in which the good of all would be represented'. In arguing and disseminating the idea that slavery killed the good inside white people, Douglass could be seen as a sower, who anticipated modern leaders such as Dr King and Nelson Mandela. Similarly, we saw in Chapter 8 how Mandela can fit the teacher and doctor.

2. See 'Florence Nightingale: The Lady with the Lamp', National Army Museum: https://www.nam.ac.uk/explore/florence-nightingale-lady-lamp.

3. Cook (1913) I 3.

4. Cook (1913) I 141.

5. Arnone and Fitzsimons (2015) 158–9, Nelson and Rafferty (2010) 2.

6. On her use of statistics, see Cook (1913) I 428–38, Arnone and Fitzsimons (2015) 159, and Magnello (2010).

7. Nightingale (1896) 214. This tallies with a quote from Indra Nooyi, one of our case studies for the teacher in Chapter 5: 'I've tried to be a lifelong student.... I can't afford to stop learning. None of us can' Nooyi (2017), quoted at the beginning of her case study.

8. See Cook (1913) I 140: 'She had wanted to receive patients of all classes, to enrol many volunteer nurses, to have opportunities for training them'; and 141: 'Her own primary object was to train nurses.'

9. Arnone and Fitzsimons (2015) 159–60. See also LeVasseur (1998) 283: 'The idea that a nurse should be trained in observation as well as in all manner of caring for the sick is an idea that stems from Nightingale. She bemoans the fact that so few nurses know what to observe, what indicates improvement, and which observations are important.... Rigorous training would remedy this situation and Nightingale would become even more of a proponent of training and education for nurses later in her life.'

10. Plato *Apology* 30a.

11. Vicinus and Nergaard (1990) 98.

12. Cook (1913) I 466.

13. Nightingale (1860) 194–5. As Nelson and Rafferty (2010) 4 point out, 'the very idea of a female profession was in and of itself an entirely radical notion in the mid-nineteenth century'.

14. 'Florence Nightingale: The Lady with the Lamp', National Army Museum: https://www.nam.ac.uk/explore/florence-nightingale-lady-lamp.
15. Cook (1913) I 290–2.
16. Cook (1913) I 466, quoted above. Cook is fond of the seed analogy when describing Nightingale's leadership. In vol. I, p. xxix, he says: 'The germinant seeds had all been sown' (sc. by 1872); vol. II part III contains an entire chapter entitled 'Sowing the seed'.
17. Although we have selected the teacher and the sower as the appropriate models for Nightingale, the navigator might also be appropriate. In an essay entitled 'Navigating the political straits in the Crimean war', Helmstadter (2010) describes the way Nightingale's time in the Crimea involved managing multiple conflicts among different parties—professional, political, and even religious: very much the job of the captain, trying to maintain cohesion on board ship. This is a good example of how a particular model might be a useful lens for looking at a specific phase in a leader's career.
18. On their friendship see Cook (1913) II 394–400 and Bostridge (2008) 389–95.
19. Bostridge (2008) 369–72.
20. LeVasseur (1998), Arnone and Fitzsimons (2015).
21. In his dialogue the *Charmides*, esp. 156c. See McPherran (2012) 203–4.
22. Bostridge (2008) 172 and 370, Magnello (2010) 117–18.
23. Nightingale (1860) 4; cf. LeVasseur (1998) 283. In the *Republic*, the person who exits the cave sees for himself, with the help of someone else's questioning. Also relevant here is Nightingale's claim, 'Let each person tell the truth from his own experience', quoted by Cook (1913) II 15 (originally from a letter to Madame Mohl, 13 December 1861).
24. For example in psychological anthropology, applied anthropology, and ethnography. See Geertz (1989) 348.
25. Mead (1961) 233.
26. Institute for Intercultural Studies, 'Biography: Margaret Mead', http://www.inter culturalstudies.org/Mead/biography.html.
27. Gardner (2011) 78.
28. Gardner (2011) 81.
29. Gardner (2011) 69.
30. Mead (1975).
31. Friedan (2010) 207–8.
32. Freeman (1983) and (1999).
33. Shankman (2009) and (2013).
34. Friedan (2010) 207–8.
35. Gardner (2011) 81.
36. Shankman (2018) 62.
37. Cassidy (1982) 54.

38. Cassidy (1982) 153.
39. Shankman (2018) 55.
40. Shankman (2018) 68.
41. Quoted by Gardner (2011) 65 as the epitaph to his chapter on Mead.
42. See Gardner (2011) 81–2: Mead didn't (have the patience to) set up institutions; and was relieved that being a woman made her less likely to be invited into administrative work.

11

Plato and Modern Leadership Models

Overview

There is not a one-to-one match between Plato's models of leadership and contemporary ways to conceptualize leaders and leadership. Nonetheless Plato anticipates many of the central ideas in the current business and political genre of leadership studies. While a full mapping of these ideas is beyond the scope of our purpose here, we do want to sketch some of the similarities and differences with key ways that current business and political thinkers have conceptualized leaders and leadership.[1]

Leadership research has gone through different phases. First, leadership was examined using the 'trait theories', among them the 'great man theory', which proposed that leadership was an innate ability. Some are born to lead; others are not.[2] If an individual has leadership traits—or the leadership gene—undoubtedly it will manifest itself no matter what the situation. 'No one believes that any more', John Gardner wrote in the 1990s. 'Acts of leadership take place in an unimaginable variety of settings, and the setting does much to determine the kinds of leaders that emerge and how they play their roles.'[3]

The focus then turned from traits to behavioural theories, which could include autocratic, democratic, and laissez-faire leadership styles. When those theories ran their course, scholars identified contingency theories of leadership, which assume that leadership varies according to situation and context, with no one specific universally effective way to be a leader. Later models drew from these three basics but turned their focus onto leadership as a change process and the leader as the primary catalyst of change.

Another phenomenon has been the emergence of 'self-help' leadership books written by experienced leaders, academics, and other 'leadership gurus'. This genre of work usually offers a definition of leadership and offers some practical advice about how to be a better leader.

The leadership models that we will link to Plato include Burns' Transformational Leadership, Collins' Level 5 Leadership, Greenleaf's Servant Leadership, and Gardner's *Leading Minds*. All of these models have been influential in both political and business circles, and each one can be traced to some of the key Platonic ideas that we have explored in previous chapters. However, first we want to return to a pair of issues that we addressed at the beginning of the book, and have been implicit in what followed. It shows us why it is fruitful to study Plato's view in the light of more recent thinking about leadership.

Two modern problems that Plato did not have

The definition problem in leadership

Leadership is an enduring subject for research, writing, and discussion. There are almost endless theoretical and fundamental explanations as to what leadership is and what makes a good leader. As Ralph Stogdill observes in his nine-hundred-page survey of scholarly research on the topic, 'There are almost as many different definitions of leadership as there are persons who have attempted to define the concept'.[4] It seems that practically every CEO of a *Fortune* 500 company has written his or her own leadership book—some bestsellers, many not—as have a host of politicians and presidents. Many of these works fall into a blueprint format and invariably portray the leader as succeeding against Herculean obstacles and barriers.

What is leadership? Can we find meaning in such a ubiquitous, perhaps overused, word? Bernard Bass, founding director of the Center for Leadership Studies at Binghamton University and founding editor of the *Leadership Quarterly*, attempted to identify the various theoretical approaches:

> Leadership has been conceived as the focus of group processes, as a matter of personality, as a matter or inducing compliance, as the exercise of influence, as particular behaviors, as a form of persuasion, as a power relation, as an instrument to achieve goals, as an effect of

interaction, as a differentiated role, as an initiation of structure, and as many combinations of these definitions.[5]

The attempt to define leadership once and for all has led to confusion and a plethora of articles trying to add or subtract various aspects of the concept from one or another model. When we read Plato, we simply do not have this problem. He used many 'models' to try and capture the many different ideas we have about leadership. We suggested in the Introduction that 'leadership' and 'leader' were best understood as 'family resemblance' terms, in a Wittgensteinian sense, and that it was pointless to try and find the one and only one model that captures all aspects of a complex idea. We suggested that we think about leadership and leaders the way we might think about games. There are many of them which have many different aspects, but it is impossible or at least not very useful to try and define 'what is a game'. While Plato might have thought that there is ultimately a single definition (or 'form') of leadership, in the *Republic* he is also writing in a practical way about justice in the state, while criticizing Athenian democracy. Therefore he doesn't make the mistake of trying to first define what leadership must be. We believe that modern theorists could take a page from Plato's book here.

The ethics and values connection

In many of the writings on leadership throughout the early twentieth century, 'values' were occasionally mentioned; 'ethics' was not.[6] Effective leadership, many believed, meant simply achieving effective results, such as the successful attainment of organizational objectives, which might be efficiency, low turnover, high profitability, innovation, and client services. These were the metrics by which many leaders were measured; the impact of ethics (and values) on the results simply was not part of the conversation. A term for this early scholarship might be 'amoral theory of leadership'.

As an example, the great man theory, focusing on the particular leader's personality trait, consequently makes no distinction between an Adolf Hitler and a Mahatma Gandhi, both of whom were effective in accomplishing many of their stated objectives. Situational theories of leadership also remained morally neutral. These theories have common characteristics. First, with a narrow focus on the leader and followers, there is no examination of the situation or the skills the leader employs. Second, these theories sought to help leaders identify ways to motivate their followers, thus making the assumption that workers needed to be prodded into productivity, and leaving any consideration of values or ethics out of the conversation. And finally, these conversations about stated objectives did not take into account whether those objectives were good or horrific. In short, the following questions have been left out of the conversation about leadership:

- Is the desired outcome desirable?
- Are the tools used ethically sound?
- Should followers be apprised as to how the leader is motivating them?
- On what basis can we determine a 'good' leader from a 'bad' leader?

Without underlying values and principles—knowing what one stands for and what will serve a company's stakeholders best—leadership does not have an ethical foundation. The focus is simply on 'getting things done', which, while important, is only a partial component of leadership. No doubt, amoral leadership theories have helped advance the study of leadership and have served as a jumping-off point for understanding the complexities of leadership, but—given that many look to business leaders to help solve some of society's problems—these theories have significant limitations.

Such a view would seem strange to Plato, who distinguishes 'leaders' from 'tyrants'.[7] Hence he would have no problem saying that of course Hitler was not a leader; he was a tyrant. For Plato, ethics and values are built into the very idea of leadership.

In the latter half of the twentieth century (and continuing into the twenty-first century), many leadership theorists began to incorporate ethics and values through ideas like 'values-based leadership' or 'responsible leadership'. Both models highlight, by their names, what has gone wrong with most of leadership studies. Nonetheless they are closer to models of leadership that Plato would recognize. On these views, to understand leadership, it is necessary to understand the *human* relationship between leader and followers. That requires first understanding one's own values, motives, ethics, strengths, and weaknesses, and then understanding the followers' values. By understanding and respecting the followers' wants and needs, and providing what is wanted and what is needed, one gains the trust, loyalty, and commitment of the followers, who will then be empowered to achieve great accomplishments.

Sometimes only focusing on values is not enough. Some of these writings did not examine the appropriateness of the goals or the rightness of the followers' values. They simply say that values are central to the leadership process. The leader must at all times appear honest, trustworthy, attuned to the people's dignity and values, inspiring, and confident. Each of these texts provides recommendations on what one must do to embody these qualities. However it is too easy to move from appearing honest, etc. to a view that rhetoric is what is important here: appearing to be honest, etc., but really dealing for oneself. But ethics requires more than this.

Responsible leadership models focus on both values and ethics. These authors make the assumption that followers are fully autonomous, ethical beings and that the leader must engage them as such. This relies on the logic of values in the sense that they are usually ethically salient. The models we will look at in more detail below all take ethics and values seriously, and would again be recognizable to Plato.

James MacGregor Burns and transformational leadership (the artist and the navigator)

'One of the most universal cravings of our time is a hunger for compelling and creative leadership',[8] writes presidential biographer and leadership scholar James MacGregor Burns in his seminal book, *Leadership*. A historian and political scientist, Burns takes a more philosophical and conceptual approach to leadership and was one of the first scholars to include an ethical/moral dimension into his leadership model and to emphasize the importance of values. 'At the highest stage of moral development persons are guided by near-universal ethical principles of justice such as equality of human rights and respect for individual dignity. This stage sets the opportunity for rare and creative leadership.'[9] Burns asserts that leadership cannot be separated from moral purpose.

Leadership, to him, is a blend of interpersonal relationships, values, morals, and motives. Burns helped turn the study of leadership away from the 'great men' theories toward a focus on the interaction and collaboration of leaders and those who follow them. He advocated for and wrote about transformational leadership, a process in which leaders and followers inspire one another to elevated moral conduct. The secret of transforming leadership and the moral and practical theme of Burns' work is that people can be lifted into their better selves. True leadership, writes Burns, not only creates change and achieves goals, but also changes those involved—both followers and leaders—for the better.

According to Burns, leadership involves power and purpose, although he downplays the universal fascination with power. Power may be a part of leadership, but not an essential part, and he hopes, in general, that people will 'disenthrall' themselves from the overemphasis on power. 'We must analyze power in a context of human motives and physical constraints', he writes. 'If we can come to grips with these aspects of power, we can hope to comprehend the true nature of leadership—a venture far more intellectually daunting than the study of naked power.'[10]

Burns defines leadership as 'inducing followers to act for certain goals that represent the values and the motivations—the wants and needs, the aspirations and expectations—*of both leaders and followers*'.[11] He believes, however, in mobilizing others when they have 'conscious choice among real alternatives'. The difference between leadership and brute power is that the former assumes competition and conflict, and the latter simply denies it. Power-wielders don't care about the motives, purposes, or values of those over whom they exert power.

Transformational leadership, according to Burns, 'occurs when one or more persons engage with others in such a way that leaders and followers raise one another to higher levels of motivation and morality'.[12] The two sides might not start out with the same purpose, but they become fused in the process. Power bases don't serve as counterweights to each other 'but as mutual support for common purpose ... transforming leadership ultimately becomes *moral* in that it raises the level of human conduct and ethical aspirations of both leader and led, and thus it has transforming effect on both'.[13] Burns cites Gandhi as an exemplar of transformational leadership given that he raised the hopes and purpose of millions of Indians and, in return, enhanced his own personality and life.

Burns expresses the hope that he will

> ... demonstrate that the processes of leadership must be seen as part of the dynamics of conflict and of power; that leadership is nothing if not linked to collective purpose; that the effectiveness of leaders must be judged not by their press clippings but by the actual social change measured by intent and by the satisfaction of human needs and expectations ....[14]

So what Platonic resonances are there in this theory? Because vision is central to the idea of transformational leadership, the most salient Platonic comparison is with the model of the artist. The transformational leader, like the artist, must have a vision embodied in a purpose that can inspire others to follow. Both models are alike in adopting a view of leadership that is simultaneously both highly moralized[15] and goal-directed ('teleological'). On Burns' model, the leader enables people to be lifted into their better selves, raising their moral aspirations; they change their followers for the better. When Plato describes the leader as an artist in *Republic* Book 6, he talks of him as someone who develops the moral virtues in his citizens, always with an eye to his own moral ideals (500d).

But we should also be alert to potential differences. One point where they seem to diverge is in the way Burns talks about a process of *mutual* development. There is interaction and collaboration between leaders and followers in so far as they inspire each other to 'elevated moral conduct'. This seems a more egalitarian approach than the model of the artist. In *Republic* Book 6, the leader first of all sorts out his own moral character and then turns to do the same for his citizens. It is not as if the citizens play any part in the process by which he attained the virtues. This is true, though we should not exaggerate the contrast. Plato did believe that potential leaders perfect their nature through the process of becoming actual leaders. At one point, he says that someone who had the potential to be a philosopher-ruler, with all the virtues and expertise that requires, would never fully realize that potential unless they ruled in an ideal state (Book 6, 497a). The process of development in which they perfect themselves involves experience of mid-level leadership in administrative and military offices (cf. Book 7, 539e), as well as their philosophical education.

Another and more striking difference between Burns and Plato lies in the role of autonomy. For many of his readers and critics, Plato does not give enough weight to personal autonomy: non-rulers in the state have no say in the values that are adopted; the leaders do not consult or defer in any way to the followers in this respect. By contrast, Burns thinks the leaders respond to 'the wants and needs, the aspirations and expectations' that the followers antecedently have. And he believes in mobilizing others when they have 'conscious choice among real alternatives'. This is not particularly Platonic. It is closely connected to the fact that, unlike Plato, Burns doesn't consider the problem of 'wiping the slate clean' (even though much damage has been done in the name of transformational leadership). Perhaps he thought that transformational leaders were leaders by choice of the followers; hence he didn't think the downside of the artist could emerge. However, we could draw the two models closer together if we adapt Plato's model of the artist into the architect, as we suggested above (Chapter 4). Here the leader does respond explicitly to antecedent 'wants, needs, aspirations and expectations' of their followers.

Although the artist is the most important point of comparison with transformational leadership, it is not the only one. The navigator is also important. Consider Burns' claim that 'at the highest stage of moral development persons are guided by near-universal ethical principles of justice such as equality of human rights and respect for individual dignity'.[16] Now think of Plato's navigator looking to the stars to guide the ship in the right direction. For Plato, the stars represent the archetypes or forms, e.g. of goodness and justice, that are central to the leader's quest in finding the right direction. The leader-navigator is someone who leads by pursuing grand moral ends (cf. the example of Frederick

Douglass in Chapter 3). Burns does not talk of Platonic forms, of course, but his reference to 'ethical principles of justice such as equality of human rights and respect for individual dignity' could be taken as a modern surrogate for the ideals to which Plato aspired.

A second point of contact between transformational leadership and the navigator is Burns' focus on the 'interaction and collaboration of leaders and those who follow them'. This recalls one of the key principles of Plato's model, where the navigator requires the cooperation of the sailors, and it is his job to inspire them into action (N6).

A third point to make is that, unlike the artist model, the navigator is more congenial to the idea that the leader takes their cue from the aspirations of their followers. When we discussed the model above, we saw that, taken literally, the image of the ship of state image implies that the passengers decide the destination. Since the passengers represent the people (the demos) the image seems oddly democratic for a philosopher like Plato to be using. But we can resolve the tension by interpreting the image in the following way:[17] the people, the followers, have certain general aspirations, which it is the leader's task to make specific. This suggests some kind of collaboration between leader and followers when it comes to determining the moral ends in question. It is not as if the leader implants values or goals in his or her followers which they in no sense had before. So the more we emphasize the passengers' role in setting the destination (something undoubtedly implicit in Plato's image), the closer we see his model tending towards Burns' theory of transformational leadership.

Finally, we should mention the weaver, because transformational leadership is also about weaving together a coalition of people who are pursuing a joint purpose. It is about integrating others into a common goal, and this recalls Plato's weaver. On this model it was crucial that all involved had a shared set of values (W2), something essential to Burns' theory.

Jim Collins and Level 5 leadership (the weaver)

Like Plato, Jim Collins doesn't give one and only one definition of 'true leadership'. There are many models or, as he puts it, 'levels'. A good leader might simply be highly capable individual (Level 1), a contributing team member (Level 2), a competent manager (Level 3), or an effective one (Level 4). Level 5 is concerned with leaders who have transformed a company from good to great.

Not many people, according to Jim Collins, have the 'seed' that is essential for becoming a Level 5 leader. Such a leader invariably 'builds enduring greatness through a paradoxical combination of personal humility plus professional will'.[18] This leader is a study in contrasts: 'modest and willful, shy and fearless'[19]—a person with the combination of a deep personal humility and a strong professional will. Collins had not gone looking for what he and his team of researchers would later term a Level 5 leader when they began studying companies in an attempt to determine what made them successful. He conducted an extensive and exhaustive study of the financial records from over 1,400 companies in the *Fortune* 500 between 1965 and 1995. He would emerge with eleven companies that, after having performed poorly for fifteen years, went on to outperform the market for another fifteen years. These companies, which included Abbott Laboratories, Kimberly-Clark, and Walgreens, were termed 'good-to-great' companies. From this data, Collins found a unique correlation between varying levels of leadership and the success of a business.

In studying these companies, Collins discovered that there are certain characteristics that make a leader 'Level 5'—or the most successful in transforming and sustaining a high-performing company. Charisma is not one of these characteristics; in fact, it is usually a liability for a company. Collins finds that leaders without the 'seed' of Level 5 leadership are usually those with monumental egos, which prevent them from transforming their companies from good to great. Thus, 'the charismatic-leader model has to die. What do you replace it with? The task that the CEO is uniquely positioned to do: designing the mechanisms that reinforce and give life to the company's core purpose and stimulate the company to change.'[20]

On the other hand, Collins notes several intangibles of a Level 5 leader. He says that Level 5 leadership is 'countercultural', which is a contrast to the commonly held belief that the transformation of a company from good to great requires 'larger-than-life leaders', such as the quite-popular CEO of General Electric (GE), Jack Welch. In fact, Collins notes that

Level 5 leadership is a catalyst for taking a company from good to great, but he adds that Level 5 also opens the doors to other factors that complement the effort to elevate a company from good to great. Instead of starting with vision and strategy, good-to-great leaders start with people first. As Collins writes, '...they *first* got the right people on the bus, the wrong people off the bus, and the right people in the right seats—and *then* they figured out where to drive it'.[21] Furthermore, good-to-great leaders establish a 'culture of discipline', in which good-to-great transformations consistently display three areas of discipline: disciplined people, disciplined thought, and disciplined action.

Level 5 leaders are true embodiments of unselfishness, placing the success and growth of their companies above all else—and they act in ways that would consequently ensure success for their respective companies in the many years to follow their absence. Humility and modesty are common findings in the CEOs Collins interviewed. When asked about the success of their companies, CEOs such as Alan L. Wurtzel of Circuit City, simply discredited themselves and replied: 'luck.' Such a response turned out to be a pattern for Collins in his findings with Level 5 leaders, which he called 'the window and the mirror'. According to Collins, the window-and-mirror concept represents how humble Level 5 leaders are. He writes:

> Level 5 leaders, inherently humble, look out the window to apportion credit—even undue credit—to factors outside themselves. If they can't find a specific person or event to give credit to, they credit good luck. At the same time, they look in the mirror to assign responsibility, never citing bad luck or external factors when things go poorly.[22]

How does Collins' approach compare with Plato's? One similarity concerns the emphasis on selflessness. In *Republic* Book 1, he stresses that leaders essentially work for others, not themselves (345c–347a). Indeed, his insistence on this point gives rise to a puzzle about what would motivate people to lead (Plato does not think people are pure altruists, even the best leaders): cf. 347a–e. So there is an extended discussion of what incentives might be required to make them lead.[23] If leaders are paid (or 'compensated' as we say), this is precisely because, as leaders they are meant to be focused on other people's good. Plato is repelled by the idea that a leader might lead because they enjoy power as such (Book 7, 521a–b). Similarly, as we have seen, Collins thinks Level 5 leaders are self-effacing.

Another point of comparison is between Collins' resistance to charisma and Plato's attitude to demagogues. Collins contrasts Level 5 leaders with charismatic 'leaders'. Again Plato would recognize this characterization as 'leaders' with 'demagogues'. Just as Collins notes that charismatic business leaders such as Lee Iacocca of Chrysler and Al Dunlap of Scott Paper Company achieved great results as CEOs, their companies went downhill rapidly after they left. They got things done but they didn't create leaders to take their place, and their sense of 'results only' leadership negated any moral good will among their stakeholders. The mark of a Level 5 leader, like Plato's sower, is that they ensure the company will sustain its success after their departure.

These two points of comparison are quite general—they pick out Plato's views about leadership that straddle a number of his models. But our last point of comparison is specific to the weaver. One of the most striking features of Collins' model is the way the Level 5 leader combines humility and assertiveness, being simultaneously 'shy and fearless'. This should immediately put us in mind of the weaver's art, which is to combine citizens of two very different types, the 'courageous' and the 'moderate' into a single web of state. So one might say the similarity between the two models is that what Plato thought would be a feature of the state—the possession of opposite qualities—is, on Collins' model, a feature of the actual leader. This would be an interesting, though qualified, comparison. But in our chapter on the weaver, we raised the question of what kind of psychology the weaver himself possesses. Our view was that the 'virtues' possessed by the citizens, courage or moderation, are imperfect. As elsewhere, Plato does not think that the perfect virtues are ever at odds with each other; it is just that the majority of people possess imperfect versions of these qualities which are not combined with their opposites. But a true leader does possess perfect courage and moderation, and so does combine them in one person—a rare achievement (W4).

There are two other similarities with the weaver model. First, the weaver is not a grandiose figure: actual weavers were humble figures in society, and to treat a weaver as a paradigm for the statesman is almost deliberately to discourage us from seeing the statesman as in any way grandiose. This chimes in well with Collins' view. Second, the weaver model prioritizes people management over everything else (contrast the artist, for instance, where vision is central): three of the four key principles are about managing people (W1, W2, and W3). (For 'selecting or discarding strands of wool', W3, read 'getting people on or off the bus'.) So the weaver foreshadows a central feature of Collins' model: good-to-great leaders start with people first.

Robert Greenleaf and servant leadership (the doctor-teacher)

It was after watching the student unrest and turmoil in the late 1960s and early 1970s that Robert Greenleaf, a retired AT&T executive, originated the concept of servant leadership, inspired by the servant character Leo in Hermann Hesse's *Journey to the East*. This concept espouses that leadership must primarily meet the needs of others. Rather than being on the self or on self-interest, the focus of servant leadership is on others, and the leader's job is to motivate and develop those around him or her. Servant leaders, according to Greenleaf, provide their followers with a vision, earn both credibility and trust, and influence others. Greenleaf's focus is on the relationship dynamics between leaders and followers, in which leaders must enhance their followers' ability to reach their full potential as human beings. Dictating strategies in a 'command and control' manner is useless, Greenleaf believes. Far better is supporting followers' ideas and actions. He first wrote about the concept in 1969, in *The Servant Leader*; he spent the next several decades until his death in 1990 refining it. Greenleaf is an innovative, complex thinker.

At the core of the idea of servant leadership is the moral principle that '...the only authority deserving one's allegiance is that which is freely and knowingly granted by the led to the leader in response to, and in proportion to, the clearly evident servant stature of the leader'.[24]

Greenleaf also devotes time and space in *Servant Leadership* as it applies beyond the individual to institutions (e.g. businesses, universities, churches, and foundations). The essential characteristics of servant leadership are listening, empathy, healing, awareness, persuasion, conceptualization, foresight, stewardship, commitment to the growth of others, and building community.

Servant leadership has much in common with Plato's idea of the doctor. In the *Gorgias*, the model is used to stress that the true leader works for the good—for the real interests—of the followers. Demagogues, by contrast, seek to gratify the citizens in the short-term in order to feather their own nests. The same idea appears in the argument between Socrates and Thrasymachus in *Republic* Book 1, where the doctor is also used to show that a leader is essentially there to serve his subjects' interests, not his own. The doctor exemplifies many of the essential characteristics of servant leadership listed in the previous paragraph: not just healing, of course, but also awareness, foresight, stewardship, and a commitment to the growth of others. It is also characteristic of the doctor to build community: recall the doctor's role in balancing different groups within the organization (D2); a good community is stable and well-balanced.

But the welfare of the patients must also be tempered, as we saw in Chapter 6 with Roy Vagelos, by the doctor also acting as a teacher. One can only serve others, if one can get others to look after their own interests, teaching what is good for them. It is a mark of a great teacher to prioritize listening, awareness, persuasion, conceptualization, some of the other essential characteristics of servant leadership. So the closest Platonic model to servant leadership is the combined doctor-teacher of the *Laws*, whom we described in Chapter 6 as listening to their patients.

Howard Gardner and thought leadership (the sower)

Plato's model of the sower, who plants seeds that may well be harvested much later, is at the centre of Howard Gardner's work on leadership. Leaders, according to Gardner, are 'individuals who significantly influence the thoughts, behaviors, and/or feelings of others'.[25] In *Leading*

Minds, he presents 'case studies' of historical leaders, including Gandhi, Margaret Thatcher, and Eleanor Roosevelt, and creates a cognitive framework for leadership, in which thoughts and images are used to influence followers (or the 'audience', as Gardner prefers). Unlike many other scholars, Gardner does not focus on various leaders' individual personalities or motivations, but instead on the 'ingredients' that have let them lead. Gardner acknowledges that the figures he has chosen[26] may not normally be linked together, since they work in different 'domains' (politics, business, and anthropology, among others) and have vastly different personalities. Yet they all are effective leaders, primarily by the 'stories' they relate (not *tell*, because speaking is not the only way to communicate). At the heart of leadership, Gardner asserts, is the individual's ability both to communicate and embody their stories, which include not only their personal experience and background but also pre-existing stories.

In his research, Gardner identifies six 'constants' of leadership. First, it is essential for leaders to have a story to communicate, and these stories are most effective when presented clearly and 'directly to the untutored mind—the mind that develops naturally in the early lives of children without the need for formal tutelage'.[27] Effective stories also provide background, include and frame future options, and appeal both to the individual ('we') identity as well as the group ('they') identity. 'Inclusionary' stories seem the best choice, but they can be divisive. Gardner gives the example of the ire directed at Gandhi from Hindus when he included Muslims in his vision and from Indians in general when he tried to include British imperialists.

Second, even the best stories will fail when the audience is unreceptive, but mediocre stories will be accepted if the audience is willing to hear them. So much depends on the interaction between leader and audience:

> The relationship between leader and audience is complex and interactive; perhaps especially in the case of leaders of nondominant groups, a dynamic interplay exists between the needs and desires of the audience, on the one hand, and the contours of the leader's story, on the other.[28]

Stories need to fit the historical context; Eleanor Roosevelt's story, that an ordinary woman could have such extraordinary accomplishments, could not have been told fifty years earlier and would have seemed unremarkable fifty years later. Nuance and sophistication in identifying the audience often are required. Gandhi, for example, was adept at presenting his story in various ways, based on whom he was addressing.

Third, in most cases, enduring leadership requires the context of an organization or institution.[29] There have been leaders who have operated outside the organization, but that particular type of leadership can be tenuous and ephemeral if the creation of an organization does not follow the initial bond between leader and followers. Gardner gives the example of twentieth-century totalitarian 'leaders' (again, Plato would have considered them tyrants not leaders), who succeeded only because of the strong political organizations they either helped create or joined up with. Leaders such as Gandhi and Churchill, however, watched their ability to command dissipate somewhat after their goals were achieved and the crises that brought them into power subsided. Gardner believes that 'the actual power of ideas and the existence of seminal work can exert effects independent of the current shape of the domain'.[30] A leader who wants to help shape his or her created organization needs to use direct forms of leadership.

Fourth, to ensure that stories ring true and find a receptive audience, the leader must embody the story (i.e. be authentic). The leader does not need to be a saint, but must not 'contradict the story by the facts of his existence'.[31]

Fifth, the multiplicity of leadership models may well include a continuum of leadership, which starts with indirect leadership (e.g. Margaret Mead's scholarship) and moves to direct leadership (e.g. the speeches and military action of world leaders). Because it is noisy and clearly evident, direct leadership can be, in the short term, the most effective.

Lastly, Gardner observes that, without the highest expertise in their particular domain, leaders will not be seen as credible. Margaret Mead became a leader of her domain because her colleagues had esteemed her work. In becoming a direct leader, however, the indirect leader risks moving away from his or her technical expertise, becoming distracted by the requirements of the 'direct', and thus, losing the power of that expertise.

Plato's model of the sower is a clear case of thought leadership: the leader is someone who sows ideas big enough to guide others and to have an enduring legacy (S1). We also saw how Plato's own embodiment of the model involved creating an institution, the Academy, that could act as a vehicle for promoting and sustaining his ideas, Gardner's third constant. This also illustrates the fifth constant, because Plato started leading in an indirect way (by doing philosophy in Athens), but then moved to a more direct role as founder and leader of the Academy. The sixth constant is also highly pertinent: the sower needs expertise to develop the ideas in the first place. Of course it is not just the sower for whom expertise is central: it also lies at the heart of the closely associated teacher model, as well as the doctor and the navigator. Furthermore, Plato worried about the way an expert has to move away from their expertise the more they engage directly with society: this is highlighted in the cave allegory, when the person returns from the light outside (the domain of their expertise) to the darkness within, i.e. when they have to struggle to see how to apply their expertise beyond the environment in which they originally developed it. (In this context it is also pertinent to recall the story of Plato's trips to Sicily.) Yet another similarity comes when we compare the fourth constant, authenticity, with the artist model: one of the key principles of this model was that the leader embodies the values that they intend to spread (A3).

However, there is a question to be asked about how close Plato's sower really is to the first constant. Gardner stresses that leaders must communicate their stories 'directly to the untutored mind'. Surely, one might protest, Plato advocates the sower model in a much more cerebral context: he is talking about what he calls 'dialectic', high-grade philosophical argument; he is not discussing stories told to untutored minds. As for the second constant, isn't Plato contemptuous of rhetorical strategies? Think of the detachment of the artist (A2): they sit alone, refusing to compromise on their ideals and being prepared to wipe the slate clean rather than accommodate to existing circumstances (A4). The second constant suggests more flexibility that Platonic leadership allows.

In fact, both objections are misguided: Plato's approach to leadership has more in common even with these aspects of Gardner's theory than might initially appear. It is true that, within the confines of the passage in which the *Phaedrus* explicitly discusses the sower, his interest is in what we would call academic learning. But if you look more broadly at Plato's approach to communication—elsewhere in the *Phaedrus*, in other dialogues, and in his own practice—we find a marked interest in 'stories' and in being sensitive to rhetorical contexts.

To start with 'stories' (as opposed to rigorously expressed philosophical theories), Plato's works are full of them. For example, the ship of state in *Republic* Book 6 is itself a mini-narrative about what can go wrong on board the vessel of democratic politics. It is a story found in poetry before Plato's time, which he then develops for his own purposes. In a more extended way, the cave allegory of *Republic* Book 7 is a story about intellectual enlightenment (and the dangers of communicating it), which again harks back to older narratives (Homer's story about Odysseus descending into the underworld) and is designed to make a vivid impression even on non-philosophers. Plato is fond of using myths in several works, especially stories about punishment after death for sins committed in this life. Such stories have much less impact now than then (another point Gardner highlights), but were used by Plato to buttress his arguments in favour of the moral life, especially for 'untutored' minds. (The *Laws* contains more such stories, designed for children as well as adults.)

Perhaps Plato's greatest and most extended narrative is the story of Socrates: the tale of his trial (in the *Apology*), his subsequent imprisonment (in the *Crito*), and his execution (in the *Phaedo*). Though there is a great deal of philosophical argument in these works, some of it quite technical, there is also a compelling story about the courage, wisdom, and dignity of his hero, confronting Athenian bigotry and retaining his composure right up to the end. (His death is vividly portrayed at the end of the *Phaedo*.) This portrayal of a philosophical martyr has resonated down the centuries. And some would say it is a narrative, which Plato used to silence rival accounts that portrayed Socrates in a very different light, e.g. as a religious heretic, or as a Spartan sympathizer surreptitiously trying to usurp Athenian democracy.[32]

All this shows that Plato was not opposed to rhetoric in itself, merely to the misuse of rhetoric by political demagogues. So there is no real tension with Gardner's second constant, any more than with the first. We discussed this when considering Douglass as an example of the navigator: it is a mistake to think Plato would have taken issue with someone who used rhetoric, in the sense of considering what would or would not make a particular audience receptive. If he had not been so concerned with this, we would not have some of the models of leadership he gives us. The navigator and artist models are both introduced in order to combat the resistance that most people (non-philosophers) will feel when confronted with his proposal for philosopher rulers. Instead of arguing the case simply by logic, he resorts to memorable images to appeal to the imagination. In general, the cave allegory shows the dangers of confronting the wrong audience with your message at the wrong time. Because he was so sensitive to this problem, he devised a series of rhetorical techniques and stories to communicate more effectively. In the *Phaedrus*, a dialogue very much concerned with the correct use of rhetoric, there is a passage (270a–272b, shortly before the writing paradox) about the need to understand the psychology of one's audience and then tailor one's message accordingly. So what Gardner said of Ghandi is also true of Plato: he too took care to present his story in various ways, based on whom he was addressing.[33]

Notes

1. This chapter is partially based on Mead, Freeman, and Spangler (2011). We are grateful to the co-authors and copyright holders for permission to recast some of this material here.
2. Or, as Malvolio said in Shakespeare's *Twelfth Night*, '...some are born great, some achieve greatness, and some have greatness thrust upon them!'
3. Gardner (1990) 6.
4. Stogdill (1974) 259.
5. Bass and Stogdill (1990) 11.
6. Material in this section is based on Wicks et al. (2010).
7. See *Republic* Book 8, 566d, with Chapter 1 n. 10.
8. Burns (1978) 1.
9. Burns (1978) 42.
10. Burns (1978) 11.
11. Burns (1978) 19.
12. Burns (1978) 20.
13. Burns (1978) 20.
14. Burns (1978) 3.

15. Plato's use of the artist model is highly moralized. However, as we saw in Chapter 4, it can be adapted so as to apply in other ways, e.g. technological.
16. Burns (1978) 42.
17. See Appendix 1.
18. Collins (2005) 140.
19. Collins (2001) 137.
20. Collins (1997).
21. Collins (2001) 13.
22. Collins (2001) 135.
23. The topic is picked up again at Book 7, 519d–521b, the passage where Plato famously claims that the people who are best suited to leadership will be those most reluctant to exercise it. For a discussion of this claim in the context of modern leadership studies, see Cox and Crook (2015).
24. Greenleaf (1977) 24.
25. Gardner (2011) 6.
26. The figures he analyzes are Margaret Mead, J. Robert Oppenheimer, Robert Maynard Hutchins, Alfred P. Sloan, Jr, George C. Marshall, Pope John XXIII, Eleanor Roosevelt, Martin Luther King, Jr, Margaret Thatcher, Jean Monnet, and Mahatma Gandhi.
27. Gardner (2011) 274.
28. Gardner (2011) 275.
29. As Jean Monnet said, 'nothing is made without men; nothing lasts without institutions' (quoted in Chapter 2 in our case study of Monnet). See Gardner (2011) 264.
30. Gardner (2011) 276.
31. Gardner (2011) 277.
32. See Cartledge (2016) 175–80. Interestingly, Cartledge seems rather sympathetic to the Athenian jury's treatment of Socrates. Clearly Plato's story does not hold everyone under its sway.
33. What applies to Plato himself also applies more generally to any leader who acts as a sower: they can lead others without always teaching them intellectually. See Chapter 10.

Conclusion

This brings our study of leadership to a close. We hope to have shown the advantages of using multiple models to examine the phenomenon in all its complexity. On our analysis, leadership might involve any of the following:

- Confronting stakeholders who are prone to give excessive weight to seemingly attractive, but short-term objectives.
- Helping an organization on its newly chosen course, bringing an unexpected kind of expertise to the task, and maintaining unity or morale when the going gets tough.
- Realizing a vision, against all the odds, and living your own life around it before trying to impose it on anyone else.
- Bringing people out of their comfort zones by appealing to their heads as much as their hearts.
- Combining a group of diverse talents and temperaments, especially hawks and doves, and unifying them with a common set of values.
- Originating ideas big enough to create a legacy, but still empowering others to adapt them as circumstances demand.

These different models can each be used to highlight what might be needed in one situation or another. Avoiding the appeal to a single formula, we can use the diversity of the models to explain why quite different people, with very little in common, can still be equally great leaders.

Of course, we have not followed a completely scatter-gun approach. As we have shown, many of the models underscore the ethical dimension of leadership. To attribute 'leadership' to someone is usually to accord them some status and legitimacy, which is not something we do with tyrants and demagogues: leaders who act as doctors or captains prioritize their followers' interests rather their own; and, in a different way, the models of the artist and the sower speak to the need to promote something larger than yourself—a vision or an idea.

Another theme running through several models is the importance of expertise. This is clear with the very first model we examined, the doctor, and it reappears with the navigator and the teacher. In both these cases the leader brings a perspective 'from the outside': the navigator looks away from the ship towards the stars; the ex-prisoner re-enters the cave to confront his fellows with tales of an alien world. But the stress on expertise raises difficulties: the expert has to lead non-experts, who may resent the message being delivered. And, aside from the content of the actual message, acquiring the necessary expertise is hugely time-consuming for the leader. For us, the task becomes ever more daunting as expertise becomes increasingly specialized. It is particularly difficult in politics, because a leader typically has to make decisions right across the spectrum.

So there is a dilemma—between becoming absorbed in technicalities and being able to communicate to stakeholders. But it is a dilemma we cannot evade.[1] In the end, the leader has to be an interstitial figure, negotiating between the very different worlds of the expert and the layperson (a point brought out very clearly in the allegory of the cave). As we have seen, Plato makes the problem very stark in the *Gorgias* and the *Republic*, but tries to soften it later on in the *Laws* by thinking more about the persuasive art of rhetoric. His emphasis on the role of listening also helps to ease the problem.

But, as we have seen from some of our case studies, the solution sometimes consists in something quite different, and more basic: getting results. In Chapter 2, we illustrated this with Roy Vagelos, who decided to 'go it alone' and distribute doses of Mectizan (the cure for river blindness) for free; when people saw his programme actually working, they began to support him. Nightingale is another example of someone who prevailed by getting results (in the Crimea), and Montessori became eminent early on because her very first school saw dramatic improvements in children's education. No amount of lecturing or sermonizing can beat this. Results are their own form of rhetoric. However, this is only a partial solution: in order to get results, you still need to carry some people with you; but to do that, you need to persuade them: a classic example of a Catch-22 situation. So the fact remains that, as well as bequeathing us a host of positive insights, Plato leaves us with a conundrum, which seems to become more difficult as expertise becomes more complex and specialized.

A final comment about the focus and purpose of this book. Obviously, we have talked a great deal about Plato. But, first and foremost, this has been a study of leadership, rather than a matter of winning plaudits for a figure from the long distant past. If you wanted to put all reference to Plato aside for a moment and summarize our discussion, you would say that we have promoted a 'family resemblance' approach to leadership, eschewing a single definition and instead separating out the different strands that make up the rope. Amid the diversity of models, two themes have been prominent: ethics and expertise. Of course, when it came to identifying the models, we turned to Plato, but the relevance of his thinking does not derive from the eminent place he happens to hold in the Western canon. It comes from the simple fact that his thought matches so well with modern perceptions and ideas of leadership and can then be used to develop them further. We have brought this out in two ways. First, his models help explain the greatness of many figures we already celebrate as leaders—among them Nobel laureates, groundbreaking politicians and CEOs, and other household names. Indeed, some of our case studies have already been used by other writers on leadership, e.g. Monnet, Douglass, and Mead.[2] Our argument would have been a lot weaker if we had needed to scour the history books to find obscure individuals who happened to fit Plato's models and then try to persuade the reader that they were shining exemplars of leadership. Second, his models turn up in some of the most recent and prominent theories of leadership, whose advocates were working without any reference to Plato. Both these two points explain why we have never needed to argue that, just because Plato is such a famous philosopher, his views on leadership ought to be relevant to us. The facts are enough to make the case.

Plato's insights, still resonant today, can also be applied to many different fields. We have looked at politics, business, science, academia, healthcare, and education. But there are others—the arts, religion, charities, journalism, to name a few. We expect that readers with experience in these fields will be able to find more applications of his ideas to their work and so further their goals. In the process, they will doubtless think of other models to add to the list.

Notes

1. As Gardner (2011) 285–6 says: 'Unless we can find or form leaders who retain some links to expert knowledge, on the one hand, and some ability to communicate to non-experts on the other, our world is likely to spin even further out of control.'
2. Monnet and Mead featured in Gardner (2011) ch. 4 and 14; Douglass in Koehn (2017) part 3.

Plato's Use of the Ship of State Image in the *Republic*

The ideal state in the *Republic*

In Chapter 3, we discussed the way Plato used the ship of state image to support some of his claims about political leadership. While these claims are embedded in his political theory, they can also be abstracted from that context. This allowed us to discuss the image in quite general terms—in such a way that readers could apply it to leadership in all sorts of contexts. But since he does use the image to elucidate his own political theory, we have written this appendix for readers who might want to know more about his views in this area.

Much of the *Republic* is about what a state would look like if it were fully just—the ideal state, which Plato begins sketching early in Book 2. He opens the whole discussion with an explanation of why human beings form states in the first place (369a–b). No one of us can exist independently; we need to work together to provide the basic necessities of life. So he imagines a very primitive association focused on the production of food, clothing, and shelter. At the very least, this would require the skills of a farmer, a builder, a weaver, and a cobbler. Then he poses a very simple question: would it be better if everyone did a bit of each task, or if each person specialized just in one of them? He takes the second option, and so founds a basic association where one person does the farming, the other the building, and so on. In so doing, he lays down a key principle for the entire work, the principle of specialization: each citizen should focus on the task for which they are most naturally suited.

Next, he starts to increase the number of trades and professions necessary for the maintenance of the state: they don't just need farmers, builders, and weavers, but also people to make their tools and materials; and where their own land is unable to provide whatever is needed for their work, they shall have to import it. But then they will need something to export by way of exchange; so they need more producers to make the goods they themselves won't use, and they need merchants, ship-builders, and sailors to sell them overseas. Thus the number and range of people needed to sustain the economic life of the state grows considerably. But all the time, Plato insists that one person should stick to one task. Eventually, he turns to security: the state will need a fighting force, but he still insists on the need for specialization, and creates a professional military, consisting of people who are by nature and temperament most suited to the military life (374a). Finally, he creates the class of leaders, the 'guardians'. (This point comes much later on, at Book 3, 412b–414b.) Again, he uses specialization as his rationale and so, without saying as much explicitly, makes his crucial anti-democratic move: like any other job in the state, political decision-making requires a specialized group of people who focus on that and nothing else. They are naturally suited for the role, by character and intellect, and then properly trained. From this perspective, democracy makes little sense: it is the political equivalent of allowing someone to do whatever job in the state they want, regardless of talent, temperament, or training.

So, by the middle of Book 4, Plato has constructed his ideal state. In outline, it consists of three classes: those who are charged with meeting the material needs of the state (the 'producers'), the military defenders (the 'auxiliaries'), and the rulers (the 'guardians'). Following the logic of specialization, Plato insists again and again that no one class should try and interfere with the job of the others, especially when it comes to ruling.

Philosopher rulers

In the central section of the work (Books 5–7), he tells us much more about the guardians. It is here that we find a proposal for which he is justly famous, that women should be allowed into the ranks of the guardians: gender is no bar to leadership, or indeed any profession in the state (Book 5, 451c–457c). Then, towards the end of Book 5, he makes another famous—or rather infamous—proposal: the guardians of the ideal state should be philosophers. Even as he announces the proposal, he says that it will arouse almost universal derision (473c7–474a4). Philosophers, you might think, are the last people to whom one should entrust power.

But there is a logic to his position. It derives from three fundamental principles. The first is that his ideal state is first and foremost a just society: his purpose in imagining it is to establish what a state would look like if we made ethics our priority. He is not giving a recipe for economic maximization, let alone for military or imperial dominance. He wants a state that is good, while also being viable and sustainable in terms of economics and security. The second principle is that of specialization: each job, including leadership, must only be done by those who are trained in the relevant field. Taken together these two principles imply that the leaders should be (among other things) moral experts. So what is it to be a moral expert? Here we come to Plato's third principle. Ethical understanding is not something you just pick up from your grandmother, or from reading a book; nor is it a matter of having gut reactions. It is a science as rigorous as any other—highly abstract, requiring logic and reasoning as difficult as anything you might find in, say, mathematics. And it is called philosophy.

Put these three principles together and you can see why Plato thought his guardians must be philosophers.[1] Most readers will still be unconvinced, but the proposal should not be dismissed out of hand, especially if one makes a (significant) emendation. What is peculiar about the proposal is the idea of a philosopher trying to rule the state. But maybe *philosophy* still has a part to play. The kind of absent-minded, abstraction-loving, head-in-the-clouds figure we associate with the philosopher does indeed sound like an improbable leader. But the ideas philosophers have generated over the centuries are another matter. There would have been no

American constitution without the British philosopher John Locke (especially his ideas on the right to property and on religious toleration); there would have been no French (or American) revolutions without Voltaire and Rousseau; turning further east, whatever your preferences, you can hardly deny the impact of Marx. But he in turn was influenced by Hegel and before him Kant. Adam Smith was not only an economist but also a philosopher. The fabric of our constitutions, the principles underlying our laws are in part philosophical. Any sustainable society requires a philosophical foundation. It is just that we do not expect the same people who produced the ideas to be running the societies built upon them.

Is the image too democratic for Plato?

At any rate, it should now be clear why Plato describes the ship of state as he does, particularly the way in which he concludes the image: just as the true navigator would be an expert in astronomy, gazing away from the hurly-burly on board deck towards the stars, so true political leaders must be philosophers focused on moral principles, however abstruse their knowledge needs to be.

In Appendix 2, we shall have a further discussion about the nature of these principles, the way Plato conceived of philosophical knowledge, and why he thought it would appear so abstruse to most people. But here we wish to raise another point, about the way the ship of state applies to politics. The image seems initially designed as a description of a democratic state, where the people decide what sort of state they want to live in, and what sorts of lives should be permitted or encouraged. The image could then be used to point out that, in order to achieve these democratically set goals, we need technical experts.

But Plato also implies that any state, including his own ideal state, can be conceived in nautical terms. (This is clear from the way it ends, comparing the ideal leader to a navigator.) But how would the image work in the ideal case? He does not seem to believe that it is up to the people to decide the ultimate goals, i.e. what sort of lives they should lead; this lies as much within the remit of the leaders as the means to achieving those goals. On board the ship of the ideal state, it would be quite permissible if the captain informed the passengers that he had chosen a different course from the one they originally wanted, simply because he thought it better for them. Taken literally (so that the ship-owner/demos decides the destination), Plato's image conflicts with his own anti-democratic thrust in the *Republic*.[2]

But there is another way of applying the image. Sometimes it is not only a matter of finding the *means* to a specific goal decided by the electorate or the stakeholders. Typically, they will have only given a very broad prescription. It might be the job of the leader to decide what counts as achieving this goal. In Plato's case, he can admit that everyone desires happiness, but (for him) it is the job of the leader to determine what counts as happiness, not simply the best means to achieve it.[3] So, if we allow that the image concerns not only the means to an end, but also what counts as achieving it, Plato's use of the image need not conflict with his anti-democratic theory. The demos still sets the ultimate goals; the philosopher-rulers determine both how to reach it and what counts as reaching it.

This may sound as if it is only of interest to Plato scholars. But if we step outside the *Republic*, we can see that it has more general interest. Consider the Brexit case, with which we started Chapter 3. It turned out that the problem was not simply how to achieve Brexit, but what Brexit actually meant.[4] What constitutes leaving the EU? Does it involve staying in the single market, the customs union, or creating some other sort of relationship (such as the EU has with Canada)? Until these questions are answered, there can be no Brexit. So the passengers may have chosen a destination (e.g. a certain island); the captain has to decide the best place on it to make landfall. In other words, the job of the leader is to determine both what the desired goal consists in and (hence) the best means for achieving it. This point can extend more widely, and apply to many different types of organization: what does it mean to be more environmentally sustainable, more innovative, or more diverse? Answering such questions may require considerable expertise; failure to address them will lead to conflict.

Notes

1. We shall discuss how Plato conceived of philosophy further in Appendix 2.
2. This problem was posed by Bambrough (1971) 194–5.
3. See *Republic* Book 6, 504e–505e with Keyt (2006) 200.
4. Theresa May notoriously ducked this issue by repeating the mantra 'Brexit means Brexit'.

Interpreting the Cave Allegory

The true objects of knowledge

When we focused on Plato's cave allegory in Chapter 5, we stressed that the core ideas behind it can be widely applied in academia and beyond: education is a matter of drawing people out of their comfort zone and exposing them to a quite different reality; this will result in the experience of a 'perspective gap', which they may find disorientating and alienating. We gave examples of this general idea in anthropology, science, politics, and business. But how did Plato himself cash out his allegory? What exactly did he mean by comparing the majority of human beings to prisoners looking at shadows on a wall, and the path to enlightenment as one of emergence from the darkness of a cave? In the interests of not overloading the Platonic section of Chapter 5, we answered these questions only in outline, saying he wanted to stress the difference between two levels of thought, concrete and abstract, and to see education as the movement between the two. For him, this had particular application to politics and ethics: most of us are all too keen to make moral judgements about particular people, actions, or situations; but we find it disorientating to look at the same issues in highly abstract and analytical terms, just as Socrates' fellow citizens resented the way he challenged them to define virtues such as courage and justice in the abstract. But Plato argued that we have to do this: in order to make good practical judgements, we first need to ascend to a much higher level of abstraction. We can then use our theoretical knowledge to help determine what to do in practice. The abstract level provides the criteria for resolving disputes, uncertainties, and dilemmas in everyday life.

The purpose of this appendix is to provide more detail about how the cave allegory supports this distinction between these different levels of thinking. So let's start over again. At the bottom of the cave, people are looking at shadows on the wall and discussing them among each other; the journey out of the cave is a matter of realizing that what we took to be reality was a mere shadow play, an imitation of something else. Ultimately, when we step outside the cave, we shall be able to contemplate the objects that constitute true reality. In the allegory these include living objects, as well as the stars, the moon, and the sun.

So what is it, according to Plato, to be a prisoner looking at shadows on a wall? This part of his theory needn't be too abstruse (although scholars still manage to disagree among each other as to his exact meaning). He is probably referring to the way people base their day-to-day judgements on experience of the perceptible objects around them; or perhaps in the moral case, they rely on the opinions absorbed from society. (In his day, this included the views disseminated by the poets; for us, it would include many sources—including journalism, TV, and social media.) The main point of the cave allegory is that we have to stop relying on these sources (sense perception or hearsay) and turn our minds in another direction.

When we ask what direction Plato has in mind, things do become a little abstruse. Ultimately, we are meant to ascend to a place where we see certain entities directly, entities that are analogized in the allegory by the objects outside the cave (e.g. the stars, the moon, and the sun). What are these entities?

A good starting-point for answering this question is Raphael's famous painting, *The School of Athens*. It represents all the Greek philosophers sitting or standing in various poses. In the centre we see the two 'greats', Plato and Aristotle. They are engaged in a conversation, both carrying copies of one of their own books: Aristotle holds his book flat and parallel to the ground; his right hand is similarly placed. Plato's book is at right angles to the ground, and he points up to the heavens with the index finger of his right hand.

Aristotle is telling us to 'keep our feet on the ground', to remain focused on the natural world using the tools of empirical science, while Plato is beckoning us to look elsewhere. In his view, the physical world is just an imitation of something else: an immaterial, transcendent reality, accessible only to pure reason. For instance, we are surrounded by physical objects of various shapes: rectangles, squares, and circles. But all of these are only approximations to pure geometrical objects (e.g. the perfect circle). When geometers study such figures, they may draw diagrams as an aid to thinking or teaching, but they are not actually studying the particular shape they see before them (which, if you examined it carefully, would not actually be perfectly square or circular); they are learning about 'the square itself' or 'the circle itself'. Such objects have no physical existence; and physical objects are approximations to them. So geometry and other kinds of mathematics are about a reality separate from the perceptible world. Perhaps, you might object, perfect geometrical figures are human constructs—just concepts in our minds. But if so, Plato could ask: why is geometry an *objective* science? There must be mind-independent objects to account for this. And, if such objects are not in the physical world, they must exist outside of it, as well as outside of our minds. Hence they are transcendent entities.

Plato extended this line of thinking to other areas: he thought that there are moral archetypes of goodness and justice, which particular good or just people merely imitate in their actions. He also believed in an archetype of beauty, of which particular beautiful objects are mere approximations. In modern discussions of Plato, these archetypes are called 'forms', and the so-called 'theory of forms' is one of his most famous contributions to philosophy.[1]

All of this has crucial implications for education. Although we are surrounded by physical objects accessible to our senses, real understanding requires us to ascend to a far more abstract level and grasp the forms instantiated or imitated by the particulars. This is what true education involves. So too in the moral world: we are surrounded by examples of people acting justly and unjustly, and of individuals voicing their opinions of each other's behaviour, but moral expertise requires an understanding of forms of goodness and justice—put in our terms, of the highly abstract principles required to support these judgements. In broad outline, this is the journey out of the cave. Plato's view is that most human beings find abstract thinking very disorientating: we feel much more at home dealing with particular cases, not least when it comes to ethics. So he uses the metaphor of light, of the almost blinding light, and the sheer difficulty of getting out of the cave, to illustrate our natural resistance to super-abstract thinking and to the idea that there exists a realm of transcendent forms.

But there is also the return journey to be considered. Once you have achieved philosophical enlightenment, knowledge of the forms, you may return to the place where you began. But, for Plato, this is no easy matter. Taking highly abstract knowledge and applying it in practice is not straightforward. So, just as there was a type of blindness associated with the ascent, there is one associated with the descent: the sense of disorientation that the theoretician will feel as they have to make their discoveries apply in practice. And that is not the only problem; another is their reception. Those who have not ascended to the same abstract perspective may simply fail to understand what is being said; they will be baffled and, as the conversation continues, increasingly frustrated, if not actively hostile.

So understanding something about Plato's forms is necessary if we are to understand what he himself meant in the cave allegory. We have only given a very brief sketch of the theory, but it should be enough to indicate how he sought to deploy the teacher model: the role of the teacher is to do whatever it takes to help people out of their reliance on particular judgements and challenge them to define the forms of justice, beauty, goodness, and the like. In the next section, we shall ask whether Plato actually thought this was a feasible model for how a political leader should relate to the citizens at large (and not only to trainee philosopher-rulers). But before we do so, it is worth pausing to see how the theory of forms relates to two of the other models we have discussed, the navigator and the artist.

In the ship of state image, the true navigator looks to the stars to set the course and is ridiculed for doing so. The stars stand for the forms—the archetypes of goodness, justice, and beauty—knowledge of which gives the philosopher-guardians their mandate for power.[2] The image captures the remoteness of this knowledge, harking back again to the sheer abstraction required, and the attendant difficulty that most people will see such knowledge not merely as abstruse, but completely irrelevant.

The forms are also involved in the artist image. The leader looks to a model, which they use to mould the character of the state and the citizens within it. When it comes to characterizing this model, Plato actually gives two different descriptions. In Chapter 4, we saw that he talks of the model in terms of a distinction between 'natural' and 'conventional' justice—between 'true' justice, existing independently of human thought, and justice as a social construct. This is a way of expounding the artist model without actually mentioning transcendent forms and instead exploiting a distinction that would have sounded more familiar to Plato's contemporaries. In general, he is somewhat reticent about mentioning his theory of forms, because he thinks most people would struggle to accept it. So he refers to the ideal as 'natural justice' as a way of making his point more accessible. But elsewhere in the passage, he indicates his more considered view, which is exactly in line with the navigator image: the model to which the artist looks is the world of forms, of which particulars are mere copies (just as physical shapes are mere approximations to perfect geometrical figures).[3] So what he calls 'natural justice' at one point is actually the form of justice, as mentioned elsewhere in the passage.

Plato's ambivalence about the teacher

When we looked at the models of the doctor, the navigator, and the artist, we were discussing models of leadership that Plato advocates very explicitly in the *Gorgias* or the *Republic*. By contrast, the teacher model is presented more discreetly: he does not showcase it as clearly as the others. This is not to say we are inventing a model that Plato never proposed. The cave allegory does give us an account of leadership, because of the way it presents the released prisoner when he returns back down: a Socrates-like figure—a public intellectual with aspirations to moral reform.[4]

But the fact remains that Plato is hesitant about advocating the teacher model of leadership. As we have just seen, he presents the ex-prisoner as someone who might try to lead the others out of the cave, but would be frustrated by their resistance. Now, you might say this is no different from the way that he handles the doctor and the navigator. Although the best leaders would imitate these models if conditions were ideal, in actual circumstances they would find themselves unable to prevail.

But at this point we come to a puzzle. If Plato viewed the teacher model in exactly the same way, we would expect him to say that in the ideal state the guardians would act like teachers to the rest of the citizens, just as they act to secure their social health or navigate them on the path to happiness. But the problem is that, on a traditional or orthodox interpretation of the *Republic*, he appears not to apply the teacher model in the ideal state: the guardians in the ideal state do not attempt to educate the rest of the citizens in the sense of bringing them up to their own cognitive level. The 'ideal' state has rigid class boundaries. Of course, the guardians will ensure that future members of their class work their way out of the cave, but they will not be attempting a general education of the citizens at large. In the ideal state, the guardians return down to the cave to rule, but not to evacuate it. The producers stay where they are.

One response is just to say that Plato did not use the teacher as a model for leadership within his ideal state. If this is correct, he changed his mind when he wrote the *Laws*: as we saw in Chapter 6, he portrays the legislator as an educator of his citizens and does not balk at the accusation that the leader is attempting to bring his citizens up to his own level (Book 9, 857d). But another response is to challenge the orthodox view of the *Republic*. Contrary to what many scholars have thought, it is possible that all the citizens of the ideal state will receive some intellectual training in ethics and justice, but it will be tailored to suit their abilities. At the time he wrote the work, Plato had particularly strong views about the level of rigour and abstraction required for moral knowledge in a political leader; and he thought only a tiny number of people were capable of this. So his guardians will not try and bring everyone up to their own level. But it does not follow from this that the rest of the citizens will have no exposure to thinking about ethical values at all. Generations of scholars and philosophers (most notably Karl Popper) have assumed that the masses in the ideal state will unreflectively swallow whatever moral truths the guardians decide is good for them. But right at the end of the *Republic*, Plato says that everyone should do whatever they can to educate themselves in matters of ethical value (Book 10, 618b–c). It's just that the cognitive level they can be expected to reach will be lower than that of the guardians.[5] When discussing the practical feasibility of the teacher model in Chapter 5, we admitted that it is unrealistic for leaders to break down the barriers between themselves and their followers entirely. But they can still do something to help their followers leave their comfort zones and to make the barriers more porous.

Notes

1. On forms in Plato's *Republic*, see Pappas (1995) 129–32 and 212–20.
2. Keyt (2006) 197.
3. The technique of talking on different levels, a hallmark of effective teaching, is something to which we shall return below. For a more detailed discussion, see Scott (2020) 38.
4. Plato is more upfront about the teacher model in his last work, the *Laws*, where he combines it with the doctor model to illustrate his idea of the political legislator (see Chapter 6). It is also worth remembering the way the *Gorgias* describes Socrates as the only true political leader in Athens, when he is referring to his work as a public intellectual (521d). Implicitly, this is to characterize the leader as a teacher.
5. Scott (2020) 115–18.

Extracts from Plato's Dialogues

In this appendix we include some of the passages in Plato most relevant to his models of leadership. The translations are by Jowett (1871), modified in places to make them more idiomatic for modern-day readers. We also provide some brief notes in italics about the context of each extract. We have already quoted the passage relevant to the navigator in Chapter 3 (*Republic* Book 6, 488a–489a), so have not repeated it here. Likewise, we have not reproduced anything from the *Laws* on the model of the teacher-doctor, because we included the relevant texts in Chapter 6.

Readers who would like to explore Plato's writings more extensively will find a complete collection in Cooper (1997). This includes a translation of the *Republic* by G. M. A. Grube (revised by C. D. C. Reeve), previously published in 1992. Another very good translation of the work is Ferrari and Griffith (2000).

The doctor

Gorgias 462b–465b

The Gorgias *is a discussion of rhetoric. In this extract, the interlocutors are Socrates, the well-known orator Gorgias, and a young man called Polus, also an orator. The passage begins with Polus asking for a definition of rhetoric. In reply, Socrates denies that it is an art, i.e. a form of expertise; rather, it is a knack of flattering the audience, which is acquired merely by experience, not systematic training. It is here that he introduces the model of the doctor as the kind of leader who aims to improve the citizens rather than to indulge them. To correspond to the model of the doctor, Socrates also uses the chef as a model of the orator: both aim merely to please their audiences or consumers.*

POLUS: What is rhetoric?
SOCRATES: Do you mean what sort of an art?
P: Yes.
S: To tell you the truth, Polus, it is not an art at all, in my opinion.
P: Then what, in your opinion, is rhetoric?
S: A thing which, as I was lately reading in a book of yours, you say that you have made an art.
P: What thing?

s: I should say a knack—a matter of experience.

p: Does rhetoric seem to you to be a matter of experience?

s: That is my view, but you may be of another mind.

p: Experience in what?

s: Experience in producing a sort of pleasure and gratification.

p: And if it is able to gratify others, mustn't rhetoric be a fine thing?

s: What are you saying, Polus? Why do you ask me whether rhetoric is a fine thing or not, when I have not as yet told you what rhetoric is?

p: Did I not hear you say that rhetoric was a sort of experience?

s: Since you value gratifying others so much, will you gratify me—just a little?

p: I will.

s: Will you ask me, what sort of an art is cookery?

p: What sort of an art is cookery?

s: Not an art at all, Polus.

p: What then?

s: I should say a matter of experience.

p: In what? I wish that you would explain to me.

s: In producing a sort of pleasure and gratification, Polus.

p: Then are cookery and rhetoric the same?

s: No, but they are different parts of the same practice.

p: What practice do you mean?

s: I am afraid that the truth may seem rude; and I hesitate to answer, in case Gorgias imagines I am making fun of his own practice. For whether or not this is the art of rhetoric that Gorgias practises I really cannot tell: from what he was saying just now, it was not at all clear what he thought of his art, but what I call rhetoric is part of something that is not very creditable.

GORGIAS: A part of what, Socrates? Say what you mean, and never mind me.

s: In my opinion then, Gorgias, the whole of which rhetoric is a part is not an art at all, but the habit of a bold and ready wit, which knows how to manage mankind: this habit I sum up under the word 'flattery'; and it appears to me to have many other parts, one of which is cookery, which may seem to be an art, but, as I maintain, is only a matter of experience or routine and not an art; another part is rhetoric . . . . And Polus may ask, if he likes, for he has not as yet been informed, what part of flattery is rhetoric: he did not see that I had not yet answered him when he proceeded to ask a further question: Whether I do not think rhetoric a fine thing? But I shall not tell him whether rhetoric is a fine thing or not, until I have first answered, 'What is rhetoric?' For that wouldn't be right, Polus; but I shall be happy to answer, if you will ask me, What part of flattery is rhetoric?

p: I will ask, and you can answer: what part of flattery is rhetoric?

s: Will you understand my answer? Rhetoric, according to my view, is the counterfeit of a part of politics.

At this point (463d), Gorgias intervenes again and briefly takes over the role of questioning Socrates from Polus.

G: Explain to me what you mean by saying that rhetoric is the counterfeit of a part of politics.

s: I will try, then, to explain my notion of rhetoric, and if I am mistaken, my friend Polus shall refute me. We may assume the existence of bodies and of souls?

G: Of course.

s: You would further admit that there is a good condition of either of them?

G: Yes.

s: Is there a condition that is not really good, but good only in appearance? I mean, there are many people who appear to be in good health, and whom only a doctor or trainer will discern at first sight not to be in good health.

G: True.

s: And this applies not only to the body, but also to the soul: in either there may be that which gives the appearance of health and not the reality?

G: Yes, certainly.

s: And now I will try to explain to you more clearly what I mean. The soul and body are two things, and have two arts corresponding to them: there is the art of politics attending on the soul; and another art attending on the body, of which I know no single name, but which may be described as having two divisions, one of them gymnastics, and the other medicine. And in politics there is a legislative part, which answers to gymnastics, as justice does to medicine; and the two parts run into one another, justice having to do with the same subject as legislation, and medicine with the same subject as gymnastics, but with a difference. Now, seeing that there are these four arts, two attending on the body and two on the soul for their highest good; flattery knowing, or rather guessing their natures, has distributed herself into four simulations of them; she puts on the likeness of one or other of them, and pretends to be that which she simulates and, having no regard for men's highest interests, is ever making pleasure the bait of the unwary, and deceiving them into the belief that she is of the highest value to them. Cookery simulates the disguise of medicine, and pretends to know what food is the best for the body; and if the physician and the cook had to enter into a competition in which children were the judges, or men who had no more sense than children, as to which of them best understands the goodness or badness of food, the physician would starve to death. I call this flattery and think it a shameful kind of thing, Polus—I'm addressing you now—because it aims at pleasure without any thought of the best. I do not call it an art, but only a form of experience, because it is unable to explain or to give a reason of the nature of its own applications. And I do not call any irrational thing an art; but if you dispute my words, I am prepared to argue in their defence.

Cookery, then, I maintain to be a flattery which takes the form of medicine; and cosmetics, in like manner, is a flattery which takes the form of gymnastics, and is mischievous, false, shameful, illiberal, working deceitfully with shapes and colours, smoothing and dressing, and making people assume a spurious beauty to the neglect of the true beauty which is given by gymnastics.

The artist

Republic Book 6, 500b–501c

Here Socrates presents the model of the leader as artist to Adeimantus, who is worried that most people will find Socrates' proposal for philosopher-rulers absurd. The image is designed to show how such rulers will be guided by a moral vision, rather than the pursuit of their own self-interest.

For someone, Adeimantus, whose mind is fixed upon true reality, has surely no time to look down upon the affairs of men, or to be filled with malice and envy, in competition with others; his eye is always directed towards things fixed and immutable, which he sees neither wronging nor being wronged by one another, but all in order conforming to reason; these he imitates, and to these he will, as far as he can, conform himself. Can a person help imitating that which he treats with such reverence?

Impossible.

And the philosopher who associates with the divine order becomes orderly and divine, as far as human nature allows; but like everyone else, he will fall victim to a great deal of slander.

Of course.

And if it becomes a necessary for him to model, not only himself, but human nature generally, whether in states or individuals, on what he sees elsewhere, do you think he will he an unskilful craftsman of justice, temperance, and every civic virtue?

Anything but.

And if the world perceives that what we are saying about him is the truth, will they be angry with philosophy? Will they disbelieve us, when we tell them that no state can be happy which is not designed by artists who imitate the heavenly pattern?
They will not be angry if they understand, he said. But how will these artists draw out the plan of which you are speaking?

They will begin by taking the state and the characters of the people within it, like a tablet. First, they will wipe it clean. This is no easy task. But whether easy or not, this will be the difference between them and every other legislator: they will have nothing to do either with individual or state, and not inscribe any laws, until they have either found, or themselves made, a clean surface.

They will be very right, he said.

Having done this, they will proceed to trace an outline of the constitution?

No doubt.

And when they are filling in the work, I suppose, they will often turn their eyes upwards and downwards: I mean that they will first look at natural justice, beauty, temperance, and so on, and then again at the human copy; and they will mingle and temper the various elements of life into a human image, taking as their reference point what Homer calls the form and likeness of the divine, when it exists among human beings.

Very true, he said.

And they will erase one feature, and put another one in, until they have made human characters, as far as possible, agreeable to the gods?

The teacher

Republic Book 7, 514a–518b

In this passage, Socrates introduces the allegory of the cave to help his interlocutor Glaucon understand the nature of education, and what it is like to lack it.

Imagine people living in an underground cave, which has a mouth open towards the light and reaching all along the cave; here they have been from their childhood, and have their legs and necks chained so that they cannot move, and can only see before them, being prevented by the chains from turning round their heads. Above and behind them a fire is blazing at a distance, and between the fire and the prisoners there is an upward track; and you will see, if you look, a low wall built along the way, like the screen which marionette players have in front of them, over which they show the puppets.

I see.

And do you see, I said, men passing along the wall carrying all sorts of vessels, and statues and figures of animals made of wood and stone and various materials, which appear over the wall? Some of them are talking, others silent.

You have shown me a strange image, and they are strange prisoners.

But they are like ourselves, I replied; and don't they see only their own shadows, or the shadows of one another, which the fire throws on the opposite wall of the cave?

True, he said; how could they see anything but the shadows if they were never allowed to move their heads?

And of the objects which are being carried in like manner they would only see the shadows?

Yes, he said.

And if they were able to converse with one another, would they not suppose that they were naming what was actually before them?

Very true.

And suppose further that the prison had an echo which came from the other side; when one of the passers-by spoke, would they not be sure to think that the voice which they heard came from the passing shadow?

No question, he replied.

To them, I said, the truth would be literally nothing but the shadows of the images.

That is certain.

And now look again, and see what will naturally follow if the prisoners are released and disabused of their error. At first, when any of them is liberated and compelled suddenly to stand up and turn his neck round and walk and look towards the light, he will suffer sharp pains; the glare will distress him, and he will be unable to see the realities of which in his former state he had seen the shadows; and then imagine someone saying to him that what he saw before was an illusion, but that now, when he is approaching nearer to reality and his eye is turned towards more real existence, he has a clearer vision: what will be his reply? And you may further imagine that his instructor is pointing to the objects as they pass and requiring him to name them: will he not be perplexed? Will he not fancy that the shadows which he formerly saw are more real than the objects which are now shown to him?

Far more real.

And if he is compelled to look straight at the light, will he not have a pain in his eyes which will make him turn away, back towards the objects which he can see, and which he will conceive to be in reality clearer than the things which are now being shown to him?

True, he said.

And suppose once more, that he is reluctantly dragged up a steep and rugged ascent, and held fast until he's forced into the presence of the sun, is he not likely to be pained and irritated? When he approaches the light his eyes will be dazzled, and he will not be able to see anything at all of what are now called realities.

Not all at once, he said.

He will need to grow accustomed to the sight of the upper world. And first he will see the shadows best, next the reflections of men and other objects in the water, and then the objects themselves; then he will gaze upon the light of the moon and the stars and the spangled heaven; and he will see the sky and the stars by night better than the sun or the light of the sun by day?

Certainly.

Last of he will be able to see the sun, and not mere reflections of it in the water, but he will see it in its own proper place, and not in another; and he will contemplate it as it is.

Certainly.

He will then proceed to argue that this is what provides the seasons and the years, and is the guardian of all that is in the visible world, and in a certain way the cause of all things which he and his fellows have been accustomed to behold?

Clearly, he said, he would first see the sun and then reason about it.

And when he remembered his old habitation, and the wisdom of the cave and his fellow-prisoners, do you not suppose that he would count himself happy because of the change, and pity them?

Certainly, he would.

And if they were in the habit of conferring honours among themselves on those who were quickest to observe the passing shadows and to remark which of them went before, and which followed after, and which were together; and who were therefore best able to draw conclusions as to the future, do you think that he would care for such honours and glories, or envy those who possessed them? Would he not say with Homer, 'better to be the poor servant of a poor master', and to endure anything, rather than think as they do and live after their manner?

Yes, he said, I think that he would rather suffer anything than entertain these false notions and live in this miserable manner.

Imagine once more, I said, such a person coming suddenly out of the sun to be replaced in his old situation; would he not be certain to have his eyes full of darkness?

To be sure, he said.

And if there were a contest, and he had to compete in measuring the shadows with the prisoners who had never moved out of the cave, while his sight was still weak, and before his eyes had become steady (and the time which would be needed to acquire this new habit of sight might be very considerable) would he not be ridiculous? People would say of him that up he went and down he came without his eyes; and that it was better not even to think of ascending; and as for anyone who tried to release another person and lead him up to the light, they would take hold of him and put him to death.

No question, he said.

The shepherd

Republic Book 1, 343b–d and 345c–e

Early on in the Republic, *Socrates and Thrasymachus debate whether rulers serve their own interests or not. To refute Socrates' appeal to doctors and sea-captains, who only pursue the interests of those in their charge, Thrasymachus cites the examples of shepherds (343b–d):*

Thrasymachus: You think that the shepherd or cowherd fattens or tends the sheep or cows with a view to their own good and not to the good of himself or his master; and you further imagine that the rulers of states, if they are true rulers, never think of their subjects as sheep, and that they are not studying their own advantage day and night. You are so wrong in your ideas about justice and injustice as not even to know that justice and the just are in reality good for someone else; that is to say, the interest of the ruler and stronger, and bad for the subject and servant; and injustice the opposite; for the unjust lords it over the truly simple and just: he is the stronger, and his subjects do what is in his interest, and minister to his happiness, which is very far from being their own.

Socrates' reply comes at 345c–e:

For I must say, Thrasymachus, if you recall what was previously said, that although you began by defining the true doctor in an exact sense, you were not as exact when speaking of the shepherd; you thought that the shepherd as a shepherd tends the sheep not with a view to their own good, but like a mere diner or banqueter with a view to the pleasures of the table; or, again, as a trader for sale in the market, and not as a shepherd. Yet surely the art of the shepherd is concerned only with the good of his subjects; he has only to provide the best for them, since the perfection of the art is already ensured whenever all the requirements of it are satisfied. And that was what I was saying just now about the ruler. I conceived that the art of the ruler, considered as ruler, whether in a state or in private life, could only regard the good of his flock or subjects; whereas you seem to think that the rulers in states, that is to say, the true rulers, like being in power.

The weaver

Statesman 305e–308b and 310e–311c

The Statesman *is one of Plato's later dialogues. By this stage in his career, he was no longer using the figure of Socrates as the principal interlocutor. Instead the main speaker is an unnamed visitor from Elea in Italy, which had been a philosophical centre long before Plato's time. The other speaker (who plays a very minimal role) is a young man called Socrates (not to be confused with the Socrates who was Plato's mentor).*
305e–308b:

ELEATIC VISITOR: Then, now that we have discovered the various classes in a state, shall I analyse politics with the paradigm of weaving?
YOUNG SOCRATES: I greatly wish that you would.
EV: Then I must describe the nature of the royal web, and show how the various threads are woven into one piece.
YS: Clearly.
EV: A task has to be accomplished, which, although difficult, appears to be necessary.
YS: Certainly the attempt must be made.
EV: To assume that one part of virtue differs in kind from another is a position easily assailable by argumentative people, who appeal to popular opinion.
YS: I do not understand.
EV: Let me put the matter in another way: I suppose that you would consider courage to be a part of virtue?
YS: Certainly.
EV: And you would think temperance to be different from courage; and likewise to be a part of virtue?
YS: True.
EV: I shall venture to put forward a strange theory about them.
YS: What is it?
EV: That they are two principles which thoroughly hate one another and are antagonistic throughout a great part of nature.
YS: How do you mean?
EV: It's a very unusual idea; for all the parts of virtue are commonly said to be friendly to one another.

YS: Yes.

EV: Then let us carefully investigate whether this is universally true, or whether there are not parts of virtue which are at war with their kindred in some respect.

YS: Tell me how we shall consider that question.

EV: We must extend our enquiry to all those things which we consider beautiful and at the same time place in two opposite classes.

YS: Explain; what are they?

EV: Acuteness and quickness, whether in body or soul or in the movement of sound, and the imitations of them which painting and music supply—these you must have praised yourself before now, or been present when others praised them.

YS: Certainly.

EV: And do you remember the terms in which they are praised?

YS: I do not.

EV: I wonder whether I can explain to you in words the thought which is passing in my mind.

YS: Why not?

EV: You fancy that this is all so easy: Well, let us consider these notions with reference to the opposite classes of action under which they fall. When we praise quickness, energy, and acuteness, whether of mind or body or sound, we express our praise of the quality which we admire by one word, and that one word is courage.

YS: How?

EV: We speak of an action as brave, quick and manly, and vigorous too; and when we apply the name of which I speak as the common attribute of all these natures, we certainly praise them.

YS: True.

EV: And do we not often praise the quiet strain of action also?

YS: To be sure.

EV: And do we not then say the opposite of what we said of the other?

YS: How do you mean?

EV: We exclaim 'How calm! How temperate!' in admiration of the slow and quiet working of the intellect, and of steadiness and gentleness in action, of smoothness and depth of voice, and of all rhythmical movement and of music in general, when these have a proper solemnity. Of all such actions we predicate not courage, but a name indicative of order.

YS: Very true.

EV: But when, on the other hand, either of these is out of place, the names of either are changed into terms of censure.

YS: How so?

EV: Excessive sharpness or quickness or hardness is termed violence or madness; too much slowness or gentleness is called cowardice or sluggishness; and we may observe that for the most part these qualities, and the temperance and courage of the opposite characters, are arrayed as enemies on opposite sides, and do not mingle with one another in their respective actions; and if we pursue the enquiry, we shall find that people who have these different qualities of mind differ from one another.

YS: In what respect?

EV: In respect of all the qualities which I mentioned, and very likely of many others. According to their respective affinities to either class of actions, they distribute praise and blame: praise to the actions which are akin to their own, blame to those of the opposite party. As a result, there is a great deal of enmity among them on many issues.

YS: True.

EV: The difference between the two classes is often a trivial concern; but when it affects really important matters, it becomes the most hateful of all political diseases.

YS: What sort of matters do you mean?

EV: Nothing less than the whole regulation of human life. For the orderly class are always ready to lead a peaceful life, quietly doing their own business; this is their manner of behaving with everyone at home, and they are equally ready to find some way of keeping the peace with foreign states. And on account of this fondness of theirs for peace, which is often out of season where their influence prevails, they become by degrees unwarlike, and bring up their young men to be like themselves; they are at the mercy of their enemies; as a result, in a few years they and their children and the whole city often pass imperceptibly from the condition of freemen into that of slaves.

YS: That's a cruel fate!

EV: And now think of what happens with the more courageous natures. Are they not always inciting their country to go to war, owing to their excessive love of the military life? Don't they raise up against themselves many powerful enemies, and either utterly ruin their native land or enslave and subject it to its foes?

YS: That, again, is true.

EV: So must we not admit that, where these two classes exist, they always feel the greatest antipathy and antagonism towards one another?

YS: We cannot deny it.

EV: And returning to the enquiry with which we began, have we not found that considerable portions of virtue are at variance with one another, and give rise to a similar opposition in the characters who are endowed with them?

YS: True.

310e–311c:

EV: The whole process of royal weaving is comprised in this one task: never to allow temperate natures to be separated from the brave, but to weave them together, like the warp and the woof, by common sentiments and honours and reputation, and by the giving of pledges to one another; and out of them forming one smooth and even web, to entrust to them the offices of state.

YS: How do you mean?

EV: Where one officer only is needed, you must choose a ruler who has both these qualities—when many, you must mingle some of each, for the temperate ruler is very careful and just and safe, but is wanting in thoroughness and go.

YS: Certainly, that is very true.

EV: The character of the courageous, on the other hand, falls short of the former in justice and caution, but has the power of action in a remarkable degree and, when either of these two qualities is wanting, cities cannot altogether prosper either in their public or private life.

YS: Certainly they cannot.

EV: So this is what we declare to be the completion of the web of political action: it is created by a direct intertexture of brave and temperate natures, whenever the royal science has drawn the two minds into communion with one another by unanimity and friendship. Having perfected the noblest and best of all the webs which political life admits, and enfolded into it all other inhabitants of cities, whether slaves or freemen, it binds them in one fabric and governs and presides over them, and so secures their happiness, in so far as any city can be guaranteed happiness.

The sower

Phaedrus 275d–276c and 276e–277a

This dialogue is a conversation between Socrates and a younger man, Phaedrus, who has a keen interest in rhetoric. Most of the work concerns rhetoric in one way or another, using examples of speeches to analyse the most important requirements of the art. But towards the end, they turn to the written word. Just prior this passage, Socrates has told the story of Theuth, the god who invented writing, but was then criticized by Thamus for its harmful potential.

275d–276c:

SOCRATES: I cannot help feeling, Phaedrus, that writing is unfortunately like painting; for the creations of the painter have the appearance of life, and yet if you ask them a question they preserve a solemn silence. And the same may be said of written words. You would imagine that they had intelligence, but if you want to know anything and put a question to one of them, the speaker always gives one unvarying answer. And once they have been written down they are tumbled about anywhere among those who may or may not understand them, and do not know to whom they should reply, and to whom they should not: and, if they are maltreated or abused, they have no parent to protect them; and they cannot protect or defend themselves.

PHAEDRUS: That again is very true.

S: Is there not another kind of word or speech far better than this, and having far greater power—a son of the same family, but legitimate?

P: Whom do you mean, and what is his origin?

S: I mean an intelligent word written in the soul of the learner, which can defend itself, and knows when to speak and when to be silent.

P: You mean the living word of knowledge which has a soul, and of which the written word is properly no more than an image?

s: Yes, of course that is what I mean. And now may I be allowed to ask you a question: Would a husbandman, who is a man of sense, take the seeds, which he values and which he wishes to bear fruit, and in all seriousness plant them during the heat of summer, in some garden of Adonis, that he may rejoice when he sees them in eight days appearing in beauty? At least he would do so, if at all, only for the sake of amusement and play. But when he is in earnest he sows in the right soil, and practises husbandry, and is satisfied if in eight months the seeds which he has sown arrive at perfection?

p: Yes, Socrates, that will be his way when he is in earnest; he will do the other, as you say, only in play.

s: And can we suppose that he who knows the just and good and honourable has less understanding, than the husbandman, about his own seeds?

p: Certainly not.

s: Then he will not seriously be inclined to 'write' his thoughts 'in water' with pen and ink, sowing words which can neither speak for themselves nor teach the truth adequately to others?

p: No, that is not likely.

276e–277a:

s: Far nobler is the serious pursuit of the dialectician, who finds a congenial soul and, by the help of science, sows and plants in it words which are able to help themselves and the one who planted them—words that are not unfruitful, but have in them a seed which others, brought up in different soils, render immortal, thus making its possessors happy to the utmost extent of human happiness.

Bibliography

Adair, J. (2013) *Confucius on Leadership*. London.

Adamson, P. (2014) *Classical Philosophy: A History of Philosophy without Any Gaps*. Oxford.

Allen, J. (2006) *Rabble-Rouser for Peace: The Authorised Biography of Desmond Tutu*. London.

Anderson, C. (2012) 'Elon Musk's mission to Mars', Interview, *Wired*, 21 October. https://www.wired.com/2012/10/ff-elon-musk-qa/.

Angier, T. (2015) 'An unjust leader is no leader', in Boaks and Levine (2015) 25–46.

Anton, J. (2011) 'Plato's philosophy of political leadership', *Philosophical Inquiry* 35: 1–7.

Arnone, J. and Fitzsimons, V. (2015) 'Plato, Nightingale, and nursing: can you hear me now?' *International Journal of Nursing Knowledge* 26: 156–62.

Aubrey, A. (2016) 'PepsiCo pledges to cut sugar as big soda comes under scrutiny', NPR website, 17 October. http://www.npr.org/sections/thesalt/2016/10/17/498274851/pepsico-pledges-to-cut-sugar-as-big-soda-comes-under-scrutiny.

Bambrough, B. (1971) 'Plato's political analogies', in Vlastos (1971) 187–205.

Barney, R. (2006) 'Socrates' refutation of Thrasymachus', in Santas (2006) 44–62.

Bass, B. and Stogdill, R. (1990) *Bass & Stogdill's Handbook of Leadership: Theory, Research, and Managerial Applications*. 3rd edn. New York.

Bauman, D. (2018) 'Plato on virtuous leadership: an ancient model for modern business', *Business Ethics Quarterly* 28: 251–74.

Bhuiyan, J. (2017) 'Uber drivers have earned $50 million in tips in just over 50 days', *Recode* web site, 22 August. https://www.recode.net/2017/8/22/16182120/uber-drivers-tips-180-days-of-change-flexibility-destinations-arrival-times-long-trips.

Blackburn, S. (2006) *Plato's Republic: A Biography*. New York.

Blank, D. (2012) 'Writing', in Press (2012) 257–9.

Boaks, J. and Levine, M., eds (2015) *Leadership and Ethics*. London.

Bollier, D., Weiss, S., and Hanson, K. (1991) *Merck & Co., Inc. (A)*. Business case 9-991-021, The Business Enterprise Trust, Harvard Business School Publishing. Cambridge, MA.

Bonazzi, M. (2013) 'Middle Platonism', in Sheffield and Warren (2013) 554–67.

Bostridge, M. (2008) *Florence Nightingale*. London.

Burns, J. (1978) *Leadership*. New York.

Butcher, M. (2012) 'Elon Musk: with jobs gone, Google will win mobile (and look out for the Hyperloop)', *TechCrunch* (blog). http://social.techcrunch.com/2012/11/19/elon-musk-with-jobs-gone-google-will-win-mobile-and-look-out-for-the-hyperloop/.

Cartledge, P. (2011) *Ancient Greece: A Very Short Introduction*. Oxford.

Cartledge, P. (2016) *Democracy: A Life*. Oxford.

Cassidy, R. (1982) *Margaret Mead: A Voice for the Century*. New York.

Collins, C. (1996) *Authority Figures: Metaphors of Mastery from the* Iliad *to the* Apocalypse. London.

Collins, J. (1997) 'The death of the charismatic leader (and the birth of an architect)', *Inc.* October.

Collins, J. (2001) *Good to Great: Why Some Companies Make the Leap . . . and Others Don't*. New York.

Collins, J. (2005) 'Level 5 leadership: the triumph of humility and fierce resolve', *Harvard Business Review* 83: 136–47.

Connors, K. (2018) *Elon Musk: The Founder of Tesla, Paypal, and SpaceX*. Published by the author.

Cook, E. (1913) *The Life of Florence Nightingale*. 2 vols. London.

Cooper, J., ed. (1997) *Plato, Complete Works*. Indianapolis.

Cox, D. and Crook, P. (2015) 'Plato's paradox of leadership', in Boaks and Levine (2015) 129–50.

Cragg, L. (2012) 'Plato, business and moral leadership', in Prastacos et al. (2012) 23–31.

Curie, M., trans. Kellogg, C. and Kellogg, V. (1923) *Pierre Curie*. New York.

Dillon, J. and Gergel, T. (2003) *The Greek Sophists*. London.

Drogin, B. (1995) 'Mandela fires wife from South Africa cabinet post', *Los Angeles Times*, 28 March. https://www.latimes.com/archives/la-xpm-1995-03-28-mn-48099-story.html.

Feloni, R. (2015) 'Pepsi CEO Indra Nooyi explains how an unusual daily ritual her mom made her practice as a child changed her life', *Business Insider*, 9 September. http://www.businessinsider.com/pepsico-indra-nooyi-life-changing-habit-2015-9.

Ferrari, G., ed. and Griffith, T., trans. (2000) *Plato: The* Republic. Cambridge.

Ferrari, G. (2005) *City and Soul in Plato's* Republic. Chicago.

Fine, G., ed. (1999) *Plato 2: Ethics, Politics and the Soul*. Oxford.

Fine, G., ed. (2008) *The Oxford Handbook of Plato*. Oxford.

Foner, P., ed. (1945) *Frederick Douglass: Selections from his Writings*. New York.

Freeman, D. (1983) *Margaret Mead and Samoa: The Making and Unmaking of an Anthropological Myth*. Cambridge, MA.

Freeman, D. (1999) *The Fateful Hoaxing of Margaret Mead: A Historical Analysis of her Samoan Research*. Boulder, CO.

Friedan, B. (2010) *The Feminine Mystique*. New York.

Friedman, M. (1970) 'The social responsibility of business is to increase its profits', *New York Times Magazine*, 13 September.

Gardner, H., with the collaboration of Laskin, E. (2011) *Leading Minds: An Anatomy of Leadership*. New York.

Gardner, J. (1990) *On Leadership*. New York.

Geertz, C. (1989) *Margaret Mead (1901—1978): A Biographical Memoir*. Washington, DC.

Gill, M. (2007) 'Establishing legitimacy for Montessori's grand, dialectical vision: an essay review of *Montessori: The Science Behind the Genius*, Angeline Stoll Lillard', *Teaching and Teacher Education* 23: 770–4.

Gill, M. L. and Pellegrin, P., eds (2006) *A Companion to Ancient Philosophy*. Malden, MA.

Gorbachev, M. (2000) *On my Country and the World*. New York.

Gorbachev, M. (2006) *The Road We Traveled, The Challenges We Face: Speeches, Articles, Interviews*. Moscow: Izdatelstvo VES MIR. http://www.gorby.ru/userfiles/file/gorbaghev_book_speeches_en.pdf.

Greenleaf, R. (1977) *Servant Leadership: A Journey into the Nature of Legitimate Power and Greatness*. Mahwah, NJ.

Grube, G., trans., revised by Reeve, C. (1992) *Plato: The Republic*. Indianapolis. Reprinted in Cooper, ed. (1997).

Haberman, M. (1976) Review of *Maria Montessori: A Biography* by Rita Kramer. *Journal of Teacher Education* 27: 188–9.

Helmstadter, C. (2010) 'Navigating the political straits in the Crimean war', in Nelson and Rafferty (2010) 28–54.

Hunter, R. (2012) *Plato and the Traditions of Ancient Literature: The Silent Stream*. Cambridge.

Ignatius, A. (2015) 'How Indra Nooyi turned design thinking into strategy: an interview with PepsiCo's CEO', *Harvard Business Review*, September issue, 80–5. https://hbr.org/2015/09/how-indra-nooyi-turned-design-thinking-into-strategy.

James, E. and Oliver, R. (2009) *Jim Kutsch: Leader with a Cause*. Business case UVA-OB-0984, Darden Business Publishing, the University of Virginia, Darden School Foundation.

Jarvis, P., Swiniarski, L., and Holland, W. (2017) *Early Years Pioneers in Context*. London.

Johnson, R. (2004) 'Looking back is not an option', *New York Times*, 28 November.

Jowett, B., trans. (1871) *The Dialogues of Plato*. 4 vols. Oxford.

Karamanolis, G. (2012) 'Academy of Athens, ancient history of', in Press (2012) 264–7.

Kennedy, J. F. (1963) Letter to Jean Monnet commending his achievements on behalf of European unity. *The American Presidency Project*. http://www.presidency.ucsb.edu/ws/index.php?pid=9365.

Keyt, D. (2006) 'Plato and the ship of state', in Santas (2006) 189–213.

Kinross, P. (2001) *Ataturk: The Rebirth of a Nation*. Phoenix, AZ.

Klein, S. (1988) 'Plato's *Statesman* and the nature of business leadership: an analysis from an ethical point of view', *Journal of Business Ethics* 7: 283–94.

Koehn, N. (2017) *Forged in Crisis: The Power of Courageous Leadership in Turbulent Times*. New York.

Kramer, R. (1976) *Maria Montessori: A Biography*. New York.

Kutsch, J. (2012) 'Dare to succeed' (speech, Blairstown, NJ, 23 October), Blair Academy, Society of Skeptics. https://www.youtube.com/watch?v=B4-1QMwU12s.

Lane, M. (2006) 'Plato's political philosophy: the *Republic*, the *Statesman*, and the *Laws*', in Gill and Pellegrin (2006) 170–91.

Lane, M. (2012) 'Politics and the figure of the politicus', in Press (2012) 235–7.

Lane, M. (2014) *Greek and Roman Political Ideas*. London.

LeVasseur, J. (1998) 'Plato, Nightingale and contemporary nursing', *Journal of Nursing Scholarship* 30: 281–5.

Lillard, A. (2005) *Montessori: The Science Behind the Genius*. Oxford.

Magnello, M. (2010) 'The passionate statistician', in Nelson and Rafferty (2010) 115–29.

Mandela, N. (1994) *Long Walk to Freedom*. Vol. I: *1918–1962*. London.

Mandela, N. (2011) *Nelson Mandela by Himself: The Authorised Book of Quotations*. Johannesburg.

Mango, A. (2004) *Ataturk*. London.

McPherran, M. (2012) 'Medicine', in Press (2012) 202–5.

Mead, J., Freeman, E., and Spangler, L. (2011) *True Leadership: Leading with Meaning*. Charlottesville, VA.

Mead, M. (1961) *Coming of Age in Samoa: A Psychological Study of Primitive Youth for Western Civilisation*. New York.

Mead, M. (1975) *Reflections: Margaret Mead*. Washington, DC: The Agency, distributed by the National Audiovisual Center. http://archive.org/details/reflectionsmargaretmead.

Meinwald, C. (2020) 'Plato', *Encyclopaedia Britannica*. https://www.britannica.com/biography/Plato.

Meredith, M. (2010) *Mandela: A Biography*. New York.

Miliband, E. (2013) 'Mandela healed the wounds of the past with compassion and generosity', *The Guardian*, 8 December. https://www.theguardian.com/world/2013/dec/08/nelson-mandela-ed-miliband.

Monnet, J., trans. Mayne, R. (1978) *Memoirs*. Garden City, NY.

Montessori, M., trans. George, A. (1912) *The Montessori Method: Scientific Pedagogy as Applied to Child Education in 'The Children's Houses', with Additions and Revisions by the Author*. London.

Nehamas, A. and Woodruff, P. (1995) *Plato: Phaedrus*. Indianapolis.

Nelson, S. and Rafferty, A. (2010) *Notes on Nightingale: The Influence and Legacy of a Nursing Icon*. Ithaca, NY.

Newman, J. (2014) 'Uber CEO would replace drivers with self-driving cars', *Time* website, 28 May. http://time.com/132124/uber-self-driving-cars/.

Nightingale, A. (2004) *Spectacles of Truth in Classical Greek Philosophy: Theoria in its Cultural Context*. Cambridge.

Nightingale, F. (1860) *Notes on Nursing: What It Is, and What It Is Not*. London.

Nightingale, F. (1896) 'A letter to Waltham', *The Trained Nurse and Hospital Review* 45 (July–December 1910; original letter published 23 December 1896).

Nooyi, I. (2017) '"Leave the crown in the garage": what I've learned from a decade of being PepsiCo's CEO', LinkedIn. https://www.linkedin.com/pulse/leave-crown-garage-what-ive-learned-from-decade-being-indra-nooyi?articleId=62963754834 28802560#comments-6296375483428802560&trk=public_profile_article_view.

Nooyi, I. and Gelles, D. (2019) 'Indra Nooyi: "I'm not here to tell you what to eat"', *New York Times.* 21 March. https://www.nytimes.com/2019/03/21/business/indra-nooyi-corner-office-pepsi.html.

Pace, E. (1987) 'Henry R. Labouisse dies; former chief of UNICEF', *New York Times*, 27 March.

Pappas, N. (1995) *Plato and the* Republic. London.

Parker, G. (2018) '10 things you didn't know about Duke Energy CEO Lynn Good', *Money Inc.* https://moneyinc.com/duke-energy-ceo-lynn-good/.

Pelley, S. (2012) 'U.S., China, Russia, Elon Musk: entrepreneur's "insane" vision becomes reality', Interview, *CBS News*, 22 May. https://www.cbsnews.com/news/us-china-russia-elon-musk-entrepreneurs-insane-vision-becomes-reality/.

Pollack, A. (1983) 'The turmoil at American Bell', *New York Times*, 8 June.

Popper, K. (1962) *The Open Society and its Enemies.* 4th edn. 2 vols. London.

Prastacos, G., Wang, F., and Soderquist, K., eds (2012) *Leadership through the Classics: Learning Management and Leadership from Ancient East and West Philosophy.* Berlin.

Press, G., ed. (2012) *The Continuum Companion to Plato.* London.

Reichenbach, H. (1938) *Experience and Prediction.* Chicago.

Russell, B. (2001) *The Problems of Philosophy.* Oxford.

Safian, R. (2017) 'How PepsiCo CEO Indra Nooyi is steering the company toward a purpose-driven future', *Fast Company*, February issue.

Santas, G., ed. (2006) *The Blackwell Guide to Plato's* Republic. Oxford.

Saunders, T. (1975) *Plato: The* Laws. London.

Scott, D. (2008) 'Plato's *Republic*', in Fine, ed. (2008) 360–82.

Scott, D. (2020) *Listening to Reason in Plato and Aristotle.* Oxford.

Shankman, P. (2009) *The Trashing of Margaret Mead: Anatomy of an Anthropological Controversy.* Madison, WI.

Shankman, P. (2013) 'The "fateful" hoaxing of Margaret Mead: a cautionary tale', *Current Anthropology* 54: 51–62 and 67–70.

Shankman, P. (2018) 'The public anthropology of Margaret Mead: *Redbook*, women's issues, and the 1960s', *Current Anthropology* 59: 55–73.

Sheffield, F. and Warren, J. eds (2013) *The Routledge Companion to Ancient Philosophy.* London.

Siegel, R. and Silverman, A. (2017) 'Pittsburgh offers driving lessons for Uber's autonomous cars', *NPR* web site, 3 April. http://www.npr.org/sections/all techconsidered/2017/04/03/522099560/pittsburgh-offers-driving-lessons-for-ubers-autonomous-cars.

Skemp, J. (1987) *Plato: The* Statesman. 2nd edn. Bristol.

Smith, J. (1979) 'Jean Monnet: a force for unity, peace', *Washington Post*, 17 March.

Smith, R. (2020) 'Aristotle's logic', in Zalta, E., ed. *The Stanford Encyclopedia of Philosophy.* https://plato.stanford.edu/archives/fall2020/entries/aristotle-logic/.

Solan, H. (2007) Review of *Maria Montessori: A Biography*, by Rita Kramer, *Optometry & Vision Development* 38: 61.

Steinmetz, K. and Vella, M. (2017) 'Uber: chaos at the world's most valuable venture-backed company is forcing Silicon Valley to question its values', *Time*, 26 June, 22–9.

Stern, M. (2011) 'Elon Musk of Tesla Motors discusses revenge of the electric car', Interview, *Daily Beast*, 25 April. https://www.thedailybeast.com/articles/2011/04/25/elon-musk-of-tesla-motors-discusses-revenge-of-the-electric-car.

Stogdill, R. (1974) *Handbook of Leadership: A Survey of Theory and Research*. New York.

Stripling, J. (2010) 'Professor in chief', *Inside Higher Ed*, 10 February. https://www.insidehighered.com/news/2010/02/10/professor-chief.

Sundstrom, R. (2017) 'Frederick Douglass', in Zalta, E., ed. *The Stanford Encyclopedia of Philosophy*. https://plato.stanford.edu/archives/spr2017/entries/frederick-douglass/.

Takala, T. (1998) 'Plato on leadership', *Journal of Business Ethics* 17: 785–98.

Taubman, W. (2017) *Gorbachev: His Life and Times*. New York.

Taylor, C. (1999) 'Plato's totalitarianism', in Fine, ed. (1999) 280–96.

Thesleff, H. (2012) 'Plato's life', in Press (2012) 8–10.

Ulanoff, L. (2012) 'Elon Musk: secrets of a highly effective entrepreneur', *Mashable*, 13 April. https://mashable.com/2012/04/13/elon-musk-secrets-of-effectiveness/.

Vagelos, R. and Galambos, L. (2006) *The Moral Corporation: Merck Experiences*. New York.

Vicinus, M. and Nergaard, B., eds (1990) *Ever Yours, Florence Nightingale*. Cambridge, MA.

Vlastos, G., ed. (1971) *Plato: A Collection of Critical Essays II: Ethics, Politics, and Philosophy of Art and Religion*. New York.

Vogt, K. (2013) 'The Hellenistic Academy', in Sheffield and Warren (2013) 482–95.

Vora, J. and Vora, E. (2004) 'The effectiveness of South Africa's Truth and Reconciliation Commission: perceptions of Xhosa, Afrikaner, and English South Africans', *Journal of Black Studies* 34: 301–22.

Whitehead, A. (1978) *Process and Reality: An Essay in Cosmology*. New York.

Wicks, A., Freeman, R. E., Werhane, P., and Martin, K. (2010) 'Leadership', in *Business Ethics: A Managerial Approach*. Upper Saddle River, NJ.

Wilkins, A. and Bristow, N. (1987) 'For successful organization culture, honor your past', *The Academy of Management Executive* 1: 221–9.

Wittgenstein, L. (1967) *Philosophical Investigations*. 3rd edn. Oxford.

Yunus, M. and Jolis, A. (2003) *Banker to the Poor*. New York.

Yunus, M. and Weber, K. (2007) *Creating a World without Poverty: Social Business and the Future of Capitalism*. New York.

Index

For the benefit of digital users, table entries that span two pages (e.g., 52–53) may, on occasion, appear on only one of those pages.